W9-BZL-491

THE
MAKING OF A
SISTER-TEACHER

THE
MAKING OF A
SISTER-TEACHER

Sister Maria Concepta, C.S.C.

UNIVERSITY OF NOTRE DAME PRESS
Notre Dame — London

LD
7251
.N9426

To Mother M. Verda Clare, C.S.C.,
Provincial Superior of the Midwest Province,
whose ideal of teacher education prompted the interest and
research that resulted in this work

PREFACE

THIS BOOK IS UNIQUE. For the first time an American religious community has placed at the disposal of a research worker the complete record of its experience in the training and assignment of teachers. Here Sister Maria Concepta, of the Congregation of the Sisters of the Holy Cross, reviews more than a hundred years of patient effort to meet demands for classroom instructors—demands that came from bishops, pastors, and parents. It was an heroic effort, as the reader will see, but until now none of us has had an opportunity to see what that heroism has implied.

The Sisters of the Holy Cross, like so many other communities, were not content merely to place a habit-garbed body in front of a class. They were committed to standards that alone could satisfy their own consciences and meet the needs of the society they served. At first, like the best of American teachers generally, they were cultivated women who tried to increase the number of cultivated women. In doing so they earned respect and affection.

But rather suddenly most of the states determined to standardize and improve teacher training methods. Although not every requirement was wisely conceived—doubtless too much emphasis was placed on pedagogy for a time—few can honestly question that the net result was better schools. Still the burden placed on the teaching profession generally, and by no means merely on the religious communities that served Catholic schools, was very heavy. How it was faced and at what cost is one major theme of this book.

A second challenge came from within the ranks of the teaching sisters themselves. This challenge was not all of a piece, but in a broad sense it is identified with the Sister Formation move-

vii

ment. The standards proposed were suggested not by state legislation but by the vocational objectives of the sisters themselves. After all they had pledged their lives to the cause of teaching for other than earthly rewards, and it was surely salutary to find out just how the pledge could be effectively redeemed. This demanded a second and no less heroic effort.

Sister Maria Concepta's study of how these dual challenges were met is placed in the context of a history that is sometimes almost romantic in flavor, although its core is wholly realistic. The reader will find out how teachers were recruited and trained, how they succeeded or sometimes failed, and how the financial strain was met. For the first time we have a clear picture of how much it has cost to train a teacher and how great the difference has been between that cost and the salaries subsequently earned.

In a sense this is a shocking book for the reason indicated. It should stir the consciences of those who profit by the services of these teachers, and it should answer some of the questions put by scholars who have been seeking information. Nevertheless the author is always aware that her community wants everything else more than a picket line or a lobby.

Sister Maria Concepta, who initiated the new graduate study program for the training of elementary school teachers at St. Mary's College, has spent many years in teacher training and supervision. She is in every sense of the term a modern American nun, which means that she is well educated, sincerely dedicated to the classroom and its objectives, deeply religious. Her determination to bring this study to a successful conclusion has resembled that of the proverbial mailman. Not even a flood that literally came within a few inches of trapping her in the community's archives, was a deterrent. For this the rest of us may be admiringly grateful.

George N. Shuster

AUTHOR'S PREFACE

THERE IS ALWAYS considerably more to the "making" of anything than appears on the surface. *The Making of a Sister-Teacher* is no exception to this phenomenon. In September, 1964, thirty-four new sister-teachers entered classrooms in the schools taught by the Sisters of the Holy Cross, representing what the press has referred to as "the sister of tomorrow." They were the first group of teachers in the Congregation of the Sisters of the Holy Cross who had completed a formal period of five years of formation: intellectually, spiritually, and culturally integrated. Not five, but 120 years had gone into their "making."

This book is not a story of the moving power and underlying spirit that is the raison d'être of a congregation of religious women dedicated to teaching and other apostolates. In the popular mind this omission might be questioned, yet such a story is left to others.

The Making of a Sister-Teacher is the story of the evolution of the informal teacher training at Saint Mary's Academy, Bertrand, Michigan, 1844, to the formal teacher-education program of the Sisters of the Holy Cross at Saint Mary's College, Notre Dame, Indiana, 1964, a saga of failures, successes, trials, and achievements. At all times it is a story of courage in the face of change and adaptation. The Holy Cross sister-formation preparation for teachers in the classrooms of the world of today is the culmination of a 120-year development of teacher education.

This book is an attempt to dispel the "mystery" concerning the religious education of sisters. The aura of mystery surrounding the hard facts of history and economics exists as much within religious communities as outside.

To do this, it has been necessary to investigate the history

ix

of the Sisters of the Holy Cross from their beginnings in Bertrand, Michigan, until the present day, to gather statistics on the personnel of the Sisters of the Holy Cross, to study the informing guides for teacher training in the nineteenth century and the formal teacher-education program that emerged in the twentieth century. The character of its first leadership determined the type of academy that emerged as the Holy Cross Academy and the training school for the sister-teacher. For the first time, the actual cost of educating a sister-teacher was computed.

I wish to make especial acknowledgement to the University of Notre Dame, Indiana, which sponsored this publication under a Carnegie grant; to Dr. George Shuster, who encouraged me to write this story for the public; to Dr. Bernard J. Kohlbrenner, who gave it scholarly direction; to Sister M. Joan of Arc (Spates), C.S.C., archivist at the general house, Saint Mary's, Notre Dame, Indiana; to Sister M. Isabelle (Jones), C.S.C.; and to Sister M. Bertrand (Sullivan), C.S.C., general treasurer.

I wish to express my gratitude to my religious superiors who made available the opportunity to study, as well as to the retired sisters at Saint Mary's Convent, Notre Dame, and at Our Lady of Holy Cross Convent, midwest provincial house, who by their continued interest and support made the study a family project.

Saint Mary's College
Notre Dame, Indiana
May, 1965

CONTENTS

LIST OF TABLES

CORPORATE TITLES OF RELIGIOUS COMMUNITIES FOUNDED BY FATHER BASIL ANTHONY MOREAU

Congregation of the Holy Cross (C.S.C.) includes the Society of Priests and the Society of Brothers, French, Canadian, and American provinces, with the generalate in Rome, Italy.

Congregation of the Sisters of the Holy Cross (C.S.C.) includes three American provinces, with the generalate at Saint Mary's Convent, Notre Dame, Indiana.

Sisters of Holy Cross and of the Seven Dolors (C.S.C.) have their mother house at Saint Laurent, Montreal, Canada.

Marianites of Holy Cross (M.D.S.C.) have their mother house at LeMans, France.

The Congregation of the Sisters of the Holy Cross (Notre Dame, Indiana) separated from the Marianites of Holy Cross (LeMans, France) and from the Sisters of Holy Cross and of the Seven Dolors (Saint Laurent, Montreal, Canada) in 1869. They were also separated (in temporalities) from the priests and brothers of the Holy Cross in 1869, but this was not fully implemented until after the death of Father Sorin (1893). Mother M. Augusta (Anderson) was elected the first superior general of the Congregation in 1882.

The words "Holy Cross" in the title of the priests, brothers, and sisters (Canada and France) have their origin from the district Sainte-Croix in the city of LeMans, France. In the title of the Congregation of the Sisters of the Holy Cross (Notre Dame, Indiana), the words "of the Holy Cross" refer to the devotion to the Holy Cross.

THE
MAKING OF A
SISTER-TEACHER

INTRODUCTION

THE SISTERS of the Congregation of the Holy Cross, French in origin, opened their first school in the United States at Bertrand, Michigan, July 16, 1844. The community conducted Saint Mary's Academy at Bertrand until historical and geographical factors forced its move to Saint Mary's, Notre Dame, Indiana. From the beginning the academy functioned in the tradition of the historic academy with a uniqueness conditioned by leadership and by the educational heritage of its founder, Basil Anthony Moreau. Mother M. Angela, the founder of Saint Mary's, Notre Dame, Indiana, was an educator in her own right. She, with Father Edward Sorin, founder of the University of Notre Dame, worked out a program of studies for academies and parochial schools. The academies became the training schools especially for elementary teachers. Saint Mary's Academy, Notre Dame, Indiana, became the center of education for teachers in the Congregation of the Sisters of the Holy Cross. In 1903 the title of Saint Mary's Academy had been changed to Saint Mary's College, at the recommendation of the North Central Association of Colleges and Secondary Schools. The title of

Saint Mary's Academy was retained for the four-year academic curriculum. In 1945 Saint Mary's Academy was moved to Twyckenham Hills, South Bend.

For more than a century, then, the same academy, now Saint Mary's College, educated the sisters who were to teach in the schools of Holy Cross in the United States, Brazil, and East Pakistan. The same college continues today to educate in a formation program the sisters who will be teachers. Their number constitutes a college within a college.[1]

Binswanger says that there is an aura of mystery about aspects of the Catholic Church in the United States as well as of its school system, an image for which the Church is responsible.[2] The purpose of this book is to dispel some of that aura, to tell the story of teacher education and training in a single congregation of religious teachers. Because the preparation of teachers is contingent upon other circumstances—the history of teacher education, leadership, the character of personnel, the program of studies, textbooks, and the cost—these will be considered at the times when they exert their influence on the education of the Sisters of the Holy Cross.

The study has limited itself to education of elementary and secondary teachers in the Congregation of the Sisters of the Holy Cross. It excludes education of college teachers, teachers abroad, teachers in the schools of nursing, and manual training staff, personnel trained in special programs for the blind, deaf, and mute. In the treatment of the subject matter certain limitations are inherent in the sources available. Archival material was lost in the fire of 1879 when the administration building of the University of Notre Dame burned.[3]

The present study is unique in that it is the first definitive study of teacher education in a single congregation of religious women. Other studies have treated the history of teacher education in the United States, the history of education of women in the United States, the history of teacher education in Indiana, and the history of the education of sisters. There are histories of religious congregations of teachers and histories of religious congregations of women teachers. To this writer's knowledge, there is no history of the education of teachers in a religious congregation of women.

There are histories of the Congregation of the Sisters of the Holy Cross and a series of seven volumes, the centenary chronicles of the Sisters of the Holy Cross, 1941–1945. None of these is definitive.

Willard S. Elsbree wrote a documented history of *The American Teacher*.[4] Elsbree's study considered the evolution of teacher education from colonial America to 1939. It is a history of evolution of informal teacher education to the formalized programs that emerged in the twentieth century. The author made a study of textbooks and curricula in the schools of America; these provided comparative data for the same considerations in the study of teacher education in the Congregation of the Sisters of the Holy Cross.

A History of Women's Education in the United States,[5] written in 1929 by Thomas Woody, professor of history of education at the University of Pennsylvania, is a definitive, documented study in two volumes, part of a series for the promotion of scientific research and educational progress. It gives a general history of education of women and a context in which the present study of an educational program for teachers inheres.

Jacob P. Dunn published a monograph of the history of Indiana, a supplement to Gordy's *History of the United States*. The work, *A History of Indiana*,[6] relates to the present study in that it tells of education in Indiana, confirms that the first schools of Indiana were Catholic schools, and treats the New Harmonie Colony (now called New Harmony), Joseph

Neef, the Pestalozzi method of object teaching and the introduction of manual training schools. There is some internal evidence that Father Edward Sorin, C.S.C., visited New Harmony, close to Vincennes, Indiana, where he spent his first months in the New World.

James A. Burns, C.S.C, and Bernard J. Kohlbrenner wrote *A History of the Catholic Education in the United States,* a general treatment of Catholic schools. The one author, a priest of the Congregation of the Holy Cross, and the other, a professor of history of education at the University of Notre Dame, are authorities on the history of Catholic education in the United States. The authors took cognizance of Saint Mary's Academy, Bertrand and Notre Dame, in their study.[7]

Sister M. Bertrande (Meyers), D.C., studied the education of sisters in sixty religious communities in the United States and in Canada. She projected a plan for integrating the religious, social, cultural, and professional training of sisters. In a personal interview with community administrators and persons responsible for the education of sisters, the author sought answers to a hypothesis that the growing sense of inadequate returns from university work manifested in most religious communities might be not in higher education per se, but in the manner in which the education was acquired. The writer was of the opinion that there had been an overemphasis of professional education in the post World War I period which posed a serious problem for religious teachers. This problem she studied in *The Education of Sisters.*[8]

Etienne and Tony Catta have published a definitive two-volume study of *Basil Anthony Mary Moreau*[9] as well as *Mother Mary of the Seven Dolors and the Early Origins of the Marianites of Holy Cross.*[10] In the former work the authors present Father Moreau as a founder and as an educator. They considered *La Pédagogie* as Father Moreau's summary of his principles, philosophy, and methodology as an educator. The life of Mother Mary of the Seven Dolors tells of the foundations of the Sisters of the Holy Cross in France, the opening of the American province, and the ultimate separation of both the American and Canadian provinces from France and from each other.

Sister Mary Carol (Schroeder), O.S.F., dealt with a related topic in a published study entitled *The Catholic Church in the Diocese of Vincennes, 1847–1877*.[11] The author studied the schools of the Sisters of the Holy Cross opened in Lowell and Mishawaka in the early 1850's, especially in Chapter V, "The Alleviation of Parochial and Educational Needs." She treated the Know-Nothing hostility which forced the sisters to leave Mishawaka. Sister Mary Carol established February 28, 1855, as the date of the first charter to a Catholic college for women in the United States. The state of Indiana issued this charter to Saint Mary's Academy, Notre Dame. She adds that the level of the curriculum was then secondary and that the first degree was granted in 1898 on the basis of a two-year post-graduate course. The author referred to a temporary setback in the educational development in northern Indiana as the result of a cholera epidemic which particularly affected the priests, brothers, and sisters of Holy Cross at Notre Dame, Indiana. Her study emphasized the isolation of and the subsequent neglect of northern Indiana by ecclesiastical authorities, a condition which Father Sorin used to explain his independence in administration.

Related to the present study is a book of historical reference, *The Diocese of Fort Wayne: 1669–1907*,[12] by Rt. Rev. H. J. Alerding. The work contained a brief sketch of the first four bishops of Fort Wayne, of the churches, schools, religious communities of men and women, and the secular clergy in the Fort Wayne area. It is undocumented.

A Brief History of the University of Notre Dame, 1842–1892[13] is a chronicle which told of the early days at Bertrand, the founding of Notre Dame, and the activities of Father Sorin—all related to this study. A definitive edition of the life of Father Sorin has never been written.

Seven volumes of centenary chronicles[14] relate directly to this study. They give the story of the first days of Saint Mary's, the mother house, the life and works of the superiors, pioneers and builders; they are chronicles of the principal foundations conducted by the Sisters of the Holy Cross. Anna Shannon McAllister wrote *Flame in the Wilderness: Life and Letters of Mother Angela Gillespie, C.S.C.* Although this is not a definitive edition, Mrs. McAllister knew her subject well. In 1936 she published the life of *Ellen Ewing: Wife of General Sherman.*[15] Ellen Ewing, a first cousin once removed from Mother M. Angela, shared with the latter much of their youth and a relationship and friendship that continued through the years. The seventh volume in the series, *This Is Mother Pauline* by Sister Francis Jerome (O'Laughlin), C.S.C., told the story of a woman who had been the educational leader during the first three decades of the nineteenth century, a period characterized by changes in certification and accreditation.

Rt. Reverend John T. McNicholas, Archbishop of Cincinnati, wrote the foreword to Volume VI of the centenary chronicles. Here he stated that Mother M. Angela stood out in bold relief in her life struggle to establish a sisterhood for the higher education of women with an independence limited only by the decisions which the Holy See imposed. "American to the core," the Archbishop continued, "this indomitable woman, following a French religious way of life, superimposed on it her own highly original method of pedagogy. She enlisted high ecclesiastics, both here and in Europe, to intercede for her at Rome. Her constant and courageous efforts were successful, but only after her death."[16] The volume is a secondary source, but in the acknowledgements it is clear that Anna Shannon McAllister had access to material, not available in the Saint Mary's Convent archives, that corroborated the chronicles used in the present study.

A story of Fifty Years by Sister M. Rita (Heffernan), C.S.C.,[17] is another undocumented annals of the Sisters of the Holy Cross, 1855–1905. Manuscripts and unpublished sources of material in the archives of Saint Mary's Convent substantiate *A Story of Fifty Years*. It could be documented because there is no evidence of lore.

Sister M. Eleanore (Brosnahan), C.S.C., wrote in popular style *On the King's Highway*,[18] the story of the Sisters of the Holy Cross from 1843 to 1931. The manuscript was read aloud to the sisters living at the time of the writing. Thirty-three years ago there were sisters who could document many of the details and who did add stories of interest. It directed the writer to prime sources.

The printed circular letters of Father Moreau[19] and Father Sorin[20] contained directives concerning schools, teachers, teacher education, and textbooks.

Wilbur M. Cunningham used the archives of the University of Notre Dame and Saint Mary's Convent to write *The Land of the Four Flags*.[21] He told the story of Bertrand, of the opening of the first school, Saint Mary's Academy, and Pokagon Mission where the Sisters of the Holy Cross taught the Potawatomie Indians. His bibliography directed the author to Fort Saint Joseph Historical Museum, Niles, where early histories of the Berrien and Cass Counties, Michigan, long out of print, were available.

La Pédagogie Chrètienne à l'usage des Joséphites de la Congrégation de Sainte-Croix,[22] a xeroxed copy of the French original by Father Moreau, is in the archives of Saint Mary's Convent. It gives the philosophy, principles, and methodology of education of the founder of Holy Cross. This was used to study comparatively "The Programme of Studies for

Academies and Select Schools"[23] and "The Programme of Studies for Parochial Schools,"[24] the work of Mother M. Angela. In turn these three works were compared with the prospectus of other Holy Cross academies to ascertain the extent of influence.

Family Portraits by Marion McCandless recounted the genesis and growth of the Holy Cross Alumnae of Saint Mary's College, from 1879 to 1949.[25] Mother M. Angela initiated the alumnae association when she summoned the postgraduates in June, 1879, to a conference at Saint Mary's; they pledged help to Notre Dame after the disastrous fire of April of the same year. Although undocumented, the work contains statistical data about graduates from Saint Mary's and sisters who became teachers in the Congregation of the Holy Cross and in other religious communities. Again, the study was useful in directing the writer to manuscripts and other prime sources.

The master's thesis of Mary Elizabeth Connolly, *Schools in California Conducted by the Congregation of the Sisters of the Holy Cross* (1953),[26] was a study of the civic activity of schools of Holy Cross. She reported oversubscribed municipal quotas of War Saving Stamps and Victory Bonds in World War II from all the Holy Cross schools in California. She said her study could not support the present-day claim (1952) of opponents of Catholic education that the parochial schools were un-American and divisive.

Mother M. Benedict (Murphy) showed in her study how Catholic girls' academies from colonial times to the First Plenary Council of 1852 contributed to the character and growth of American education. She pointed up the isolation of the Catholic school in the midwest and slow rise of the parochial schools.[27] Burns and Kohlbrenner noted that forty per cent of the parishes had parochial schools in 1883; fifty years later there was a gain of only twenty per cent.[28] Brother

Austin Flynn maintained that poverty was the reason for this slow gain.[29] Their claim supported one of the findings of this study: The Sisters of the Holy Cross closed many parochial schools because of isolation and poverty.

William K. Dunn published in 1958 his study *What Happened to Religious Education?*[30] Among his conclusions he held that the Massachusetts law forbidding sectarian textbooks, as enforced by Horace Mann, who wanted to keep religion in but sectarianism out of education, spread to all the original colonies and the District of Columbia. By 1861 the public schools had abandoned formal doctrinal training. The Catholic parochial school system gradually unfolded because of this. The early growth of the schools of the Sisters of the Holy Cross was a part of this unfolding.

In 1905, A. E. LaFontaine, the Superintendent of the Catholic schools of the Diocese of Fort Wayne, reported to Rt. Rev. H. J. Alerding, bishop of Fort Wayne on the state of education in the diocese.[31] The report contained the syllabus used in the parochial schools, the textbooks approved, the conditions of physical plants, statistics on personnel, teacher qualifications, and sample tests for teacher certification. There were three separate reports for the years 1905, 1906 and 1907. They included the course of studies of the Priests of Holy Cross and the Sisters of the Holy Cross in academies. In fact, the "Programme for Academies," planned by Mother M. Angela, was printed verbatim. The reports were valuable because they told how teachers were certified.

Joseph A. Kershaw and Roland N. McKean studied an applied analysis of the supply and demand for good teachers and the relationship of good teachers to salary. The authors developed a case for additional salary differences by showing, as in the case of doctors and scientists, that other professions have a structured salary scale related to the market for a given professional skill. The authors showed that well-trained teachers of vital subjects such as mathematics, physics, and English were already in short supply because of heavy demands outside the schools and the cost of necessary inservice education in the schools. The authors proposed a new type of salary schedule, one that took account of supply and demand. They showed how, by means of a structured salary scale, schools could attract and could keep the teachers needed.[32] The study supports the thesis that inservice teacher education will become prohibitive unless salaries in parochial schools increase or private schools receive subsidies.

Four books show the development and the growth of the Sister Formation Program. *The Mind of the Church in the Formation of Sisters*[33] contains the proceedings of the first series of conferences on formation following the directive of Pius XII to adapt to new conditions but to preserve always those values that do not permit any change.[34] *Spiritual and Intellectual Elements in the Formation of Sisters*[35] reported the proceedings of the second series. The thesis of these addresses was that sister formation is more than sister education. The latter must always be an integral part of a total formation program.[36] *Planning for the Formation of Sisters*,[37] the third book of the series, presented statistics of schools, teachers, and pupils currently (1956) and projected (1966). Planning for formation of teachers must take place in the context of the present and of the future. *The Juniorate in Sister Formation*[38] was a guide and a source book for planning years of further training apart from the postulancy and novitiate.[39] For a sister to become involved in the active work of the congregation on a level of professional competence with her peers, further study is necessary.

Winifred R. Long and Carol E. Enzler compiled and classified advanced studies on Catholic education and closely related subjects published between 1958 and 1963. Thirteen graduate research projects on teacher education have been done during this period. None, however, is a study of teacher education in a specific congregation of religious women.[40]

The Everett Curriculum[41] was the result of a three-month study by educators from communities and colleges. They worked at Everett, Washington, on a college curriculum designed to educate sisters as sisters. The curriculum is at present being revised.

The Holy Cross Sister Formation Program is the culmination of a one-hundred twenty-year development of teacher education. It is a curriculum comparable to that proposed by the Everett Curriculum, yet distinctively one in keeping with the aim and spirit of Saint Mary's College, Notre Dame. The present book is the story of the evolution of the informal teacher training at Saint Mary's Academy, Bertrand, Michigan, 1844, to the formal teacher-education program at Saint Mary's College, Notre Dame, Indiana, 1964.

In reviewing related literature one becomes aware that a study of teacher education in the Congregation of the Sisters of the Holy Cross has never been done. However, there is statistical information on the number of teachers, the number of schools in which they have taught, and the number of students they are currently teaching to make possible this study. Chapter I will consider the establishment of the sisters in the United States from 1843 to 1855. Chapter II will consider Holy Cross education as affected by Rev. Basil Anthony Moreau in La Pédagogie Chrètienne à l'usage des Joséphites de la Congrégation de Sainte-Croix and by Mother M. Angela (Gillespie), C.S.C., in her "Programme of Studies for Select Schools and Academies." The latter was the model on which the Holy Cross academies were patterned. These were the training schools for teachers considered in Chapter III. Chapter IV investigates the history of certification and accreditation (1900–1964) and its concomitant influence upon the teacher education of the Sisters of the Holy Cross, under the long professional leadership of Mother M. Pauline (O'Neill), C.S.C., (1895–1931) and Sister M. Madeleva (Wolff), C.S.C., (1934–1961). Chapter V studies the formal teacher education in the Congregation of the Sisters of the Holy Cross (1944–1964) culminating in the Sister Formation Program. The first group of teachers to have finished this five-year program entered the teaching field in September, 1964. Chapter VI presents conclusions and suggestions for further study of the increasing challenge and demands made upon religious teachers in Catholic schools.

References

[1] Survey of the Educational Status of the Congregation of the Sisters of the Holy Cross (1844–1964). AGH.

[2] Robert B. Binswanger, "The Dilemma Facing Roman Catholic Schools in the United States with Respect to Current Financial Considerations" (Unpublished doctoral dissertation. Harvard University, 1961), p. 64.

[3] Interview with Rev. Thomas T. McAvoy, C.S.C., Archivist, University of Notre Dame, February, 1964.

[4] Willard S. Elsbree, The American Teacher (New York: The American Book Company, 1939).

[5] Thomas Woody, A History of Women's Education in the United States (New York: The Science Press, 1929).

[6] Jacob P. Dunn, A History of Indiana (New York: Charles Scribner's Sons, 1916).

[7] James A. Burns, C.S.C. and Bernard J. Kohlbrenner, History of Catholic Education in the United States (New York: Benziger Brothers, 1937).

[8] Sister Bertrande (Meyers), D.C., The Education of Sisters (New York: Sheed and Ward, 1941).

[9] Etienne and Tony Catta, Basil Anthony Mary Moreau (Milwaukee: Bruce Publishing Company, 1955).

[10] Etienne and Tony Catta, Mother Mary of the Seven Dolors and the Early Origins of the Marianites of Holy Cross (Milwaukee: Bruce Publishing Company, 1959).

[11] Sister Mary Carol (Schroeder), O.S.F., The Catholic Church in the Diocese of Vincennes, 1847–1877 (Washington, D.C.: Catholic University of America Press, 1946).

[12] Rt. Rev. Herman Joseph Alerding, The Diocese of Fort Wayne: a

Book of Historical Reference, 1699–1907 (Fort Wayne, Indiana: Archer Printing Company, 1907).

[13] *A Brief History of the University of Notre Dame du Lac, Indiana, 1842–1892* (Chicago: Werener Company, 1895).

[14] *Centenary Chronicles of the Sisters of the Holy Cross. Songs of the Rood*, Vol. I (Paterson, N.J.: St. Anthony Guild Press, 1941); *Superiors General*, Vol. II (Paterson, N.J.: St. Anthony Guild Press, 1941); *Pioneers and Builders*, Vol. III (Hammond, Indiana: W. B. McConkey Company, 1941); Sister M. Francesca (McDougal), C.S.C., *Our Mother House*, Vol. IV (Hammond, Indiana: W. B. McConkey Company, 1941); *Our Provinces*, Vol. V (Privately printed, 1941); Anna Shannon McAllister, *Flame in the Wilderness*, Vol. VI (Paterson, N.J.: St. Anthony Guild Press, 1941); Sister M. Francis Jerome (O'Laughlin), C.S.C., *This Is Mother Pauline* (Paterson, N.J.: St. Anthony Guild Press, 1945).

[15] Anna Shannon McAllister, *Ellen Ewing: Wife of General Sherman* (New York: Benziger Brothers, 1936). This biography was important to the present dissertation because of her sources, 2500 original letters from Mr. P. Tecumseh Sherman and his mother, Ellen Ewing. The daughter of General Hugh Ewing lent the author 200 family letters corroborating archival material at Saint Mary's Convent, especially those which refer to the early history of Saint Mary's and Notre Dame. Chronologically Mrs. McAllister's study covers the Ewing family from 1796 to 1888. In her acknowledgements in the preface the author makes no reference to any use of the archives at Saint Mary's or at Notre Dame. Ella, Ellen, and Eleanor Ewing Brown are one and the same person. The college records list her as Eleanor; familial archival material in the convent archives bear the name Ella or Ellen.

[16] McAllister, *op. cit.*, p. ix.

[17] Sister M. Rita (Heffernan), C.S.C., *A Story of Fifty Years* (Notre Dame, Indiana: Ave Maria Press, 1905).

[18] Sister M. Eleanore (Brosnahan), C.S.C., *On the King's Highway* (New York: D. Appelton and Company, 1931).

[19] *Circular Letters of the Very Reverend Basil Anthony Mary Moreau*, trans. Edward L. Heston, C.S.C. (Notre Dame, Indiana, 1943).

[20] Edward Sorin, *Circular Letters of the Very Reverend Edward Sorin* (Notre Dame, Indiana: Ave Maria Press, 1894).

[21] Wilbur M. Cunningham, *The Land of the Four Flags* (Grand Rapids, Michigan: William B. Eerdmans Publishing Company, 1961).

[22] Basil-Antoine-Marie Moreau, (La) *Pédagogie Chrètienne à l'usage des Joséphites de la Congrégation de Sainte-Croix* (LeMans: Imprimèrie Julien, Laniel et Cie., 1865).

[23] *Teachers' Guide for the Use of the Sisters of the Cross* (Privately printed, n.d.).

[24] *Ibid.*

²⁵ Marion McCandless, *Family Portraits* (Hammond, Indiana: W. B. McConkey Company, 1952).

²⁶ Mary Elizabeth Connolly, "Schools in California Conducted by the Sisters of the Congregation of the Holy Cross" (Unpublished master's thesis. Department of Education, San Francisco College for Women, 1953).

²⁷ Mother M. Benedict (Murphy), *Pioneer Roman Catholic Girls Academies* (New York: Columbia University Press, 1958).

²⁸ Burns and Kohlbrenner, *op. cit.*, pp. 144–145.

²⁹ Brother Austin (Flynn), F.S.C., "The School Controversy in New York, 1840–1842, and its Effect on the Formulation of Catholic Elementary School Policy" (Unpublished doctoral dissertation. Department of Education, University of Notre Dame, 1962), p. 8.

³⁰ William K. Dunn, *What Happened to Religious Education?* (Baltimore: The Johns Hopkins Press, 1958).

³¹ A. E. LaFontaine, *Report of the Superintendent of the Catholic Schools of the Diocese of Fort Wayne* (Fort Wayne, Indiana: 1905, 1906, 1907).

³² Joseph A. Kershaw and Roland N. McKean, *Teacher Shortages and Salary Schedules* (New York: McGraw-Hill Book Company, Inc., 1962), preface, pp. vii–viii.

³³ *The Mind of the Church in the Formation of Sisters*, edited by Sister Ritamary, C.H.M. (New York: Fordham University Press, 1957).

³⁴ *Ibid.*, p. vii.

³⁵ *Spiritual and Intellectual Elements in the Formation of Sisters*, edited by Sister Ritamary, C.H.M. (New York: Fordham University Press, 1957).

³⁶ *Ibid.*, p. vi.

³⁷ *Planning for the Formation of Sisters*, edited by Sister Ritamary, C.H.M. (New York: Fordham University Press, 1958).

³⁸ *The Juniorate in Sister Formation*, edited by Sister Ritamary, C.H.M. (New York: Fordham University Press, 1960).

³⁹ See Glossary, p. 231, for terms.

⁴⁰ Winifred R. Long and Carol E. Enzler, "Recent Doctoral Dissertations on Catholic Education," *National Catholic Educational Association Bulletin*, LX:4 (May, 1964), pp. 2–43.

⁴¹ *Report of the Everett Curriculum Workshop*, Sister Formation Conference of the National Catholic Educational Association, (Seattle, Washington: Heiden's Mailing Bureau, 1956), p. 138.

CHAPTER I

HOLY CROSS BEGINNINGS IN THE UNITED STATES: 1843-1855

FOUR FRENCH sisters of the Congregation of the Holy Cross established the first American foundation in 1843 at the invitation of Rt. Rev. Celèstin de la Hailandière, bishop of Vincennes, deep in the wilderness of Indiana.[1] Although this area was strictly missionary territory, French and Americans had permanently settled there in numbers, especially along waterways and stage coach routes. South Bend on the Saint Joseph River was busy with inland trading.[2]

Missionaries were not new in this area. As early as 1680, Jesuit missionaries had labored among the Indian tribes in the area of Lakes Superior and Michigan. Father Claude Allouez, S.J., built three chapels at this time: one at Pokagon Village, another at the lakes of the future Notre Dame, and a third at the fort of the Potawatomies. These missions remained open under Jesuit instruction until the English destroyed Fort St. Joseph in 1759, taking the survivors as prisoners to Quebec.[3] In 1830 Leopold Pokagon, chief of the Potawatomies,[4] asked that a blackrobe once more be sent to the Indians.[5] Rev. Gabriel Richard, vicar general of the diocese of Cincinnati, and congressman from the state of Michigan in 1823, obtained from the Kentucky mission Rev. Stephen Theodore Badin,[6] who built a log chapel on Saint Mary's Lake, Notre Dame. He purchased from the United States government a section of land with the intention that a university be built on it, but transferred the property to the Bishop of Vincennes on the condition that the latter would assume the debts. In 1842 Bishop de la Hailandière transferred the title of this land to Father Edward Sorin, religious superior of the priests of Holy Cross who were then in Indiana. Father Badin, living with the Indian chief Pokagon, attended not only the Miami and Potawatomie Indians but also a French village and two future sees, Fort Wayne and Chicago.[7] He died in Cincinnati in 1853. His body was re-interred in 1906, in the log chapel of the University of Notre Dame, where it rests today. Waterways, stage coach routes, trading posts, French and Indian villages and missions are marked on the maps of Ralph Ballard.[8] They testify to the antiquity and intensity of the trade and traffic in the region where the Congregation of the Sisters of the Holy Cross took root.

In coming to America the original band of sisters had intended to do missionary work with the Indians and to be housekeepers for the priests of the Congregation of Holy Cross. From the beginning Father Edward Sorin, the religious superior of the sisters as well as of the priests and brothers in this country, realized the necessity of opening a novitiate to meet the needs of an educational establishment in the wilderness and to augment the number of sisters in the United States. Bishop de la Hailandière had in 1843 invited the Sisters of Providence to establish a school in the southern part of Indiana. But he did not believe that the young missionary diocese over which he had pastoral jurisdiction could support a second novitiate for religious teachers.[9]

Parc Aux Vaches, a fur trading post, lay in the Territory of

Michigan on a north bend of the meandering Saint Joseph River only six miles from Notre Dame, Indiana. It was outside the juridical control of Bishop de la Hailandière; Rt. Rev. Paul LeFevre, bishop of Detroit, administered this mission territory. The first trader, Antoine Le Clerc, Sr., had settled Parc Aux Vaches in 1763, leaving in 1800 for Milwaukee, where he made a fortune as a full-time trader.[10] John Kinzie, trader and silversmith, operated the post from 1794 until leaving for Chicago in 1803. His leadership was replaced by that of Joseph Bertrand, a French fur trader. He had married Magdalen Bourassa (baptized Madeline), probably the adopted daughter of Chief Topenebee.[11] Parc Aux Vaches was renamed Bertrand in 1835;[12] Madeline Street honored his wife.

Because of its favorable situation, Bertrand gave promise. It was a possible threat to the supremacy of Chicago as a trade center.[13] It was a rival of nearby Niles and Buchanan. In fact, Bertrand was more accessible than South Bend to the thoroughfares and trails in the decade of 1830 to 1840. With a population of more than 1000, Bertrand enjoyed a rush of settlers in 1836 to 1837, reaching the height of its prosperity in 1838. Bertrand had accessibility and the advantage of regular mail delivery: lake travel to Saint Joseph, Michigan, then a transfer to one of the finest stage coach lines in the heart of the hinterland, the Sauk Trail.[14]

The first sisters of the Holy Cross enjoyed the favor and patronage of Joseph Bertrand, who probably acted as an agent for Leon Bourassa, from whom Father Sorin purchased a house for the young community.[15] At Pokagon Village, Silver Creek, Michigan, they taught the Indian children from 1845 to 1852. Madeline Bertrand died October 14, 1846, two years after the sisters had established themselves in Bertrand. Shortly afterwards Joseph Bertrand moved to Saint Mary's, Kansas, where he died in 1865.[16]

But why should a prosperous trader who had told his friends that his annual income in 1834 was $16,000, leave the village of Bertrand, which provided such a fortune? Speculators had bought up large areas of land in the environs of Bertrand, re-offering the land for sale at prohibitive prices. The people of Bertrand refused to be duped by these operators. They bought land closer to Niles and to Buchanan. Soon the mail coach no longer made frequent stops at Bertrand; the once-promising town found itself off the principal transportation routes. "Speculation more than anything else ruined Bertrand."[17] The school which the Sisters of the Holy Cross had opened there would likewise have developed very differently under the influence of such isolation had not another event occurred concomitantly.

Because Bishop de la Hailandière had refused Father Sorin the permission to establish the novitiate of the Sisters of the Holy Cross in the diocese of Vincennes, his successor, Bishop Jean Etienne Bazin, also withheld his sanction. But with the death of the latter, Rt. Rev. Maurice de St. Palais made it possible for Father Sorin to move the novitiate to Notre Dame. The bishop of Detroit looked unfavorably upon this move, especially since he had entertained hopes that the community at Bertrand would become a diocesan community under his episcopal jurisdiction. In 1854 Father Sorin moved the orphans and dependent children from Bertrand to Holy Angels Academy, Mishawaka, Indiana, having in mind to move the novitiate there also.[18]

Of the unhappy year at Mishawaka there are no archives; however, fragmentary pieces of correspondence tell a harrowing tale of poverty as well as persecution by the Know-Nothing Party. So strong was the prejudice that the sisters could not purchase food from local markets. Parents kept their children away for fear of recrimination.[19] Another plan was devised. Historic and geographic factors were to shape the selection of the site of the mother house of the Congregation of the Sisters of the Holy Cross.

The Rush estate lay a mile and a quarter west of Notre Dame on the Saint Joseph River. Father Sorin purchased one hundred eighty-five acres of the property; he moved to this site two houses from Bertrand and one from Mishawaka. Here on August 15, 1855, Saint Mary's Academy and Saint Mary's Novitiate opened, the cradle of teacher training for the Congregation of the Sisters of the Holy Cross. The sisters remained in Bertrand with kind benefactors and neighbors until their effects were moved in September, 1855.[20]

Because Saint Mary's Academy, Notre Dame, Indiana, continued in the pattern of Saint Mary's Academy, Bertrand, Michigan, one must return to the latter to know something of the clientele, the curriculum, the faculty, and the cost of this first school in the hinterland of Indiana, a wilderness difficult for a people in the complex culture of today to understand.

The archives record simply the occasion of the opening of the first school of the Congregation of the Sisters of the Holy Cross at Bertrand:

Bishop Hailandière would not permit the sisters to remain at Notre Dame for manual labor only, as the object of their coming to America was not domestic work but also teaching. Their first school therefore opened at Bertrand. The house was a small frame building presented by Mr. Joseph Bertrand. They took possession July 16, 1884. An accomplished lady, Miss Catherine Shea, offered to teach for them gratuitously for a year. Two postulants, Misses Mary Sweeney and Mary Dougherty, assisted her.[21] Both were well educated.[22]

From the beginning of 1844, the sisters were obliged to receive some little orphan girls. The first year they had four; the following year six; and in 1846 there were eight.[23] At Bertrand the sisters received a few pupils, but being cramped for room and having no persons of talent or experience, and no pecuniary resources, the house could hardly develop.[24]

The archives of Saint Mary's College contain a registration of every class since the first of 1844. Correspondence from parents reveals the circumstances and conditions under which many orphaned children were received.

Recently restored (1963), the tombstones in the cemetery at Bertrand give silent testimony to the plagues and hardships which threatened the life span of the women of these decades. Whole families were wiped out with cholera. Women frequently died in childbirth. A widower often sought the sisters to mother and to teach not only his own children but the children of his brothers or sisters, doubly orphaned in an epidemic. Children survived diseases only to be maimed for life with deafness or muteness. All of these types are to be found in the early registers (1844–1846) of Saint Mary's Academy, Bertrand.

Alice Owens was typical of the many orphaned or handicapped children whose fathers brought them to the sisters for care and education. She entered Saint Mary's Academy in 1858 when she was ten years old.[25] Senior Sisters of the Holy Cross recall Alice, whose modest tombstone in the community cemetery tells little of her story. But a letter in the archives is a preface to her life spent with the Sisters of the Holy Cross, who cared for her in the infirmary in her last days.

After a trial of nearly three weeks, writes her guardian grandfather (Elyria, Ohio), we find it utterly impossible for us to take care of Alice. . . . we return her to the care of your institution. . . . We had the impression that Alice would be some help to her Grand Mother (sic), that hope is entirely dissipated. . . . Alice will be 18 years old the 20th inst. I am at this time the owner of a house and lot worth say from 3000 to 4000 dollars, clear of incumbrance. Whatever of property may be left, when myself and wife are gone, Alice, if living, through her mother, will be legally entitled to one-third part, be the same more or less.[26]

A mute, educated in the deaf and dumb department of Mishawaka and Saint Mary's Academy, Alice made her home at the latter until her death in 1922.

The earliest days (1844–1854) at Saint Mary's Academy, Bertrand, are sketchily drawn in chronicles written years later. It is perhaps fairly safe to turn to internal evidence, particularly in the correspondence between parents and the sisters, from which to reconstruct "beginnings." In 1844, in a letter from Detroit, Mr. Louis Antoine Beaubien asks the sisters to educate his two orphaned children in exchange for a piece of land later sold for fifteen thousand francs.[27]

In a letter to Father Moreau, LeMans, France, Father Sorin describes the confirmation of Catholics in Bertrand in November, 1847:

His Lordship officiated pontifically and the ceremonies were as grand as possible. After dinner the prelate visited the sisters, who had come to meet him at the entrance of their grounds with their fifty girls in procession and a banner at the head.[28]

In three years the enrollment had changed from eight to fifty, and another building had been erected to provide for this growth. This structure had been made possible through a gift of five thousand francs from the Propagation of the Faith and seventy-seven acres of land from the inhabitants of Bertrand.[29]

Another letter exchanged between Rev. P. Farrelly, Joliet, Illinois, and Mother M. Angela (Gillespie), directress of the academy in 1854, requests:

Two young ladies in this part of the country are desirous of entering your academy at the termination of the present vacation. They seem to be about the age of seventeen or eighteen. The one is Miss Carey; the other is Miss Kilroy. The latter is an orphan, and Mr. Carey will pay for her as for his own daughter.[30]

Robert Harves writes from New Orleans, 1856:

As for the Foulkes Bill i (sic) cannot obligate myself personaly for that but as soon as their estate is settled and i get the money in

my hands i will Hand it over to the President (Mother Angela).
. . . If you think proper to send the Foulkes children home with
my daughter, i will pay their Traveling Expences. . . . if you do
not think proper to send them to me you must use your own
discretion as to their welfare for I am not able nor willing to
spend any more money for them.[31]

Records show that the Foulkes children were kept at Saint
Mary's because they were orphaned and their guardian had
died but recently.[32]

From St. John's Cathedral in Milwaukee, Rev. Patrick
Donahoe wrote:

The bearer of this note Peter Le Strange, an honest man, wishes
to send his orphaned daughter to your school. . . . he has no
money at present having bought a good farm and paid for it.
. . . You may rely on his word for the Amt (sic) required or the
Amt he agrees to pay.[33]

Bertrand opened its doors to rich and to poor alike. This correspondence testifies to the small amount of actual cash trans-
action for tuition and to the barter that characterized much
of the payment. "I have many orphans to look after," wrote
Mr. T. O'Reilly from LaSalle, Illinois:

Margaret is one of eight half orphans for whose pious and ardu-
ous training I am no little concerned. . . . I wish her to receive
a tolerable and good training. A solid rather than a brilliant education, I greatly prefer. She reads rather indifferently, writes
tolerably, has a meagre knowledge of grammar, and quite a
little of geography. Of history and arithmetic, she knows almost
nothing yet these are the requirements which I most regard in a
young girl's schooling and which I wish her to learn above all
others. She tinkles a little on the piano, but if her talents will not
permit her to apply to the latter without detriment to the
former, then I want no piano. I see by the Catholic Almanac
that you have raised your terms from $60 to $70, but I hope in
the present case you will let it stand at the good old terms.[34]

Mr. O'Reilly drew up a formal contract whereby three of his daughters—Maryana, Frances, and Elizabeth—would be cared for by the sisters until the minors had reached the age of twenty-one. The quaint terms read as follows:

It has been agreed between Thomas O'Reilly and the Reverend Edouard Sorin that the three daughters of the said Thomas O'Reilly shall be received into the institution of the sisters at Bertrand as orphan apprentices until the age of twenty-one years, the oldest being seventeen, the second thirteen, and the youngest ten on the condition that their portion of the farm of 60 acres valued at four hundred dollars shall pass to the community. It has likewise been agreed upon that on their leaving the community at the age of twenty-one they shall have nothing returned to them except their feather-beds.[35]

Another interesting file of correspondence points up the high value which was placed on the education of young girls, the little available cash to finance such education, and the manner in which the problem was most frequently solved. John M. Woods (Alton, Illinois, 1870) signed an insurance policy on his own life,[36] made out to his daughter Ada, but for her education. Catalogues list Ada Woods as a student until 1872. In 1879 Ada wrote from Belvidere, Illinois, to tell of the death of her father. The file closes with the payment of her tuition in full in 1879, and the return to Miss Woods of that amount of the policy which exceeded her indebtedness.[37]

Because all the costs of operation were paid by the University of Notre Dame, all the income from the tuition at Bertrand likewise went to the University.[38] Ready cash was not available in either institution, still subsidized by funds from the mother house in LeMans. It is not uncommon to find costs of operation at Notre Dame and Saint Mary's bartered for in terms of schooling. Alexis Coquillard, prominent early citizen of South Bend and successful business man, wrote off debts due him in terms of education. Receipts show that in exchange for lumber, flooring, shingles, iron beds, and such basic necessities, this benefactor educated not only his own daughters but also daughters of friends and relatives.[39]

The sisters did all the manual work attached to the operation of the school at Bertrand and the laundry at Notre Dame. Their services were augmented uniquely by those who contracted to serve the sisters. Joseph Nicolas Louppe gave his services

. . . for one hundred years to the sisters at Saint Mary's Academy, Bertrand, Michigan, in exchange for the consideration of being kept for the same space of time . . . claiming nothing more for services than . . . to be sheltered from the troubles of the world.[40]

This promise Joseph executed with fidelity and service until his death in 1887.

Bridget and Patrick Foy added to a similar contract all their possessions: a mortgage of $272.50, 103 bushels of corn, forty-three bushels of potatoes, one yoke of oxen, a cow, two two-year old steers, a one-year old heifer, a wagon, a pair of bob sleds, six loads of hay, one hundred pounds of flour, half a barrel of salt, a plough, a shovel plough, a log chain, and sundry articles of furniture—all valued at $250.90.[41] The contract was later nullified by the consent of both parties, but the barter in commodities was commonplace. Widows, also, taught in exchange for a home and the care of their children.[42]

Because of the wide range in age groups and the varied background, it is highly probable that the course of study at Saint Mary's, Bertrand (1844–1847) coincided with that described by Elsbree.

Prior to the organization of the graded system of schools, the course of study consisted of whatever textbook material the pupil could absorb in the course of a school year, together with the additional information, if any, which the school master provided. Each succeeding year the course of study was resumed at the point in the textbook where it had left off the preceding term.[43]

But with the formal introduction of boarders in 1848 the enrollment was sufficient to warrant grouping by ages. The prospectus advertised separate facilities for juniors and seniors.[44] Meanwhile Father Moreau, founder of the Congregation of Holy Cross, had recommended (1845) the solemn distribution of prizes at the end of each scholastic year, a custom prevalent in the French school system.[45] There are many today who remember nostalgically similar ceremonies as well as the weekly awarding of points. Another French influence served to sharpen the subject matter and to raise the standards of achievement. Priests and lay professors from Notre Dame conducted the oral examinations at the end of each session. Promotion to a higher class was dependent upon performance.

From the prospectus of 1851 it is clear that the curriculum included those subjects most frequently taught in the established schools of the East (see Appendix, page 222). Bertrand had a course of study comparable to that which Elsbree describes as used in the common schools of Cincinnati in 1848.[46] In the first curriculum of the academy there were included the fifteen highest scored subjects which Woody found offered in female seminaries (162 institutions) from 1742 to 1871.[47] Incredibly cradled on thirty acres of clearing in the heart of primeval forest, reading, spelling, writing, English grammar, mental philosophy, rhetoric, French grammar and literature, arithmetic, algebra, plane geometry, moral philosophy, geography, natural philosophy, chemistry, botany, astronomy, and history made up the first curriculum. Saint Mary's, Bertrand, from its inception offered music, music theory, harp, guitar, drawing, design, and history of art (1845–1850). These, however, are not included in the highest scored subjects in Woody's curriculum.[48]

Reference is made in the early correspondence concerning the textbooks which were available to the first teachers. There were the textbooks written by Father Moreau principally for the schools conducted by the Brothers of Saint Joseph.[49] Except for one reference to them, there is no other evidence of their use in the academy of Bertrand. Moreover, a bill from

Bill for Textbooks and 1000 Academy Prospecti, 1861

Mother Provincial
of the Sisters of the Holy Cross
St. Mary's Academy, Ind.   Bought of Peter F. Cunningham

24	History of U. States (Quackenbos)	20.00
24	Quackenbos' Natural Philosophy	20.00
24	Quackenbos' Advance Rhetoric	20.00
30	Bullion's Analytical Grammar	13.50
48	Cornell's High School Geo[graphy] and Atlas	64.00
24	Cornell's Intermediate Geo[graphy]	12.00
24	Fredet, Modern History	15.00
12	Davies New Algebra	7.20
1	Key to Do[or]	.40
24	Brocklesby's Astronomy	12.00
1	Barnard's School Architecture	1.25
1	Barnard's Normal School	1.25
1	Kame's Criticism Boyd	.87
1	Kame's Elementary Criticism	1.12
1	Day's Rhetoric	.56
1	Abbot's Teacher	.88
1	Northent's Teacher	.87
1	American Words	1.25
1	Root's School Amusement	.80
6	Fasquelles' French Course	6.75
	Printing 1000 Prospectus [sic]	25.00
	Box and Postage to Depot	1.25
		$225.95

Philad[elphi]a   Aug. 27, 1861

Peter F. Cunningham of Philadelphia for textbooks purchased in 1861 gives the names of books in use at this time.[50] The titles are also found in Woody's list of textbooks mentioned in academy and seminary catalogues (1780–1870).[51]

In the rare-book room of Saint Mary's College Library there are textbooks used by Lydia Rohrer in 1856. These were a gift from her daughter Mrs. Flora Shiveley Beitner of South Bend. They include Davies' *Elementary Algebra: Embracing the First Principles of the Science* (1856); Fredet's *Ancient History from the Dispersion of the Sons of Noe to the Battle of Actium* (1851); Fulton's *Practical System of Bookkeeping by Single and Double Entry* (1856); Hervey's *Rhetoric of Conversation: Bridles and Spurs for the Management of the Tongue* (1853); Olmsted's *Compendium of Natural Philosophy* (1851); Olney's *School Atlas and Supplement* (1844); and the Brothers of the Christian Schools, *The Third Book of Reading Lessons* (1853).[52]

As we previously mentioned, the village of Bertrand had been isolated by the Northern Indiana and Southern Michigan Railroad because of the highhandedness of speculators. With the opening in 1851 of a railroad between South Bend and Chicago there was an increase in enrollment at the academy, but Bertrand was no longer on the daily mail route. This disadvantage in communication was offset by the opening of a post office at Notre Dame the same year, a favor secured by Henry Clay. Father Sorin became the first postmaster.[53] Because Bertrand was still accessible, but not as it had formerly been, a prospectus was printed to attract students to its enlarged quarters.

ST. MARY'S ACADEMY, BERTRAND, MICHIGAN

Under The Direction Of The Sisters Of Holy Cross

This institution is beautifully situated in a healthy and pleasant location on the bank of the St. Joseph River, four miles from Niles and six from South Bend. A daily line of stages running from the former town to the latter, and passing through Bertrand, forms the connection between the Michigan Central and Southern Railroads, and renders access to the academy easy from all parts of the country.

The above engraving represents the east side of the buildings of St. Mary's. On the west of the academy the grounds slope gradually to the clear, bright waters of the St. Joseph's. Here a fine bathinghouse is being erected for the use of the pupils. The grounds on this side are also enriched by two fine mineral springs, which were, doubtless, the cause of the selection for the first house upon this particular spot.

The main academy building has been lately much enlarged, and arrangements have been made to render it still more spacious.

At all times the sisters guard with maternal vigilance the pupils entrusted to their charge, regarding them as a precious deposit, for which they will be responsible to their parents and to God. For the preservation of order the pupils are divided into Senior and Junior circles, having separate playgrounds, classrooms, dormitories, etc.

The Institution possesses a fine Philosophical and Chemical Apparatus, Globes, and a Planetarium. All means are employed to excite laudable emulation in the minds of the pupils, and strict attention is paid to the religious instruction of Catholic children. Pupils of all denominations are received and there is no interference with their religious opinions, but discipline requires that all should conform with decorum to the public worship of the Catholic Faith.

In case of sickness, due notice is given to parents who, should they prefer leaving their children at the academy, may rest assured that they will receive excellent medical attendance and careful nursing. A skillful physician connected with the College of Notre Dame, visits the institution weekly, or oftener, if necessary. This gentleman, Thomas McKinnis, M.D., will also during the course of each session, deliver three lectures on Hygiene before the pupils of the academy.

The scholastic year is divided into two sessions of five months;

the first commencing on the 1st of September; the second, on the 1st of February.

A private examination is held at the end of each and the examination closes with a day of public exhibition, at which suitable rewards are bestowed on the most worthy. No pupil is received for a shorter period than five months, for which payment must be made in advance. All letters, written or received, are examined by the Directress.

Regulations For The Wardrobe

Every pupil must be furnished with six towels, six napkins, six pairs of cotton hose, the same number of woolen hose, six chemises, six pairs of drawers, four nightgowns, four caps, two pairs of gloves, three pairs of shoes, one pair of rubbers, two knives and forks, one large and one small silver spoon. The uniforms for winter consist of a dress and cape of mazarine blue merino, and bonnet trimmed with dark blue. The summer dress and cape must be of azure blue delaine or lawn, and bonnet trimmed with white. No particular dress is required for school days. The uniform is worn on Sundays and Wednesdays.

Pupils intending to remain for a short time at the academy are not obliged to take the uniform.

Pockets must be inserted in all dresses of pupils.

Terms

Entrance Fee	$ 5.00
Board and Tuition per Session	35.00
Washing and Bedding	7.50
Music and Piano per Session	10.00
Use of Piano	10.00
Guitar	10.00
Latin	10.00
French	6.00
German	6.00
Drawing and Painting: Water Colors	6.00
Drawing and Painting: Oil	10.00
Flowers	3.00
Fruits	3.00
Apparatus	2.50

At St. Mary's the Sisters of Holy Cross have also opened a school for deaf-mutes. Terms: $100.00 per annum. Visits are not permitted except on Wednesdays, excepting those from a distance. Letters should be addressed to Sister Directress of St. Mary's Academy, Bertrand, Michigan.[54]

Evidence in correspondence testifies to the implementation of the curriculum as stated in the 1851 prospectus. The archives abound with letters from fathers regarding the education of their daughters. Mr. William Egan wrote, September 17, 1852, from New Orleans to the directress of studies at Bertrand:

Bridget also mentioned that she would like to learn drawing. She may do so, sister, if you think proper. We put full confidence in your protection of our children. . . . Please to send me the bill as soon as ready and I will be punctual and please do not be too exact in giving the girls what will keep them warm and comfortable as they require more attention than if they had been raised in a cold climate.[55]
The studies my daughter will wish to pursue will be English and instrumental music.[56]

In a letter of February, 1853, concerning his daughter, Mr. F. J. Flanagan gave indirectly one of the attractions that the young school offered as far east as New York:

In her studys (sic) as named on the list, I desire no alteration except as regards the study of French, which I consider very necessary and useful, to be familiar and thoroughly acquainted with, in our connection with the world, independent of my liking the language itself for its beauty of softness. . . . I have always thought that the earlier the conveniences to learn to speak French, the better, provided the teacher is French by birth and education.[57]

Then in a human-interest postscript the proud father added:

Permit me to call to your attention that Catherine Jane is one of the best and fastest knitters of her age I ever saw. She has always knitted her own stockings and my socks. You might occasionally employ her in that way usefully.[58]

The earnest concern of fathers for the education of their daughters characterizes the correspondence of these first decades and reflects the responsibility of the man as head of the family. The absence of women's correspondence and the receipts for tuition signed by fathers and guardians silently testify to the facts of a history in which women did not enter into business transactions. In a file of letters from parents concerning their daughters, 1852 to 1856, the Kennedy correspondence is a gem of paternal solicitude. Dates on the letters and envelopes show that two months by pony express separated the father in El Dorado, California, from his motherless daughters at Saint Mary's, Bertrand, and his son at Notre Dame. Registers indicate that the girls transferred to the "new" Saint Mary's, Notre Dame, in the school year 1855–1856. A letter to Sarah is quoted here in its entirety. This and other letters contain postscripts from Sarah's suitor, Urban Monsimer, who found it difficult to get his love letters through the mail censorship. Monsimer offered to permit Sarah to continue her studious life if she married him (he was a school teacher by profession). He would pay for her music lessons even if she rejected him. Receipts of the following year attest that Sarah took piano lessons and Mr. Monsimer paid for them![59]

Miss Sarah M. Kennedy
St. Mary's Imm. Conc.
Notre Dame P.O.
St. Joseph's Co. Ind.

Kelsey, El Dorado Co. Cal.
March 2, 1856

My dear Daughter,

Your letter of the 10th of Jany, to which this is an answer, is more grammatical than those received previously; however, you are still deficient in punctuation and construction, I will merely say here that whenever you have written a sentence which is not perfectly plain to your understanding, you should examine every word of it and see whether it fulfils the functions which grammar gives it. If it be a verb, for instance, see whether you have given it a nominative and whether it is in the person and number required by said nominative etc. etc. calling to memory the rules which regulate verbs; if a noun, see in what case it is and if in the nominative, be sure you have given it verb, and if in the other cases, find the governing words; and so on with other words.

I received your Christmas letter and Ann's and answered both separately by the last mail, registering the answers on account of their importance. Have you received them? I sent $200 on the 20th of last December. Ask M. Angela whether they have been received. You have no doubt received my daguerreotype, which M. Monsimer forwarded and registered on the 20th of Jany, as well as a letter to you. By the mail of the 15th of the same month, I received your daguerreotypes.

I did not receive any letter from Ann by the last mail, nor have I yet received any from James. Give them both my love and tell James to write. I am very anxious to see some of his writing.

I am in pretty good health and so is your friend. The weather is warm and the sky is clear; we have had no rain yet, but we have ditch water.

Poor old Ned was very glad to hear from you. He is now a sober man, does a great deal for the Church and boards our Priest. Mr. Monsimer sees him every second Sunday, and then generally takes his dinner with him. Ned . . . sends you his compliments, as well as to Ann and James.

I now come to the main object of this letter, the proper plans to be adopted for the further development of your mental and corporal faculties, about which I have already several times written to you, without obtaining a satisfactory answer. In order to give you a proper understanding of the matter, I will divide the various branches which enter into the education of a young lady, whether they relate to the body or the mind, into three classes: the necessary, the useful, and the ornamental.

1st, by the necessary, I understand everything that a woman should know, no matter what her condition or prospects may be. These things are with respect to the mind: reading, writing, grammar, arithmetic, and in a word, a common education, to which a Catholic must add the rudiments of her religion; and with regard to the body: cooking, washing, ironing, and sewing, or housekeeping in general. These things you must not consider as a matter of choice, but of duty; nor do I wish you should apply yourself to the useful or ornamental, unless the Sisters conscientiously think you can do so without any detriment to necessary accomplishments. For the present I presume you are tolerably proficient in the necessary, and I will therefore pass to the useful branches.

2nd, by the useful, I understand professional labor of the head or hands such as teaching, dress-making, millinery, mantua making, or any other money making business. A woman may sometime or other be left to her own resources; and then, if she understands a useful trade, she can be independent, but otherwise, she will have to work for wages and perhaps suffer. In order to insure success in a trade or profession, a natural taste and aptitude are necessary. It is therefore a matter of choice for you. I am thankful for your dutiful affection which refers the choice to me, but this is not what I want. Tell me what trade, if any, you would rather learn. If, instead of a trade, you should prefer studying so as to enable you to teach, don't be afraid to tell me, so I will do my best for you. But as the latter choice would require a great outlay of money, if you make it, I will request you to send me the separate opinions of two or three of your teachers, concerning the probability of your ever being able to manage a school; for many learned persons cannot teach.

3rd, by the ornamental, I understand with respect to the body, all sorts of fancy work; and with respect to the mind the languages, living and dead, except the maternal tongue; drawing, painting, music, etc. I have a great objection to all these accomplishments, which is, that many young ladies apply themselves to these whilst they neglect the useful and even the necessary things. After leaving school, many think that their parents or husbands

should buy them pianos and other costly things, when perhaps they cannot afford it. I think, however, that you would not be unreasonable. I know that you are anxious to learn music and I have no objection to it, for you may make money hereafter by teaching the Piano, and I trust the elect of your heart will be able to buy you one. I cannot pay for your music, but you can manage that—I will gladly therefore allow you to learn it, provided that Mother Angela incloses a note saying that in two years you could learn enough to tune the instrument and perfect yourself (without danger of any error) after leaving school, and showing also that you could learn it without material detriment to the necessary or useful branches. Mr. Monsimer thinks it would take a quarter of an hour for the lesson and the practice might take place during recreation.

You seem anxious to return to me at the end of your two years in order to help me. Your affection touches me. But I have no home and an unmarried, motherless young lady would be too much exposed here. Unless therefore you can obviate this difficulty, I may not be able to see you for a long time, if ever, for with the burden of the schooling of three children, it may take me ten years to make a raise, and I therefore, will have to find a safe place for you, at the end of your two years, until you become of age, or get married, or until I make a pile. Think of all this, my dear Daughter, and write to me all that you would like to do about it, as well as the useful and ornamental branches above explained. Be not afraid to displease me.—If your choice is independent, I know that you will cheerfully abide by my decision,—Write without delay.

One thing more, My Dear Daughter, I have an especial confidence in the Blessed Virgin and I request you to pray devoutly to her that she may enlighten you and enable you to give a clear answer after making a good choice.

My respects to your teachers and to your Superior or President, Mother Angela; and rest assured of my paternal love,

Henry Kennedy[60]

My Dear Sarah,

You are aware that I esteem you highly and love you affection-
ately—Should your feelings toward me be similar and should you
accept my heart and hand which I now offer you we could very
well obviate all the difficulties your father speaks of. You and I
would give him a home here where Ann could also come and
stay with all safety after her schooling. I would gladly spend
to further your education and thus help your father, even if you
chose to learn a trade. But if you chose a studious life, then (I)
would let you know what branches to study during your two
years, as there are many things that I could teach you myself after
our marriage and your return here. I would not have made this
premature proposal, had not your present circumstances convinced me of its propriety. For you see, if we fully understand
each other at once, we can make our plans so as to more highly
adorn your mind and heart and thus to enhance your own happiness, your father's, and mine also, if I prove acceptable. If you
reject me, I will still pay for your music as I promised, but if you
accept me, I will do everything in my power for you and strain
every nerve for your happiness—Answer this, Dearest; pray to our
good Mother, the Blessed Virgin, for me and for yourself; and
meanwhile rest assured of my best and sincerest love.

Urban J. B. V. Monsimer[01]

Mr. Kennedy's letters, too, tell us something about the
manner in which parents were informed of their daughters'
progress at Bertrand. In a letter, September 8, 1855, Mr.
Kennedy made a genial recommendation to Mother M.
Angela, then directress of studies.

The school could improve upon its method of stating class standing. Sarah obtained seventh place in history, geography, and
grammar. This would be a tolerably fair place in a class of twelve
or fifteen but poor in a class of eight or ten. Would it not be
better if the number of pupils in the class be stated so that a

correct opinion of the relative strength and ability of my daughters may be ascertained.[62]

The albatross of class rank had not as yet been hung around the neck of the American system of rating!

From the earliest days at Bertrand art and music held an important place in the curriculum. The French who came to this country were from the beginning impressed with the American love for music. In the archives of the University of Notre Dame there is a letter to Father Moreau from Father François Cointet at Notre Dame in which he points up his observation of this American penchant:

I understand why Father Sorin asked with such entreaty for a musician. In America one hears everywhere of nothing but music. Whoever has ever so little a fortune cannot do without a piano or some other instrument. The Protestant churches as well as the Catholic ones almost all have organs. . . .[63]

To interpret properly the magnitude of the undertaking and the courage of the first personnel, it is necessary to understand how unformed the Congregation of the Sisters of the Holy Cross was at this time. Four French women became the first Sisters of the Holy Cross in 1841 in LeMans, France. They ranged in age from 17 to 43. None of these had intended to join a teaching community, nor did they teach in later years. Unsettled conditions in the French government, the urgent demands of bishops in America for missionaries—these were contributing causes why all four were in America by 1843. Two other French women received the religious habit in France, joining those in America in 1844. This marked the end of any band which was completely French in origin. The first group of three women to receive the religious habit in the United States had all been born in Ireland, where they received their education. The first American to join the community received the habit in LeMans, France, in

1844 but did not persevere.[64] Such factors are not likely substance for the faculty of the embryonic Saint Mary's Academy which in twenty years would be acclaimed the mecca of education in the young West.[65] The state of Michigan granted a "liberal (arts) charter" in 1850 to Saint Mary's Academy, Bertrand.[66] One might well ask what qualifications the early faculty of the academy had to meet the standards required by such a charter.

The first four Sisters of the Holy Cross who came to Notre Dame in 1843 were missionaries at heart. Soon it was clear that the mandate to "teach all nations" must include profane as well as sacred knowledge. The school at Bertrand opened in 1844 with two lay teachers, Miss Catherine Shea, a governess from Ireland,[67] and Miss Ann Molloy,[68] later Sister M. Francis. Both experienced, they taught secular subjects, especially music, to the older students.[69] The sisters, undaunted by a language barrier, spoke the universal language of love as they cared for every physical need of the students. They instructed their charges in the culinary and practical arts required of a "lady" of the times. Their inservice training in the first year included classes in English, scripture, and other subjects basic in the curriculum of the common schools of early nineteenth century America. From the beginning they profited by proximity to Notre Dame.

The priests and other professors (Father Sorin (sic), F. Cointet, Father Gouesse, T. Marivault, Professor D. O'Leary, and St. Michael E. E. Shaw) were generous about coming to Bertrand to instruct the sisters in scripture and secular studies.[70]

Father Badin preached both at Notre Dame and at Bertrand; he also taught the Catholic students catechism twice a week.[71]

Father F. Cointet, scholar and graduate of the College of Chateau Gontier near LeMans, France, regularly visited and instructed the sisters at Bertrand. Master of five languages,

Father Cointet spoke impeccable English.[72] Such contacts as these were a part of the training of the first teachers in a region where there was not as yet any public school.[73]

The training for teaching at this time was universally one of apprenticeship. The young sister learned theory and practice simultaneously under the direction of an older member of the congregation.

When Bertrand opened its doors to boarders and set up an academy curriculum, Father Moreau sent from Canada a sister experienced in establishing this type of school.[74] Educated in France in a classical course, Mother Marie du Sauveur spoke English fluently.[75] This fluency she had achieved in the classes conducted at Saint Laurent by Soeur Marie du Coeur-de-Jésus, "qui avait étudié l'anglais aux Etats-Unis," and Mlle. Fanny Guygins, "qui dirigèrent les classes d'anglais trois fois la semaine."[76] She gave the sisters training in teaching scripture and art, helped them with their classwork, and insisted on their educational advancement.

The archives contain a list of assignments for the year 1850. Of the fifty members then in the Congregation of the Sisters of the Holy Cross, fourteen are listed as teachers, primarily teachers of art, music, and French. One sister's work for the year 1850 was uniquely spelled out: "Maîtresse d'arithmétique et de francais, surveillant pendant les récréations à Bertrand."[77] The same listing shows three members assigned to study, one "étudiant le reste du temps," the counterpart of the contemporary "part-time study."[78] The sisters had come from France, Ireland, Germany, Canada, and the United States. They included two widows and six former "maîtresses d'école."[79] Three teachers were assigned to study music and art for one year at Saint Mary's College, Louisville, Kentucky;[80] the artist went abroad for advanced study two years later.[81] Those destined to teach lived at the University of Notre Dame, where they had the opportunity for secular studies. Professors at the college gave lectures in the neighboring towns and served the sisters as chaplains and as teachers at Bertrand.

Thus with an "idea of a university," with a philosophy of education, a psychology, and an axiology, Father Moreau planned his first institutions of learning in France, in Canada, and in America. The missionaries who founded Notre Dame were priests educated in the tradition of this founder; they were chaplains to the sisters at Bertrand; they were teachers at the first Saint Mary's Academy.

Lay teachers have occupied a prominent place in the academic life of the Saint Mary's faculty from 1844 to the present day. In the mid-nineteenth century young widows who had had means and genteel background frequently turned to teaching as a means of livelihood. They usually were well educated in music or art, the hallmark of a young lady's education. Notre Dame had opened in 1854 Saint Edward's Hall, a separate department for boys under thirteen years of age. A similar department for young girls made up the minim (prep) department of Saint Mary's Academy.[82] These two schools were an attraction for young mothers eager to give their children educational opportunities comparable to their own. These young women taught with the sisters on the first Bertrand faculty. The majority of sisters continued to perform the auxiliary services so important in boarding schools, to perform those homely comforts which endeared them to the student body. There remain today alumi and alumnae from both sides of the Dixie Highway who cherish the memory of sisters who did not teach them formally, but whose contacts, whose example, and whose motherly care made life at Notre Dame and Saint Mary's warm and homely.

From 1854 to 1863 a group of distinguished lay teachers, six in number, taught in the minim department at Notre Dame, two of these teachers later becoming sisters of the

Holy Cross. Not until 1863 did the sisters under Mother M. Angela replace the secular faculty at Notre Dame.[83]

Similar conditions existed at Bertrand, where widows taught while their children attended Saint Mary's and Notre Dame. Some of the finest teachers of the young faculty joined the congregation. While sending her son to Saint Edward's, Mrs. E. M. Guthrie, graduate of St. Lewis Seminary, Lexington, Massachusetts, taught literature and rhetoric at Saint Mary's until 1870, when she became Sister M. Ignatia. It is difficult to establish the date when Mrs. Guthrie came to Saint Mary's Academy; however, an 1853 schedule of classes lists her as teacher of rhetoric, sixth period. Ledger A of accounts, 1852, lists in the expenditure column: "Birdseed, 18¢, Mrs. Guthrie."[84] She will play a significant role in the "era of the academies."[85]

Mrs. Harriet Redman Lilly entered the Congregation of the Sisters of the Holy Cross at Bertrand, where she began a long career of forty-seven years as a distinguished teacher of music. Mrs. Lilly, a convert from Anglicanism, had been educated in England. Her family included Dr. S. Arnold, composer of Anglican church music; Dr. M. Arnold, organist at Tetworth; another, organist in Chichester Cathedral. Her uncle, Dr. George Arnold, a graduate of Oxford and for many years organist at the Cathedral of Winchester, taught Mrs. Lilly. As Sister Mary Elizabeth, she developed at Bertrand a department of music which, within a decade, was to bring internationl recognition to the music conservatory of Saint Mary's Academy, Notre Dame.[86] Mrs. Harriet Arnold Redman, Mrs. Lilly's mother, also came to Bertrand as teacher and prefect. The family was a musical acquisition. They moved in, Chickering piano, violin, harp, and all. Mrs. Redman cared for Mrs. Lilly's two children, Edward and Edith, both of whom attended the academies at Notre Dame and at Bertrand. Gifted musicians, taught by their mother and relatives, they both joined the Congregation of Holy Cross. Father Edward Lilly, C.S.C., was an accomplished violinist; Sister M. Cecilia (Edith Lilly) taught piano, violin, harp, and organ for many years when her mother was head of the department of music at Saint Mary's in the decades of 1870 and 1880. With a prophetic sense of destiny, Mother Elizabeth (title given to administrators at that time) wrote a history of the Lilly family for her daughter, Sister M. Cecilia. She added a postscript in her Spencerian hand, commenting on the family tree: "This little record may be useful. *Keep it.*"[87]

Neal Gillespie, first graduate from the University of Notre Dame, 1849, became the first American-born Holy Cross priest. His sister, Eliza Gillespie, entered the Sisters of the Holy Cross in 1853. She was superior and directress of Saint Mary's Academy, Bertrand, from February, 1854, until its transfer in August, 1855, to Saint Mary's, Notre Dame. At this time, Mr. and Mrs. William Phelan also moved to Saint Mary's in 1855 to aid their children in the pioneer educational institutions to which they both belonged. This marked a turning point in the fortunes of the young academy, which had struggled for ten years and achieved standards incredible for the time and the region of the country. Already its enrollment included students from coast to coast, from California to Texas to Massachusetts. It was to presage the international character of the student body of Saint Mary's College today.

While a strong professional group of lay teachers was allying itself with the pioneer undertakings of the sisters, recruits from Ireland, "well-educated young women,"[88] joined the congregation. The community chronicles for 1854 include this commentary: "Between 1852–54, a number of valuable subjects joined the community."[89] Then follows a list of fifteen sisters, many of whom were administrators and builders of the congregation.[90]

Reference has been made to the oral examinations which were given at the end of each session, presided over by the priests and lay professors of Notre Dame. Father Moreau had recommended the introduction of this grading evaluation, a practice solidly entrenched in the French educational system of the early nineteenth century and one that persists to this very day. Of all the European school systems, perhaps none more than the French emphasizes oral and written examinations as the criteria of determining awards and diplomas.

Father Sorin, too, attached great importance to oral examinations. In his interest in the scholastic progress of the school he never missed an occasion to be one of the examiners if he was in the United States at the time. There are many sisters, former graduates from Saint Mary's Academy or College, who remember the grueling experience of the semester orals.

Sister M. Eleanor, author of *On the King's Highway*, a history of the Congregation of the Sisters of the Holy Cross, was herself a graduate of Saint Mary's College. She knew the ordeal first hand. In her inimitable storytelling style, Sister recounts the first record (1854) of public student examinations by the "college men" from Notre Dame:

The prelude to the commencement, famous for those days, was the beginning of a custom continued almost to the present, . . . the graduates' final examinations conducted orally by the priests and other professors from Notre Dame. Some of us who went helplessly . . . as lambs to this intellectual slaughter in our own school days can well enter into the feelings of the St. Mary's girls of Bertrand in that momentous June when the innocent joy of an evening's recreation in the garden with Father Sorin was suddenly blasted as effectually as if by an exploding bomb in their midst. . . . On the morrow he would come with some of his best professors to examine the graduates orally.

In spite of his assurance that his professors were "perfect gentle-

men," . . . it was a subdued and longfaced crowd of girls that
filed into the study for night prayer and the succeeding study
hour. The girls were not the only ones shocked that night. The
presiding sister watched with curiosity and then with growing
alarm, brown and blond and red heads bent industriously over
desks. The prefect of discipline got a shock when the sister at the
end of the hour had no reports to give for lack of application or
other misdemeanor. Next day, however, the miracle was explained, and these sisters, who had been fearing an epidemic of
serious sickness, breathed normally once more and again put on
their disciplinary manners.

At recess on that infamous Monday morning, some one espied
the carriage from Notre Dame wheel into the avenue. By some
occult means of news-spreading, the school was in a ladylike
panic before the occupants of the carriage alighted, a panic which
ended respectably in hands folded tight behind backs planted
stiffly against the kindly support of desks. Even in the room of
the "mutes," some one had scrawled across the blackboard the
cruel words, "College men here."

The modern girl who thinks that her grandmother, away back
in the dark days before equal suffrage and higher education for
women, knew only household accomplishments and music and
knitting, may be somewhat surprised to read the following
account of one of the examinations held on that day. The learned
mathematician, Professor Denis O'Leary, according to Mother
J. Elizabeth

gave his own problems to be worked out by each girl in turn.
The girls, getting interested in the work, soon forgot their
fright; and for two hours, professor and pupils were so fasci-
nated by their labors in this essential study that they all failed
to remember the other classes that were to be examined, until
the warning Angelus bell reminded them that time really has
wings.

Between the ordeals intervened a turkey dinner, at which
Professor O'Leary did some mathematical carving. In history
and in the other subjects the girls covered themselves with glory

to such an extent that "a spectator might not have been able to decide which showed the most knowledge, professors or pupils." Some of us hope the historian of our own days may be able to say as much; but certain memories are stirring uncomfortably, as we type these words, of later examinations when we at least had no question in our minds as to which group had the major share of information.[91]

To give an adequate financial appraisal of early Bertrand, the value of property, the receipts and expenditures, is impossible. Until 1869 the administration was an integral part of the Congregation of Holy Cross: priests, brothers, and sisters. The early school building of Bertrand, for example, had been purchased through the agency of Joseph Bertrand. All the income from boarders at Saint Mary's, Bertrand, was forwarded to Notre Dame. In return for receipts they financed all expenditures. All debt was a corporate community debt. As we previously mentioned, the Propagation of the Faith gave the young community several sums of money for maintenance. The mother house in LeMans, too, lent funds at a low rate of interest to the American mission. This much is certain: the lack of funds threatened the existence of the congregation for the first twenty years. Circular letters from Father Moreau, correspondence of Father Sorin, and early account books of the sisters themselves are replete with references to the precarious fiscal state of the institutions. The number of schools opened and closed in a given decade are indicated in the list of Schools and Orphanages of the Sisters of the Holy Cross, Appendix, page 203. In most instances between 1844 and 1855 the reason for closure was indebtedness.

In a letter to a priest in Bourbonnais, Illinois, Father Sorin explains his reluctance at that time (1859) to open any more parochial schools, giving as his reason the sad commentary of those institutions which were unable to support teachers in their school and hence were forced to close.[92] Academies operated by the sisters fared better. Private lessons in music and in art frequently were the greatest source of income. This was not peculiar to the Sisters of the Holy Cross. In the southernmost portion of Indiana the Sisters of Providence were facing similar problems. Their chronicles, too, emphasize the importance of the fine arts in the financial support of the "female seminaries" in Indiana.[93]

The diary of Mother Mary Compassion, who had come to Bertrand in 1845, tells of the dire poverty of the sisters. It is in her notes that many human interest stories of community history are found. When two sisters walked six miles to Notre Dame to get bread, their supply exhausted, Mother Compassion makes the following comment, "The bread would have made an anchorite envious."[94] She adds that Father Cointet then gave the sisters five dollars to take care of any emergency in the future.[95]

Pére Victor Drouelle made the regular canonical visit to Bertrand in 1848. The following is part of his official report:

This establishment was placed on a ground of eighty acres, eight of which only are clearing. All the buildings are of wood, poorly built, hot and stuffy in summer and cold as ice in winter, if they do not keep the stove perpetually burning in all the rooms. The poor sisters are obliged to draw water from the river at a great risk of breaking arms and legs during winter, especially because the river bank or the approach is so steep, covered with ice and snow. . . . Vocations here, as with the brothers, are generally Irish and present the same characters and dispositions. The society of the sisters is called to give the same service and more than that of the brothers. I do not doubt that they will prosper, but the progress will be slow and difficult. It is necessary to put the sisters in a condition to build a suitable house and secure for them necessary furnishings, which would require an expense of twenty thousand francs. That is to say, many more years of sufferings for them. However, they are thrifty and it is true to state that they are dressed in rags and tatters. All of the appointments and provisions are furnished by (Notre Dame) du Lac which is a distance of five miles from Bertrand. The sisters have a horse and carriage for this purpose. In spite of their extreme poverty, they find a way to teach, dress and instruct a dozen unfortunate orphans. . . . In order to put this house in a condition of earning money and of doing well, the father superior has had come, in return for a salary which is not yet agreed upon, a very capable English teacher, so that the sisters with this help, can open a boarding school for young girls, the prospectus of which I send you. What will be the result of this trial? No one knows as yet, but I can say I find it opportune. . . .

Bertrand has no material administration. All is done at du Lac. The sisters work for the university when they have fulfilled the duties of their own house.[96]

The poverty of the sisters was a poverty shared by priests and brothers alike. In a letter to Father Chappé, Father Sorin tells of a brother whose foot was frozen. He used the only cash he had on hand, fifty cents, to get him to South Bend for medical aid. He then reiterated his plea for more financial help from France and for a supply of winter clothing.[97]

Archives of St. Mary's list the first property purchase and its cost. Financial ledgers show individual accounts of students, receipts, and expenditures.[98] Tuition for boarders in 1855 was $42.50 per session, i.e., $85 a year.[99] This included board and room, tuition, laundry, and linens. There were enrolled at this time 103 students, sixty of them resident.[100] As mentioned previously, the records show that much of the tuition was paid in the form of barter for necessities, mortgages on property, and liens on life insurance policies. The Coquillard[101] and Byerley[102] families of South Bend were great benefactors. Joseph Bertrand, wealthy in his own right and doubly so through his wife, who inherited vast acres of land at the death of Chief Topenebee,[103] had befriended the Bertrand establishment from the beginning.

There are annual reports of finances of the Sisters of the Holy Cross beginning with 1869, when the community was separated in temporalities from Notre Dame on the recommendation of Rome. Prorated costs of teacher education are available only from 1931, when for administrative purposes the community was divided into provinces. Accrual accounting today has replaced the cash in, cash out, French peasant bookkeeping system of the past and has made accurate cost studies possible.

References

[1] Vincennes Papers (Moreau to Hailandière). February 3, 1845. A copy of minutes drawn up by Rev. Basil Anthony Moreau and his council. They reveal that in a visit to LeMans, France, 1842, Bishop Hailandière signed a contract with Father Moreau for priests, brothers, and sisters of Holy Cross in the Vincennes diocese. According to Article No. 2 of the contract, the members of the congregation were to obey the superior general at the mother house (LeMans), but regard Bishop Hailandière as their local superior. Bishop Hailandière resigned in 1847; he was succeeded by Rt. Rev. Jean Etienne Bazin (1847) and Rt. Rev. Maurice de St. Palais (1848–57). Archives, University of Notre Dame. Hereafter cited as AUND.

[2] Leon M. Gordon, "The Influence of River Transportation," *Indiana Magazine of History,* XLVI:3, (1950), 284–289.

[3] Rt. Rev. H. J. Alerding, *The Diocese of Fort Wayne: a Book of Historical Reference, 1669–1907* (Fort Wayne, Indiana, 1907), p. 70.

[4] There are varied spellings of "Potawatomi." Even the official treaties in the National Archives have inconsistencies. In the 1821 Treaty with the Ottawas, etc., the spelling is Pottawatamie; in 1826, Potawatomies; in 1832, "Treaty with Potawatomi"; in public law 87–205, September 6, 1961, "A judgment in favor of the Potawatomi Nation of Indiana." For consistency the most common spelling "Potawatomi," singular, and "Potawatomies," plural, will be used in this text.

[5] G-II (A chronicle of community history written at Saint Mary's Convent, Notre Dame, Indiana, 1834–1879), p. 61. Archives, General House, Saint Mary's Convent, Notre Dame, Indiana. Hereafter cited as AGH.

[6] Rev. Gabriel Richard sent Rev. John Frederick Rezé to the Pokagon Indians. He remained during the month of July, 1830. He was replaced the same year by Rev. Stephen Theodore Badin. The first thirty entries

of Father Badin's Baptismal Register were signed by Father Rezé.

[7] Alerding, op. cit., p. 72.

[8] Ralph Ballard, Map of Indian Trails (Niles, Michigan, 1939) Reprints of originals.

[9] G-II, 26, AGH.

[10] Alfred Mathews, History of Cass County, Michigan (Chicago, 1882), p. 58.

[11] That Madeline Bertrand was a full-blooded Potawatomi, the daughter of Chief Topenebee, is doubtful. More recently discovered evidence points that Joseph Bertrand's mother was an Indian (marriage certificate from Cour Superieure, Montreal Superior Court). His second wife was Magdalen Bourassa. Her brother married Marguerite Bertrand. Their son, Leon Bourassa, sold property to Father Edward Sorin according to the Abstract of Title to the Bertrand property, where the first Saint Mary's Academy was established. In Father T. Badin's record of baptisms (1843) there is the account of the conditional baptism of Luc (Leon) Bertrand, age 22, son of Magdelen and Joseph Bertrand.

[12] "Bertrand," Files of Fort Saint Joseph Museum, Niles, Michigan, p. 2.

[13] Matthews, op. cit.

[14] Edward B. Cowles, comp. Berrien County Directory and History (Niles, Michigan, 1871), p. 29.

[15] Community Chronicles claim that Joseph Bertrand gave the sisters their first home, but the deed of the property shows that Father Sorin purchased it for three hundred dollars from Leon Bertrand in 1845.

[16] Register Sepultura of the Potawatomi Mission, Saint Mary's, Kansas (signed Augustine C. Ward, S.J., archivist).

[17] Cowles, op. cit.

[18] G-II, 28, AGH.

[19] G-I (A chronicle of community history written at Holy Cross Convent, Notre Dame, Indiana, 1841-1908), p. 73, AGH.

[20] G-I, 29, AGH.

[21] G-II, 9, AGH.

[22] G-I, 13, AGH.

[23] G-I, 30, AGH.

[24] G-I, 29, AGH.

[25] Sister M. Emerentiana (Nowland), C.S.C., Notes on Deaf Mutes, pp. 18-21, AGH.

[26] Chaney to Mother M. Angela, April 24, 1864, AGH.

[27] G-I, 196, AGH.

[28] Sorin to Moreau, 1847, AUND.

[29] G-II, 31, AGH.

[30] Patrick Farrelly to Mother M. Angela, 1854, AGH.

[31] Robert Harves to Mother M. Angela, 1856, AGH.

[32] Saint Mary's Academy Register, 1854, n.p., AGH.

[33] Patrick Donahoe to Sorin, 1856, AGH.
[34] O'Reilly to Sorin, 1854, AGH.
[35] Records of Bertrand Administration, Vol. V: Contracts, 1, AGH.
[36] Ibid.
[37] Ada Woods to Mother M. Angela, 1879, AGH.
[38] G-II, 102, AGH.
[39] Brother Laurence to Sister M. Columba, 1858, AGH.
[40] Contract made by Louppe with Sisters of the Holy Cross, 1851, AGH.
[41] Contract made by Foy with Sister M. Charles, 1866, AGH.
[42] G-I, 60, AGH.
[43] Willard S. Elsbree, The American Teacher (New York, 1939), p. 219.
[44] G-II, 119, AGH.
[45] L'Abbe Charles Moreau, Le très réverend Père Basile-Antoine Moreau, prêtre du Mans, et ses oeuvres (Paris, 1900), I, 277.
[46] Elsbree, op. cit., pp. 220–221.
[47] Thomas Woody, A History of Women's Education in the United States (New York, 1929) I, 563–565.
[48] Ibid.
[49] Rev. David H. Verhalen, "Father Moreau's 'Christian Pedagogy,'" Bulletin of the Educational Conference of the Priests of Holy Cross, XXX (December, 1962), 60.
[50] The original copy of this bill is found in the Archives of the General House, Saint Mary's Convent, Notre Dame, Indiana.
[51] Woody, op. cit., pp. 552–562.
[52] Rare Book Room, ASMC.
[53] A Brief History of the University of Notre Dame du Lac, Indiana: 1842–92 (Chicago, 1895), p. 79.
[54] G-II, 68, AGH.
[55] William Egan to Directress of Studies, 1852, AGH.
[56] Ibid.
[57] F. J. Flanagan to Directress of Studies, 1852, AGH.
[58] Ibid.
[59] Kennedy File, 1852–1856, AGH.
[60] Ibid.
[61] Ibid. The letter above is Mr. Monsimer's proposal to Sarah. It was probably dictated to her father, because, although signed by Mr. Monsimer, it is in Mr. Kennedy's hand.
[62] Ibid.
[63] François Cointet to Moreau, 1848, AUND.
[64] Reception Register, I, 1841–1844, AGH.
[65] Chicago Sun, June, 1875, G-I, AGH.
[66] An act to incorporate St. Mary's Academy, at the village of Bertrand in Berrien County, No. 314, April 2, 1850, AGH.
[67] G-II, 196, AGH.

[68] Community Register, I, 3, AGH.
[69] Records of Bertrand Administration, Vol. III: Visits, 60, AGH.
[70] Sister M. Emerentiana, C.S.C., "The Origin of the Congregation of the Holy Cross," p. 51, AGH.
[71] G-II, 59, AGH.
[72] *The Life of the Rev. F. Cointet: Priest and Missionary of the Congregation of Holy Cross* (Cincinnati, 1855), p. 52.
[73] Alerding, *op. cit.*, p. 492.
[74] *Annales de la Congrégation des Soeurs de Sainte-Croix et des Sept-Douleurs* (Saint-Laurent, P.Q., 1930), I, xxix.
[75] G-II, 58, AGH.
[76] *Annales de la Congrégation, op. cit.*, I, 97.
[77] Victor Drouelle to Sorin, 1850, AGH.
[78] *Ibid.*
[79] Community Register, I, 1–5, AGH.
[80] G-I, 16, AGH.
[81] G-II, 118, AGH.
[82] G-I, 26, AGH.
[83] Microfilm, Reels 11, 13, AGH.
[84] Ledger A, 1849–1864, AGH.
[85] Beginning with 1855, commencement programs included historical plays. Sister M. Ignatia (Guthrie), C.S.C., was the author of them. For the centenary of the founding of the Congregation of the Sisters of the Holy Cross, 1941, the play "Anima" was revised and presented by Sister M. Francesca (McDougal), at LeMans Hall, St. Mary's College. AGH.
[86] Ella Ewing Brown, "Memoirs of Sister M. Elizabeth Lilly," AGH.
[87] *Ibid.* (Underlining in the original.)
[88] Records of Bertrand Administration, Vol. III: Visits, 2, AGH.
[89] G-I, 23, AGH.
[90] Sisters M. *Euphrasia (Mahoney); Augustine (Murphy); *Euphrosine (Pepin); *Arsene (Bourdais); *Patrick (Richards); Edward (O'Neill); *Bertha (McDermott); *DeSales (O'Neil); Felicitas (Molloy); *Euphemia (McConvery); *Ambrose (Corby); *Assisum (Flynn); *Emily (Rivard); and *Angela (Gillespie). An asterisk (*) indicates that the sister held an administrative position in the community.
[91] Sister M. Eleanor (Brosnahan), C.S.C., *On the King's Highway* (New York, 1931), pp. 197–199.
[92] Sorin to Pastor of St. Philomena's Parish, Bourbonnais, Illinois, 1859, AGH.
[93] Sister Mary Borromeo (Brown), *History of the Sisters of Providence of Saint Mary-of-the-Woods* (New York, 1949), I, 531.
[94] Mother M. Compassion (Gleason), C.S.C., Diary: May 6, 1845–March 13, 1913, I, n.p.

[95] *Ibid.*
[96] Records of Bertrand Administration, Vol. III: Visits, 2, AGH.
[97] Sorin to Chappe, 1844, AUND.
[98] Ledger A, ASMC.
[99] *Ibid.* See Appendix, p. 224.
[100] *Ibid.*
[101] Alexis Coquillard to Sister M. Columba, 1858, AGH.
[102] Records of Bertrand Administration, Vol. VI: Benefactors, 2, AGH.
[103] Wilbur M. Cunningham, *The Land of Four Flags* (Grand Rapids, Michigan, 1961), p. 116.

CHAPTER II

HOLY CROSS
EDUCATION

To UNDERSTAND in part the character, the growth, and the
spirit of the educational system of the Congregation of
the Sisters of the Holy Cross we turn to the philosophy, principles of pedagogy, and curriculum of Basil Anthony Moreau,
its founder and an educator and administrator of vision, with
a modernity enlightening to the contemporary teacher. These
are best reflected in his *La Pédagogie,* Catta's *Life,* circular
letters, and the textbooks of Father Moreau.

In the prospectus which he drew up for the school in Le-
Mans, July 6, 1836, Father Moreau wrote:

You may inform those parents who wish to send their children
away to school at LeMans that I intend to establish a boarding
school at Sainte-Croix, LeMans, in which French, Greek, and
Latin will be taught. . . .[1]

We hope to join, in a short time, a secondary school to this
primary boarding school, so that those who finish in our elementary classes may find in our secondary boarding school the
means of completing their education. But, to attain this end,
we must first form professors qualified to satisfy the exactions of
the law; and we would have these in such numbers that each

one would have to teach but a single branch. For this purpose we have sent some young ecclesiastics to Paris to follow the higher courses. These will soon be ready to teach the languages, mathematics, and the natural sciences.[2]

Gary MacEoin says of this move:

Sending these students to the Sorbonne ranged Father Moreau publicly on the "progressive" side in a bitterly controversial issue. For he was proclaiming that Catholic education must incorporate the best elements of the secular system, that the schools he hoped to establish could attract top students only if the teachers were fully qualified.[3]

At a time in the history of France when the Jesuits were deprived of their teaching rights, Father Moreau turned to the nascent community of Brothers of Holy Cross to staff Catholic schools. If France was to survive the debacle of the French Revolution, Christian education for its youth would be needed. In the early days of the Congregation of Holy Cross the political situation in France was unstable and shifting. Early schools in Canada and the United States were opened in periods when suppression in France prevented priests, brothers, and sisters from entering into the teaching phase of the apostolate. These historical reasons account for Father Moreau's great concern for education evidenced in the circular letters to the community at large. In the preface to *The Brothers of Holy Cross* Rev. James J. Trahey clarifies the erratic history of religious educators in France.

One hundred years have come and gone since France, June 22, 1804, modified the law of August 18, 1792, by which she suppressed all the religious orders within her territory. The imperial edict of 1804 provided that a religious community might, on examination and approval of its statutes, be legally organized. A few years later the French government became friendly to the religious orders, and the result of this friendship we (Congregation of Holy Cross) all know. . . .

The preceding remarks will find their appropriateness in the fact that the religious congregation, the history of one division of which we are about to trace, had its origin in France, was legally authorized by a decree of Louis XVIII, June 23, 1823; and was expelled from France by the "Law of Associations" passed in 1901.[4]

The situation was made more complex because the enforcement of the education laws vacillated with the change of politics in a strong centralized department of education. One of the battles of the Church in France during the last century was the effort of Catholics to be granted the authority to establish and to maintain their own schools.

The political situation which existed was anything but stable and constantly shifted from one position to another with regard to the Catholic pressures for their rights, and liberties. Depending upon which group was in power, the fortunes of Catholics either progressed or floundered. . . . Father Moreau plunged his young society immediately into the battle, notwithstanding the almost insurmountable obstacles. . . .[5]

By the edict of 1804 the French Ministry of Education permitted religious educators to teach in secondary schools. In a circular letter to his sons and daughters in Holy Cross (April 15, 1849) Father Moreau asked that all members join in thanksgiving for another privilege.

M. de Falloux, a man whom the religious world has learned to respect and admire and who ranks among the most generous defenders of true liberty and sane doctrine, has been made Head of Public Instruction in France. . . . Upon the recommendation of the Deputy of Le Sarthe. . . . he granted me, with a kindness I shall never forget, that complete teaching liberty which we had coveted so long. . . .[6]

In 1849 Sainte-Croix was granted full teaching rights, which meant that the young men there could finish their studies in rhetoric and philosophy; that is, until they were nineteen or twenty. Thus, Father Moreau's school at the mother house was authorized as a full-fledged college a year before the French government gave the first small concession to private schools in general.[7] The victory meant that in eleven years, the school at LeMans progressed from a primary school (1838) for boys to the age of fourteen or fifteen, to a secondary school (1839) for students to the age of sixteen or seventeen. Finally in 1849 Sainte-Croix emerged as a college in the best of French tradition.

Even though we base our philosophy course on the data of faith, no one need fear that we shall confine our teaching within narrow and unscientific boundaries. No; we wish to accept science without prejudice, and in a manner adapted to the needs of our times. We do not want our students to be ignorant of anything they should know. . . . We shall never forget that virtue, as Bacon puts it, is the spice that preserves science.[8]

Mindful that an ambitious curriculum could not be implemented without a superior faculty, Father Moreau continues:

We cannot fail to recognize the special protection of His Providence in the fact that we now have all the teachers necessary for our project and that He has crowned with success all the candidates whom we presented for the various examinations since receiving full teaching rights. Out of eight candidates who took the examination for teachers, six passed with very high grades. Four professors of our college went to Paris and returned with their baccalaureate diplomas. . . . The District Committee of Laval which, since 1830 has obstinately refused to accept our Brothers as public school teachers, unanimously decided, in extraordinary sessions on May 17, to admit them for the future, provided they comply with the ordinary legal requirements.[9]

Father Moreau issued his first circular letter to the brothers of Notre Dame de Sainte-Croix, LeMans, November 8, 1835.

It contained exhortations concerning the opening of boarding schools. There were directives about relations with civil authorities, parents, and the students themselves. This was but the first in a series of letters (188) directed to the priests, brothers, and sisters. The sisters were included for the first time in a January, 1845, letter.[10]

(La) Pédagogie Chrétienne à l'usage des Joséphites de la Congrégation de Sainte-Croix[11] and *Nouveau livre de lectures*[12] contain Father Moreau's principles of education and his methodology. If one does not read the letters and works of Father Moreau in their entirety, if one does not interpret them in the context of the French struggle of the times, one may well err in judging his primary objectives of education. True, in his preface to *La Pédagogie*, Father Moreau does state:

I had in mind in writing it *(La Pédagogie)* the formation of the will and the development of religious perspectives in the student . . . being persuaded that society has more need of virtuous men than of learned men. Knowledge does not produce virtue, nor does virtue produce knowledge, but rather augments and properly regulates its use.[13]

For Father Moreau this did not in any measure lessen the objective of education to train and to enlighten the intellect. "Piety without knowledge would make a teacher useless and would compromise the honor of his apostolate."[14] Father Moreau was not to be victim of the age-old polemic: Is the training of the will or the intellect the primary objective of education? He saw no dichotomy in the objectives of the professional and religious educator. These objectives were written into the rules and constitutions of the Sisters of the Holy Cross. It is stated thus: "The primary object of the sisters as teachers is the intellectual formation of the students."[15] He held that a solid foundation in the sciences, both sacred and profane, was necessary in order to present the truth and reality of life. He insisted that teachers should continue at all times to study and to improve. He exhorted them to better their methods of teaching, to keep up with state schools in France of that time.[16] More than one hundred years later Pope John XXIII was to remind Christian educators of the same responsibility when he urged religious teachers to bring to their apostolate the same professional excellence which should characterize those in state schools.[17]

La Pédagogie is divided into three parts: (1) Teachers and Students, (2) School Administration, and (3) The Formation of the Christian Life. These discussions are so contemporary in spirit that even today they are the topics of discussion in the educational conferences of the teachers of Holy Cross. Father Moreau sees no conflict in a teacher's life and the life of a religious. There is no threat to either one where the proper balance is maintained.[18] With a profound understanding of psychological differences, he counsels the teachers of Holy Cross to work individually and understandingly with all types of students. "Though these principles of action are important and necessary," he continues, "they will not suffice to give you a complete knowledge for the instruction and education of youth, a knowledge which you will have to acquire."[19]

La Pédagogie contains many wise counsels:

Do not think that it is age, size, tone of voice, or threats which give a teacher authority and inspires respect in his students. . . . It is an even, firm, and moderate character, one of self-possession, one which never acts through caprice. These qualities maintain order and establish discipline.

Further:

A teacher must continually nourish her mind in order to have a superior knowledge of the subject to be taught. She must be moved by zeal to serve all without distinction. She must maintain the dignity of the woman of faith. She should strive to build up a relationship of love with her students, remembering that "friendship is bought by friendship." The teacher must establish rapport with parents and civil authorities. She must study to perfect the art of communication, seeking to use terms and references which are intelligible to the student; otherwise there can be no teaching. The religious teacher must pray always for guidance. Finally, she must be courageous and decisive.[20]

We read that in preparing lessons and duties it is not enough to know the matter itself. Order, method, clarity, and exactness in thought as well as in expression will enable you to teach the slowest students. Come down to the level of the students with ideas and comparisons. Most important of all, motivate your students if you wish them to learn.

Try to convince students that you are their friends; your only goal is their progress. . . . Respect the feelings of the extremely sensitive student.[21]

Father Moreau had a basic principle of discipline. "It is better to reward than to punish.[22] For this reason the first schools and first teachers emphasized rewards of all kinds. The traditional gold and silver medals, the exhibitions, the pupil oral examinations, and the point system in the schools of the Sisters of the Holy Cross—all were practices in which they had been instructed by their first directors of education.

Father exhorts his religious to consider the individual differences in their students: if the child is spoiled, give easy, meaningful corrections; if proud, correct with courtesy; if opinionated, speak to him quietly until he comes to acknowledge his faults; if jealous, win his friendship; then act with profound patience.[23]

At the close of Part I of *La Pédagogie* Father Moreau writes:

It is ordinarily at the ages of twelve, thirteen, or fourteen—when (your students) are most in need of guidance—that they are leaving school. . . . I have dedicated a chapter at the end of this section to an explanation of the manner in which the brothers might assist in the continuation of religious training during these critical years after the boys have left school.[24]

The appended chapter outlines a program which could serve as the structure for a modern CYO, with laymen working under the supervision of the brothers.[25]

In the third part of La Pédagogie, devoted to the formation of the Christian life, hymns to be sung for every occasion make up a large part. They are singularly similar to the contemporary Gelineau psalms.

Finally, Father Moreau was far in advance in his methods of teaching. Every subject in the curriculum of his time is presented with general and specific methods. The principles are based on psychology. They are as Pestalozzian as Pestalozzi. Object teaching,[26] the necessity of grading,[27] the analytical method of deductive teaching,[28] all basic principles of Pestalozzi, were an integral part of good methods. Pestalozzi recognized three separate aspects of the natural organism of the child: the head, the hand, and the heart.[29] Father Moreau's maxims relate to the same threefold consideration of a student, to which he adds that of the soul or the spirit.[30]

Rev. Thomas Barrosse, C.S.C., in an article entitled "Father Moreau and the Question of a Holy Cross Education," posed the question whether Father Moreau wanted anything distinctive or different about Holy Cross education. The Society of Jesus, for example, has its ratio studiorum regulating the education it gives on the secondary level. All this is implied in an expression "Jesuit-trained." Did Father Moreau have such a distinctive pattern in mind in his repeated aims to be envisioned and methods to be employed in education?[31] In the circular letters Father Moreau makes frequent attempts to unify, to make homogeneous, the kind of education given in Holy Cross schools. In France he recommended that the same textbooks be used and a unified program of studies be followed. Father Barrosse believes that the founder did not intend an official pattern for a characteristically Holy Cross education, but that he did wish Holy Cross educators to give their students something over and above a good Christian education, viz., a family spirit.[32]

In the constitutions, rules, circular letters, and especially *La Pédagogie* there is evidence that Father Moreau was explicit and even emphatic that a family spirit exist among priests, brothers, sisters, faculty, students, and parents.

Father Barrosse writes:

If we admit that this (family spirit) is the distinctive mark Father Moreau wished to see characterize us, we must next examine whether he implied that it should color our apostolates, in particular our teaching, and whether he (Father Moreau) may want it to include or extend to our students or even to be imparted to them.[33]

In a circular letter dated December 27, 1837, Father Moreau wrote, "Here at Sainte-Croix charity reigns and unites the one hundred and more whom Providence has brought together."[34]

Of this spirit the Cattas say:

On the testimony of former students, a great family spirit reigned in the house (Sainte-Croix). Good news and bad news was shared in common. The spirit of solidarity extended also to the families of the students. Very early in his career, Father Moreau was convinced that the families of the students should be in contact with the administration of the college. At the beginning of 1858, he organized a "family council" composed of the parents of twelve students in the college, to offer suggestions on all matters calculated to improve the school at Sainte-Croix. The council met a minimum of four times each year. . . . In these gatherings the parents were requested to make their observations on the discipline and curricula of the school, to present and to solve all questions relating to the physical and moral well-being of the student body, to make known the reaction of public opinion to the administration and progress of the school and, lastly, to indicate to the director of the house anything which, in his relationships with the students, their parents, or different outside persons, might seem useful for the improvement and expansion of the school. It is certain that at that time, very few educational establishments maintained any similar contacts with the families of their students. The results of these meetings are not known; nevertheless, we must conclude that they contributed in no small degree to the good will with which Notre Dame de Sainte-Croix was constantly favored by the families of LeMans and the vicinity.[35]

To give prestige to Sainte-Croix, Father Moreau inaugurated an honorary academy, to which he invited prominent figures such as Dom Gueranger, Frederic Ozanam, and Montelambert. The members of the academy met every two weeks to decide which student papers would be read at the trimestral assembly. Programs for these events would also include plays, music, original verse, experiments in physics, and often a lecture by some dignitary.

Father Moreau used the press to interest laymen in the role of Holy Cross in Christian education. In 1838 he established the Association of St. Joseph. Thirteen years later it existed in eighty-six parishes besides those in LeMans.[36] Probably of greater value than the financial help made possible by the dues of the members was the rapport established between each Holy Cross school and the community it served. *Etrennes Spirituelles,* a yearly publication, included an almanac, simple meditations, a moral guide concerning plays, novels, and the use of snuff (sic), commentary on current events, and a report of the activities of Holy Cross around the world.[37] This publication went to every member of the Association of St. Joseph.

At Sainte-Croix, then, under Father Moreau's educational leadership, a family spirit bound the students with one another and with the priests, brothers, and sisters who cared for them.[38]

The Cattas comment:

Institutions like Sainte-Croix offered to the younger generation an atmosphere entirely different from that created by the imperial lycees and colleges and permeating all secondary schools depending on the university. Public education had retained that "military character" which had been stressed by Madame de Stael and Alfred de Vigny. Between them and the schools opened by congregations there was a striking contrast, and this was one of the reasons for the success of the Catholic schools.[39]

Although these references apply to the school at LeMans where Father Moreau spent most of his time, it takes little imagination to believe that he wished the same spirit to prevail in all the schools of the congregation.

In his January 5, 1846, circular, Father Moreau reminds the teachers they are to use the catechism adopted by the diocese wherein they are employed.[40] He counseled the members of the congregation to respect the liberty of instruction which the government had given them, being careful not to offend in matters where principles were not involved. To this end, he directed the teachers to withdraw from the primary schools *The History of France* by the Brothers of De La Salle (editions prior to 1850) as well as *The Writing Manual*, both of which primary school inspectors reported were hostile to the government.[41] Father Moreau in 1853 recommended specifically the adoption of two works by Father Louis Champeau, C.S.C., *The Principles of Public Reading* and *Etiquette*.[42] In the following year he added another of Father Champeau's works, *Voyage astronomique*, and two of M. Mariotti, inspector of primary schools, *Livre de lecture du premier âge* and *Pétite arithmétique*.[43] By 1862 a circular letter announced the recommended books for the coming year. It included many written by members of the Congregation of Holy Cross: *Reader* and *Pedagogy*, both by Father Moreau; *Meditations for the Laity*, perhaps also from the pen of Father Moreau; *Complete Lexicon of Greek Roots* and *Greek Exercises* by Father Charles Moreau; *Etiquette* by Father Louis Champeau; and *Speller* by Father Pierre Galmard. Also included in the list were texts not written by members of the congregation: *Catechism of Bellarmine, Selected Dialogues, Collection of Fables* by Fabliau, *Principles of Elocution*, and *Meditations for Houses of Education*.[44] In the same circular Father Moreau stated emphatically that no French schools should introduce any other reader than that which he had had printed for that purpose.[45] This was a child's reader of four hundred pages, published in 1838; it went through eight editions in twenty-seven years.[46]

The first priests and brothers of Holy Cross who came to the United States received an education at the mother house at LeMans or its environs during the decades of 1830 to 1850.

The first French sisters, too, had lived at Sainte-Croix and had known personally Father Moreau, to whom they were devoted as their spiritual father and founder. Father Sorin visualized Notre Dame du Lac, Indiana, in kind and in degree as a "Sainte-Croix." He wished to make Notre Dame a great Catholic university in the new world. His dream for a Saint Mary's academy for girls was equally portentous. Hence, his pleasure when the promising Eliza Gillespie, the future Mother M. Angela, entered the young community in 1853. After a novitiate in France, Mother M. Angela returned the same year to Bertrand as superior and directress of the academy. On the return voyage she and Father Sorin made plans for the schools in America. Unity, not uniformity, was to be the hallmark of Holy Cross education.

Adaptations from the French ideal to the American ideal and spirit are evident in the two programs which they drew up: "The Programme of Studies for Academies and Select Schools" and "The Programme of Studies for Parochial Schools." In these plans there are curricula, there is a recommendation for uniform textbooks, but there is more. There is a built-in adaptability to the needs of the type of school and the character of its personnel. See the Appendix, page 222, for the Programme of Studies of Saint Mary's Academy, Notre Dame, for c. 1851.

There are repeated references in Holy Cross archival material to a program of studies drawn up for academies and parochial schools. The first rules of the Sisters of the Holy Cross, *Régles particulières aux Marianites,* give detailed procedures for teachers, prefects of studies, health, and discipline.[47] These rules passed through a series of translations and revisions. By the end of the nineteenth century the constitutions of the congregation treated more generally teachers and teacher training; a program of studies was printed in book form.[48] That this program was implemented and adapted to the academies from 1855 to 1900 can be substantiated by catalogues published by Saint Mary's Academy during this period.[49] This was a pattern for all community academies.

"The Programme of Studies for Academies and Select Schools" consisted of three primary classes, three preparatory classes, and four academic classes. In the primary course catechism, spelling, reading, writing, oral arithmetic, and object lessons made up the curriculum.

The preparatory course introduced Bible history, progressive and practical arithmetic, analytical and practical grammar, geography, United States history, map drawing, globe reading, reading, and spelling. The last year of the preparatory course introduced physiology, Latin, French, or German.

The academic course of four years following the preparatory course consisted of the third senior class, second senior class, first senior class, and graduating class. The recommendations for the academic course were followed closely by Saint Mary's Academy, Notre Dame. The accompanying outline of study from the catalogue of 1862 gives the curriculum.[50] Not only were the subjects listed but also the texts to be used.

PROGRAMME OF STUDIES
FOR
SELECT SCHOOLS AND ACADEMIES

*****

PRIMARY COURSE

___

Third Junior Class
Catechism (taught orally), Spelling, Reading, Writing, Oral Arithmetic and Object Lessons

Second Junior Class
Catechism, Spelling, Reading, Writing, Robinson's Arithmetic, Primary Geography, Bullion's Elements of Grammar (taught orally)

First Junior Class
Catechism, Bullion's Elementary Grammar, Excelsior Geography (No. 2), Spelling, Robinson's Arithmetic, Reading and Writing

___

PREPARATORY COURSE

___

*Junior Preparatory and + Third Preparatory Classes
Catechism, Sadlier's Bible History, Robinson's Progressive Practical Arithmetic, Bullion's Analytical and Practical Grammar, Excelsior Geography (No. 3), Map

Drawing, Robinson's Mental Arithmetic,
Excelsior Fourth Reader, Sadlier's
Excelsior Speller

Second Preparatory Class

Catechism, Sadlier's Bible History, Bullion's Analytical and
Practical Grammar, Excelsior Geography (No. 3), Barnes'
United States History, Map Drawing and Use of Globes,
Robinson's Practical and Mental Arithmetic, Excelsior
Speller, Dictation, Excelsior Fifth Reader

First Preparatory Class

Catechism, Sadlier's Bible History, Bullion's Analytical and
Practical Grammar, Excelsior Speller, Robinson's Higher
Arithmetic, Robinson's Mental Arithmetic, Martin's Physi-
ology, Cornell's Physical Geography, Latin, French or
German commenced

ACADEMIC COURSE

Third Senior Class

—1st Session—

Reeve's Bible History, Perry's Instructions, Quackenbos'
Rhetoric, Ganot's Philosophy, Fredet's Ancient
History, Davies' University Algebra,
Bailey's Etymology, Languages

—2nd Session—

Reeve's Bible History, Perry's Instructions, Quackenbos'
Rhetoric, Davies' University Algebra, Fredet's
Ancient History, Ganot's Philosophy,
Bailey's Etymology, Languages

Second Senior Class

—1st Session—

Reeve's Bible History, Perry's Instructions, Quackenbos' Rhetoric,

Davies' Legendre Geometry, Avery's Complete Chemistry,
Fredet's Modern History, Davies' University Algebra,
Wood's Botany, Book-keeping, Languages

—2nd Session—

Reeve's Bible History, Perry's Instructions, Rhetorical Analysis
of Prose and Poetry, Geometry, Modern History,
Chemistry, Languages

First Senior Class

—1st Session—

Noethan's Church History, Perry's Instructions, Jevon's Logic,
Davies' Legendre Geometry, Wood's Botany, Dana's Geology,
Jenkins' Literature, History of France, Languages

—2nd Session—

Noethan's Church History, Perry's Instructions, Logic, Geometry,
Botany, Literature, Geology, History of England
(Burke's Lingard), Languages

Graduating Class

—1st Session—

Noethan's Church History, Wilmer's Christian Religion,
Young's Astronomy, Haven's Mental Philosophy,
Criticism of Standard Authors, General
Literature, Trigonometry, Languages

—2nd Session—

Noethan's Church History, Wilmer's Christian Religion, Hill's
Moral Philosophy, Trigonometry, Botanical Analysis,
Criticism of Standard Authors, Languages, a
General Review of all the Studies of the
Course

———

Penmanship, Elocution, Composition, Laws of Hygiene, and
Botanical Analysis taught throughout each course.

The above plan of studies was for all private schools of Holy Cross. Subsequent "Programmes of Studies" which appear in the Saint Mary's Academy catalogues show modifications. These follow from the direction of Father Moreau. In a circular letter to the sisters in February, 1860, he sets the agenda of the Committee on Studies for the next Chapter:

(1) What class books have been used up to the present? Are there reasons for preferring some to others? (2) Draw up a definitive list of the works to be adopted for the future in primary and secondary teaching. (3) What observations are to be made on *La Pédagogie* and *New Reader?* (4) Have examinations been taken and the records sent to the General Administration?[51]

In the first years of Saint Mary's Academy, the enrollment was not large enough to warrant a full program of ten years; i.e., there were not always ten classes.[52] Students were taken at any time of the year, tested, and placed as qualified.[53] In 1868 the prospectus stated that the combined primary and preparatory courses could be completed in six years, but "it may require seven years."[54] In the same year, to complete a classical course as opposed to the English course, two more sessions were added. By 1880 the primary course was extended to four years, the preparatory to three years, the academic to four years, and the classical an additional year (4–3–4 or 4–3–5).[55] The first degree was conferred in 1898 on a 5–3–4–1 program.[56] The first four-year college course was offered in 1902;[57] the first 4–4–4–4 program appeared in 1910.[58]

The experimentation with the number of years in a given curriculum was not unique to the plan of the Sisters of the Holy Cross for its academies. It reflects strong French influence: public examinations to which parents, friends, and faculty were invited. Advancement depended upon achievement; it varied in different subjects.

Cubberley discusses the varying lengths of curricula in public and private schools in the United States, remarking that "parts of our schools system at first possessed no fixed limits or length of course."[59] Sometimes a three-year high school was superimposed on a six-year elementary course of study.[60] But by 1890 the 8-4 plan had become common except in New England and the South. At the same time, educators were beginning to question the haphazard way in which the curriculum had evolved in a democracy. President Charles W. Eliot, of Harvard University, presented a series of three papers (1888, 1892) at regional and national conventions of the National Educational Association attacking the lengthening of the years of the courses of study in the public and private schools. His topics—"Can School Programs be Shortened and Enriched," "Shortening and Enriching the Grammar School Course," and "Undesirable and Desirable Uniformity in Schools"—opened up a discussion on the respective places and purposes of elementary school, high school, and college.[61] Kandel, too, describes the broad, encyclopedic, and flexible curricula of academies. Wesleyan Seminary in 1856 had a three-term program.[62] Phillips Exeter Academy for years offered a 4-3 English program and a 4-4 classical one.[63] Saint Mary's Academy and College did not have a 4-4-4-4 program until 1910. The forces which brought about this change, accreditation, will be discussed in Chapter IV.

The program for parochial schools differed little from that taught in the private schools. It lacked modern language courses, music, and art, generally taught in private lessons in academies. The course which followed the algebra of the seventh and eighth grades was termed "university algebra." However, algebra and philosophy were optional. Interviews with sisters who attended schools conducted by the Sisters of the Holy Cross (1884) helped to bring to light the content of such a course as philosophy taught in the elementary school.

It was actually a general science course, sometimes called physiography, at other times, natural philosophy.

After the two programs, one for academies, the other for parochial schools, the guide develops "Work in the Primary Course."[64] The section includes: (1) teaching of the alphabet, (2) spelling, (3) reading, (4) grammar, (5) arithmetic, (6) fractions and decimals, and (7) geography. In the primary grades history and geography were treated simultaneously as complementing one another. "Many interesting points of history can be brought in with study of the different cities and countries. The children should always be encouraged to seek information at home and elsewhere regarding the history and geography of every place."[65]

The guide gives not only the subjects taught and the texts used but also the amount of material "to be covered" in the first and second semester; e.g., *Excelsior Geography,* first session, from the beginning to page 37, with map reading; second session, from page 37 to Europe. *Davies Algebra,* first session, from the beginning to "Extraction of Roots"; second session, from the "Extraction of Roots" to "indeterminate coefficients."[66] There is strong evidence of textbook teaching, typical of the school system of the second half of the nineteenth century.[67] The fact that the teachers used the same textbooks recommended for specific courses in most parochial schools and in all community academies was an aid to teacher mastery of content. Elsbree points out that the multiplication of textbooks in the years when textbook teaching was "the method" presented difficulty for the teacher who was expected to teach many or all of the subjects in the curriculum.[68]

For obvious reasons textbooks recommended by Father Moreau in his circular letters would not meet needs in the United States. But the value which Father Moreau placed on uniform texts may well have quickened the pace with which Mother M. Angela began to write and to edit books for the Sisters of the Holy Cross.   .

The dossier of correspondence concerning the publication of textbooks with D. J. Sadlier and Company of New York City is incomplete. There is a dearth of publication data in the archives of the University of Notre Dame, which may readily be explained by the fire of 1879, when much archival material was destroyed. Sixty letters and three contracts over a period of thirty-one years (1869–1900) testify that the books which Mother Angela had written or edited were still in use in the Catholic schools in the United States during this time.

The earliest Sadlier correspondence in the archives of the general house is dated 1869. This is an agreement between Father Sorin and Mother M. Angela for equal division of all royalties from the proceeds of sales of books written or compiled by persons at either Notre Dame or Saint Mary's.[69] *The Metropolitan Sixth Reader: the Book of Oratory,* however, has an 1867 copyright. The frontispiece bears the inscription "By a Catholic Teacher," as did the entire series.[70] The preface likewise states that with the exception of the *Readers* of the Christian Brothers, no other text for Catholic schools is available.[71]

Early correspondence extant in the archives of the University of Notre Dame relevant to this topic are letters from Mother M. Angela to Orestes Brownson. In a letter dated October 21, 1859 (Elizabeth, New Jersey), Mother Angela makes reference to the advanced readers for younger classes, adding that she is carefully choosing selections so that when pupils leave school, they will know what good literature really is.[72]

Another letter, January 2, 1860, reads in part:

Mr. O. A. Brownson—
  Most honored Sir
  . . . Truly do I appreciate your generous reply. . . . I now avail myself of your kindness by asking if I should select from Emerson and Carlyle—and what extracts: May I also obtain a notice of

these authors from your pen? In the 4th Reader I wish to preface all selections by a notice of the Authors.

I feel deeply indebted for your kind offer of correcting the proof sheets. I have no definite arrangement with my publisher as I have been waiting to receive answers from other religious institutions in order to know what number may reasonably be presumed will adopt the Readers. . . . I have heard favorably from the Visitandines, Sisters of Mercy, Ursulines, and Notre Dame. Archbishops Kenrick and Purcell, Bishops Young, Duggan, Luers and Rt. Rev. Dr. Spalding have sent me their candid approbation of the Prospectus. How much I would like to see you before the 4th and 5th ms are issued.

I will write to Mr. Sadlier with regard to the publishing this week.

Friend and servant in X
S. M. of St. Angela

St. Mary's Academy
Notre Dame P.O.
   Ind.
     January 2, 1860
N.B. Will you send me a name for the Readers?[73]

In April of the same year another letter between Mother M. Angela and Orestes Brownson shows that Mother M. Angela was continuing work on textbooks.

Mr. O. A. Brownson
  Most esteemed Sir
  Permit me to remind you of your exceedingly kind offer to revise our Series of Readers for Catholic Schools. Three of the Books—1st, 2nd, and 4th—I have sent to Messrs. Sadlier. Shall I authorize them to send you the proof sheets? At the same time I hope you will make or suggest to me more freely any change you think necessary in order to make them what our Catholic schools require. I do not feel competent to arrange them and was induced to do so solely from the great need I felt there was, and is, for a higher class of Catholic school Books. . . .

I leave our Readers to your charity and zeal in the cause of education. I have the honor to remain with profound respect

Your obedient Servant

Mother M. Angela

April 24th 1860[74]

A contract signed March 7, 1870, between Mother M. Angela and D. S. Sadlier included terms for the renewal of the agreement of 1860. Although this contract is not extant, some of its provisions can be found. Sadlier would assume all publication costs of the *Metropolitan Series of Readers and Spellers,* granting the author ten percent annually on the wholesale prices of sales.[75] Another contract signed by Father Sorin, January 26, 1877, approved a previous agreement made in July, 1875, with William H. Sadlier for the *Excelsior Readers, Spellers, and Geographies.* Five percent of the royalties was to be paid to both Notre Dame and Saint Mary's. The contract further required that the books be regularly revised and improved to keep them acceptable textbooks for Catholic schools.[76]

An 1877 letterhead of the Sadlier Company showed fifteen Catholic textbooks published by the Company. Mother M. Angela was the editor or compiler of all but one, *Illustrated Bible History.*

A letterhead dated December 27, 1879, bears testimonials from John Cardinal McCloskey, archbishop of Baltimore; Rt. Rev. James P. Purcell, archbishop of Cincinnati; the Academy of the Sacred Heart, Manhattanville, New York; and Sister M. Xavier of Heythuizen, Holland. These testimonials endorse the adoption of *Excelsior* readers, spellers, and geographies.[77]

The receipts for royalties are incomplete, again partly because of the loss of Notre Dame archives. In an account, however, between William H. Sadlier and the Sisters of the Holy Cross, January 1, 1879, the royalty amounted to

$4,080.52; January 1, 1879, to July 1, 1882, for *Metropolitan Readers*, $609.64.[78]

Excerpts from Sadlier letters follow:

January 15, 1881, . . . Last year we paid you $508.01 for *Sadlier Readers;* this year $567.74, an increase of 12%. This year it will be much larger as the Readers are becoming increasing popular.

Enclosed please find statement of copyright returns for the past six months amounting to $673.74. We are well pleased with the showing considering the increased competition.

Enclosed please find check for $650 copyright royalty from January 1, 1889 to January 1, 1890. I have proportioned this as well as possible as to the expense of the new improvements in the readers, as agreed. Competition is so great. The sales are relatively small.[79]

The Sadlier file contains excerpts of letters of this nature, with the average amount of royalty approximately $500 a year. The Sadlier Publishing Company changed hands four times during the period of this correspondence. Officially, the Holy Cross business with the publisher was terminated in 1906.

The textbooks edited by Mother M. Angela served their purpose in the years when the controversies about textbooks were a part of the history of Catholic education in the United States. Mother M. Angela drew on her rich education, her experience, and her study of French literature to make classic selections high in the level of reading interest. As the textbook industry advanced, more books came into circulation. From 1855 on there were attacks on the quality of the books, as well as editorials against "Catholic textbooks." Many of these attacks came from the Catholic press itself. The Sadlier dossier contains an editorial from the newspaper, *Church Progress,* written by Rev. Charles Kuhlmann. He attacks the Sadlier books as *Barnes and Company Readers* "doctored by a Catholic teacher"; *The Sadlier Geographies and Speller* as

"Monteith's in a Catholic dress." He asks pastors and superiors to examine the books carefully before adoption.[80] By the turn of the century the Sadlier books had outlived revision, since new methods of teaching necessitated new approaches. Yet the books remained in use until the early part of the twentieth century. The first *Sadlier Geography* published without the name of "A Member of the Order of Holy Cross" was the 1917 edition of Book III, edited by Frank X. Sadlier.[81]

The textbooks were closely related to the requirements of the two programs of studies which Father Sorin and Mother Angela had drawn up for the schools of Holy Cross.

Thus, Father Moreau—as teacher, educator, administrator, and founder—gave to the teachers of Holy Cross a philosophy of education, clear objectives, an organized curriculum, and recommended textbooks. He encouraged a family spirit among the three branches of the congregation, their school faculties, their students, and their families. Both Father Sorin and Mother M. Angela, aided by intrepid pioneers, implemented and adapted his educational plans to the Holy Cross schools in the United States. Father Moreau directly counseled the Sisters of the Holy Cross in their educational efforts; Holy Cross priests gave the community encouragement and supervisory aid. Through the leadership of Mother M. Angela an education in the French tradition was to be Americanized in a network of Holy Cross academies and schools in the United States.

References

[1] *Circular Letters of the Very Reverend Basil Anthony Mary Moreau,* trans. Edward L. Heston, C.S.C. (Notre Dame, Indiana, 1943), I, p. 5. Hereafter cited as *Circular Letters.*

[2] Canon Etienne Catta and Tony Catta, *Basil Anthony Mary Moreau,* trans. Edward L. Heston, C.S.C. (Milwaukee, 1955), I, p. 353. Hereafter cited as Catta, *Life.*

3 Gary MacEoin, *Father Moreau, Founder of Holy Cross* (Milwaukee, 1962), p. 60.

4 James J. Trahey, C.S.C., *Brothers of Holy Cross* (Notre Dame, Indiana, 1909), p. 5.

5 William Norris, C.S.C., "Fr. Moreau and the Apostolate of Education," *Basile Moreau* (LeMans, 1962), pp. 53–54.

6 *Circular Letters,* I, p. 161.

7 Falloux Law of 1850.

8 *Circular Letters,* I, pp. 161–162.

9 *Ibid.,* I, p. 162.

10 *Ibid.,* I, p. 88.

11 Basile-Antoine-Marie Moreau, (La) *Pédagogie Chrétienne à l'usage des Joséphites de la Sainte-Croix* (LeMans, 1856). Hereafter cited as *La Pédagogie.*

12 Basile-Antoine-Marie Moreau, *Nouveau livre de lectures* (LeMans, 1865).

13 *La Pédagogie,* preface.

14 *Ibid.,* p. 8.

15 *Constitutions of the Congregation of the Sisters of the Holy Cross* (Notre Dame, Indiana, 1962), article 247, p. 74. The present rule of the Congregation of the Sisters of the Holy Cross has had six editions since 1854. In all these editions the primary object of the sisters as teachers is the development of the intellect. The first rule reads: "Comme Institutrices (La Préfête d'Etudes et La Préfête de Discipline) elles doivent se proposer pour but de leurs efforts le dévelopment intellectuel et moral des Elèves." Regle XIII, Des Maîtresses d'Ecole, article 167, p. 266.

16 *Etrennes spirituelles,* 1842, pp. 38–44.

17 Encyclical Letter of Pope John XXIII, "Il Tempio Massino," July 2, 1962. Published in *Sister Formation Bulletin,* X, (Autumn, 1962), pp. 1–9.

18 *La Pédagogie,* preface.

19 *Ibid.* p. 43.

20 *Ibid.,* pp. 41ff.

21 *Ibid.,* pp. 59–60.

22 *Ibid.,* p. 64.

23 *Ibid.,* pp. 43ff.

24 *Ibid.,* p. 126.

25 *Ibid.,* p. 1.

26 *Ibid.,* p. 106.

27 *Ibid.,* p. 64.

28 *Ibid.,* p. 102.

29 Willard S. Elsbree, *The American Teacher* (New York, 1939), p. 108.

30 Moreau, *Nouveau livre de lectures,* p. 9.

31 Thomas Barrosse, C.S.C., "Father Moreau and the Question of a Holy

Cross Education," *Bulletin of the Educational Conference of the Priests of Holy Cross*, XXX, 68.

[32] *Ibid.*, p. 77.

[33] *Ibid.*, p. 73.

[34] *Circular Letters*, I, p. 11. At this time there were but sixty-one members in the entire community; therefore, the number must include students.

[35] Catta, *Life*, II, pp. 216–217.

[36] *Ibid.*, I, p. 741.

[37] *Ibid.*, I, p. 740ff.

[38] Barrosse, *op. cit.*, p. 73.

[39] Catta, *Life*, I, p. 642.

[40] *Circular Letters*, I, p. 109.

[41] *Ibid.*, I, p. 263.

[42] *Ibid.*, I, p. 278.

[43] *Ibid.*, I, p. 315.

[44] *Ibid.*, II, p. 255.

[45] *Ibid.*, II, p. 254.

[46] Catta, *Life*, II, pp. 96–97.

[47] *Régles particulieres aux Marianites* (LeMans, 1854).

[48] *Teachers' Guide for the Use of the Sisters of the Holy Cross* (Notre Dame, Indiana, n.d.).

[49] *Catalogues of St. Mary's Academy, Notre Dame, Indiana, 1860–1900*, ASMC. Hereafter cited as *Catalogue*.

[50] *Catalogue*, 1862, ASMC.

[51] *Circular Letters*, II, p. 422.

[52] *Catalogue*, 1860, pp. 7ff.

[53] *Ibid.*, 1863, p. 5.

[54] *Ibid.*, 1868, p. 6.

[55] *Ibid.*, 1880, p. 6.

[56] *Ibid.*, 1898, p. 8.

[57] *Ibid.*, 1902, p. 7.

[58] *Ibid.*, 1910, pp. 29ff.

[59] Ellwood P. Cubberley, *Public Education in the United States* (Boston, 1934), p. 550.

[60] *Ibid.*

[61] *Ibid.*, p. 551.

[62] Isaac L. Kandel, *History of Secondary Education* (Boston, 1930), p. 415.

[63] *Ibid.*, p. 415.

[64] *Ibid.*, pp. 10–21.

[65] *Ibid.*, p. 21.

[66] *Ibid.*, p. 25.

[67] Elsbree, *op. cit.*, pp. 216ff.

[68] *Ibid.*
[69] Sadlier Correspondence, 1869, AGH.
[70] By a Catholic Teacher, *The Metropolitan Sixth Reader: The Book of Oratory* (New York, 1867), frontispiece.
[71] *Ibid.*, preface.
[72] Mother M. Angela to Brownson, 1859, *Brownson* papers AUND.
[73] *Ibid.*, 1860.
[74] *Ibid.*
[75] Sadlier File, 1870, AGH.
[76] *Ibid.*, 1875.
[77] *Ibid.*, 1879.
[78] *Ibid.*, 1879, 1882.
[79] *Ibid.*, 1881, 1884, 1891. (In a recent correspondence with William H. Sadlier, Inc., F. Sadlier Dinger claims that all past correspondence is missing; they have no information regarding these books. The Congregation of the Sisters of the Holy Cross, however, is in possession of many of the books, not a complete set of all editions.)
[80] Charles Kuhlmann, editor, *Church Progress*, (Marchall, Illinois), May 1, 1886, p. 4.
[81] *Sadlier's Excelsior Geography Number Three* (New York edition), revised edition of the *First Catholic Geography in America*, edited by Frank X. Sadlier (New York, 1917).

CHAPTER III

ACADEMIES OF HOLY CROSS: 1855-1900

THE PHILOSOPHY, principles of practice, and the methodology of Holy Cross education as envisioned by Father Moreau and developed in the United States by Father Sorin and Mother M. Angela can best be exemplified in the academies which opened under Holy Cross auspices in the middle nineteenth century. Historically it was the time when the academy as an institution in the educational development in America enjoyed its golden age. These academies were the source of teachers for private and public schools alike.[1]

The academy had evolved from the Latin Grammar School, which as an institution had failed to meet the needs of a rapidly changing democratic society. A more practical curriculum for youth, not college-bound, characterized the academy from the beginning. Retaining Latin, and sometimes Greek, the curriculum now emphasized English, oratory, declamation, rhetoric, and literature. Arithmetic, algebra, geometry, trigonometry, and astronomy, natural and moral philosophy were the common offerings of a school that now opened its doors to girls as well as to boys. In curriculum the academy built upon the subjects taught in the common schools, not running counter to—as the Latin Grammar School had done—but complementing and supplementing the elementary school.[2]

Privately owned, the tuition academy became a representative educational institution in a transition period of American history characterized by great progress, increased population, heavy immigration, and a westward movement.[3] Some academies offered opportunities to work; hence a more democratic enrollment characterized the school. As an institution, the academy played an important part in the broadening of education opportunities for the middle class. Essentially religious, it was a transition from the denominational colonial school to the secular high school of today; from higher education of men only, to education of women, and eventually coeducation. The academy was the normal school in embryonic form.[4] It is difficult to ascertain where and when the American academy had its beginnings, but that it was rooted in the East and particularly the Northeast is conceded by historians.[5]

The curriculum of Franklin's academy included writing, drawing, arithmetic and accounts; some of the first principles of geometry and astronomy; English language, composition (style to be based on 'reading some of our best authors—Tillotson, Addison, Pope, Algernon Sidney') and pronunciation (declamation, speeches, orations, 'the tutor assisting at the rehearsals, teaching, advising, and correcting their accent') ; universal and national chronology, ancient customs, morality, religion and politics, ancient and foreign languages, Latin, Greek, French, German, and Spanish selected according to professional needs, sciences of observation and experimentation. . . .[6]

By the beginning of the nineteenth century Phillips Andover (Massachusetts, founded in 1778) and Phillips Exeter (New Hampshire, founded in 1781) were the two academies which furnished the model and inspiration of many later institutions in the northern states, both east and west.[7] By

1830, 950 incorporated academies and many unincorporated academies had mushroomed in the United States.[8] At the crest of the wave of academies in 1850 there were 1007 academies in New England, 1636 in the Middle Atlantic states, 2640 in the southern states, 753 in the Upper Mississippi Valley states, and a total reported for the entire United States of 6085, with 12,260 teachers and 263,096 pupils.[9]

The Sisters of the Holy Cross opened their first academy in 1844 in Bertrand, Michigan. Saint Mary's Academy was typical in that it was privately owned, enrolled girls only, and prepared teachers for the common school system as well as the parochial school system. It was atypical in that it was a denominational school, but it did admit members of all faiths. It did not require them to take instructions or to attend daily church services. It did require attendance at, but not participation in, Sunday worship.[10]

Saint Mary's was the only institution of higher learning within a radius of many miles.[11] In 1855 the academy moved to the state of Indiana. Here for a half century factions in the northern and southern parts of the state warred over the legality of tax-supported secondary education. A Yankee element predominated in the North; a southern element controlled the central and southern portion of the state.[12] The Supreme Court of the state of Indiana declared local taxes for education unconstitutional in 1854. Academies were established, and seventy-two opened after 1850.[13] Not until 1867 were local taxes legalized to make way for the public high school which grew out of the institution of the academy.[14] The latter differed from the former chiefly in the matter of support and control.

Earlier tax-supported schools had died out with the decline of zeal for education after about 1750. Academies were mainly dependent upon private energy and benevolence for support. Public-spirited citizens, private stock companies, and denominational organizations administered the academies under a board of trustees holding corporate powers through a charter given by the state.[15]

Saint Mary's Academy was organized and administered in a similar manner. In the Articles of Incorporation of Saint Mary's Academy the board of trustees who appeared before Judge S. Stanfield of the Ninth Judicial Circuit included Edward Sorin, Mathruin Salou (Mother M. Ascension), Eliza Gillespie (Mother M. Angela), Julia Rivard (Sister M. Emily), Prosperiana Chanson (Sister M. Circumcision), and Margaret Mahoney (Sister M. Euphrasia).[16]

To the national scene and particularly to the Indiana scene the problems peculiar to the history of the Church in America were added. A very large element of Catholic immigrants put a hard strain on the Church in the matter of education. Rt. Rev. Francis J. Macelwane, in speaking of this period of Catholic education, claims that adequate training of teachers was impossible. To meet the need of the hour, religious communities frequently sent out postulants to take charge of classrooms, hoping with the aid of their experienced teachers to meet with some success.[17] But pupils differed in racial origin, in social standing, and in financial means. Pride of country, as well as sectional pride of the North and the South, was a rival of love of the Church.[18] Language presented great difficulties, especially to those whose native tongue was not English; e.g., Germans, Poles, and French. Irish immigrants were, of course, spared this handicap.

The schools in which the Sisters of the Holy Cross taught were schools where all these problems could be found in whole or in part. The heterogeneous backgrounds of the sister teachers made possible the staffing of schools where there was a demand for a foreign language, the native language of the parents and the teachers. For this reason the foreign-born sisters were not reduced to the level of the pupil, a condition which existed in many schools. Often the sisters did not have the mastery of English, but learned it as they taught. The sisters opened parochial schools for the German, Polish, and Belgian people, a kind of school which was a part of the American system until the first World War.[19]

In definitive studies of the history of education, Woody, Elsbree, and Cubberley, among others, emphasize leadership as a measure of success, of curricula quality, and of teacher training. It is feasible to turn, then, to the sister of the Holy Cross who gave academic impetus to the community in its pioneer days, Mother M. Angela.

Eliza Maria Gillespie was born of John P. Gillespie and Mary Madeleine Miers, February 21, 1824, in Brownsville, Pennsylvania. When Eliza was twelve years old, her father died. The family then returned to the mother's home in Lancaster, Ohio, close to Thomas Ewing and his wife, granddaughter of her uncle, Neal Gillespie, Sr. The family was a closely knit family of wide interest and experience: the Gillespies, Ewings, Blaines, Browns, Walkers, Shermans, and Bigelows. In her youth Eliza's intellectual tastes were omniverous. Her rich temperament loved all that was gay, good, beautiful, and delightful. She received her early education at Saint Mary's Female Literary Society, Somerset, Ohio; she was graduated from the Academy of the Visitation, Georgetown, Washington, D.C., in 1842.

In the previous year Mrs. Madeleine Gillespie, her mother, had married Mr. William Phelan. The latter soon recognized the business talent, social grace, and spiritual quality of Eliza. He gave her opportunities to share with him the multiple duties of a businessman of means. "She learned bookkeeping, developed a natural business acumen, and became practiced in the organizational management of Mr. Phelan's army of farm hands, tenants, and large staff of house servants."[20]

Eliza's only brother, Neal Gillespie, returned to teach and

to enter in 1850 the Priests of the Congregation of Holy Cross, a year after his graduation from Notre Dame. Eliza herself had had teaching experience in her home town of Lancaster and at Saint Mary's City, Maryland, in 1852. Not until she was twenty-nine years of age did she renounce the world of balls, fox hunting, diplomatic contacts, and political campaigns. Because of her active participation in charitable works, teaching poor children, sewing for various civic institutions, and leading in activities of the Church, no one was surprised at her decision.

In 1853, en route to Chicago to enter the novitiate of the Sisters of Mercy, Eliza stopped to visit her brother at Notre Dame; but she stayed to join the Sisters of the Holy Cross at Bertrand, Michigan.[21] Receiving the habit in 1853, Eliza became Sister M. Angela. She went to France the same year to make her novitiate, returning a professed member of the community. It was on her return voyage, as we have seen, that she and Father Sorin drew up the prospectus for academies, parochial schools, and manual training schools.

Her abilities were evident. The same year, 1853, she became superior and directress of studies at Saint Mary's Academy, Bertrand, Michigan. It was she who supervised its moving to Saint Mary's, Notre Dame; it was she who as educational administrator, teacher, and nurse for thirty-four years gave the young community the leadership which was to mark its development into a teaching and nursing religious congregation of women.

The year and a half which Mother M. Angela spent at Bertrand as directress was an era of phenomenal growth. In 1852 forty-six boarders attended the school at Bertrand. Sister M. Elizabeth writing in her diary in 1854 records:

In the next years there was an increase of about thirty-five boarders at the end of the scholastic year. Public examinations and an exhibition took place. The satisfaction expressed by all gave encouraging hopes for the future . . . the number of postulants had increased also so that they were separated from the rest of the community . . . shortly they moved into a house purchased by Rev. Father Superior (Father Sorin).[22]

Mother M. Angela drew on her experience as a student at Georgetown Visitation, as well as Father Moreau's plan of studies, to set standards of scholarship and a reputation for culture unknown to the people of this undeveloped territory. Her fingers gave everything she touched a quality of elegance.[23] It is evident from diary notes that the teachers were aware of Mother's ideal and imitation to some degree of Georgetown Visitation education.[24]

So it was not surprising that the fifth commencement of Saint Mary's Academy and the last at Bertrand in 1855 was a memorable one. A family friend from Lancaster, Ohio, Rt. Rev. Joshua Young, bishop of Erie, gave the commencement address.[25] *The Boston Pilot*, July 21, 1855, carried an account of the ceremony. It paid tribute to the directress of the academy, to the quality of the graduating program, and to the success of the students. It hailed the school as the "educational mecca of the West."[26]

The program of commencement was an all-day affair. There were students who received awards, premiums, and rank for every subject in the curriculum. The ceremonies were held on the academy lawn overlooking the Saint Joseph River. Parents and friends who came were served a dinner in the outdoor expanse of a clearing, fragrant with briar roses and honeysuckle.[27]

The musical numbers reflected the classic education of the two European-trained music teachers, Mrs. Redman and her daughter, Sister M. Elizabeth; the literary selections, the quality of education of Mother M. Angela and Mrs. Emily Guthrie.

For some time, despite the material progress of Bertrand,

Father Sorin was uneasy about the attitude of the bishop of Detroit toward the presence in his diocese of a novitiate not under his episcopal jurisdiction. A recent ruling of the Sacred Congregation of Faith on the employment of women in religious houses of men made the establishment of the novitiate at Notre Dame precarious. The activities of the Know-Nothing-Party in Mishawaka made the transfer there impossible. For some time Father Sorin had been negotiating with John Rush for one hundred and eighty-five acres of land along the Saint Joseph River, one mile west of Notre Dame. A verbal agreement had been made. Then the owner began to vacillate on terms. On the strength of the verbal agreement, Father Sorin and five brothers immediately broke the dam which held the spring waters of the lakes of Notre Dame. They flooded the ravine and divided the Rush property. Sister M. Euphrosine's diary states, "The owner came to terms within an hour. The property was purchased for eight thousand dollars."[28] The deep stagnant water of the lakes, long the suspect of the source of typhus and cholera, was released into the Saint Joseph River. Cholera epidemics which had ravaged the community of priests, brothers, and sisters terminated.[29] The annals of 1854 tell of twenty-one deaths in a two-week period.

Studies that have been made of the diocese of Vincennes and later of Fort Wayne are restrained and tolerant of the way in which Father Sorin administered the religious family of Holy Cross temporally and spiritually.

During the 1850's the three communities, including the Holy Cross priests, brothers, and sisters, were under the immediate supervision of Edward Sorin, who in a remote area felt impelled to carry on his splendid work almost independently of diocesan or congregational superiors. The task was no easy one but he went on courageously.[30]

The same writer points out that the entire northern portion

of the diocese of Vincennes had been neglected and that proper surveillance had become increasingly difficult. The diocese was divided in 1857, and Rt. Rev. John Henry Luers became first bishop of Fort Wayne.[31] In *The Diocese of Fort Wayne* reference is made to administrative problems which plagued the young community.

The period (1844–1864), although blessed with a measure of success, was wanting in the sense of stability which cannot be enjoyed . . . when full episcopal approbation is withheld. . . . There was no censure on the community, but the atmosphere had not the clearness of perfect understanding.[32]

Mother M. Angela attracted to Saint Mary's a clientele which was to include her family and friends, her parents moving there in 1855. Their gift of a farm in Lancaster, Ohio, their former home, made possible the purchase of the Rush estate. Mrs. Harriet Redman, her daughter Mrs. Lilly, and her two children were personal friends of Mother M. Angela, moving to Bertrand from Lancaster, Ohio. The Shermans, the Ewings, the Alexanders, the Dunbars—all sent their children to Saint Mary's and to Notre Dame. During the Civil War, daughters of officers from the North and the South patronized the academy. General William Sherman visited his two daughters, Minnie and Lizzie, at Saint Mary's during the war.

In the memoirs of Mother M. Angela Mrs. Ellen Ewing Brown writes with an awareness of the effect of the leadership of Eliza on her personal family and on her religious family, a leadership which stamped the character of Saint Mary's, Notre Dame.

Mrs. Lilly, her two children, and her mother, Mrs. Redman, a family of musicians, came from Lancaster, Ohio. . . . Grandma Redman was for years an outstanding teacher at Saint Mary's until old age crippled her hands. Eddie Lilly and Edie Lilly were both gifted musicians (both joined the order of Holy Cross) but they died young. Mrs. Guthrie, afterwards Sister M. Ignatia, was a talented writer of historical dramas. Mrs. Judge Arrington of Chicago was a convert; she visited her three children at Saint Mary's and Notre Dame, Alfred, Flora, and Genevieve. There are many who come to Saint Mary's and to Notre Dame on her account. All her sister's children, the Ewings, one Agnes Ewing who became Sister Mary Agnes (C.S.C.) and her sister's two grandchildren, Agnes Brown and Henry Brown; her cousins the Tongs from Carroll, Ohio, who came to live in South Bend and were pupils at Saint Mary's and Notre Dame . . . three of them joined the community, Sister M. Florentine (C.S.C.) and the twins, Sister Presentatione and Sister Purificatione (C.S.C.), her first cousins, Father Frank Bigelow (C.S.C.) and his sister, Sister M. Blanch (C.S.C.); her cousins Julia and Maggie Walker; Fenelon, Louise, and Ella Blaine; Miss Braddock, great granddaughter of General Braddock, Revolutionary War (sic), went to school at Saint Mary's and later became Mother M. Praxedes (C.S.C.); her cousins, Tom, Charles, and Sherman Steele (Notre Dame) ; Marie and Florence Steele (Saint Mary's). It was Mother M. Angela who noticed John Zahm as an altar boy out West (sic). She brought him to Notre Dame where he became a distinguished scientist and priest of Holy Cross. His three sisters joined the Sisters of the Holy Cross. . . . There were many others that we never heard of. I know these only as a member of the family and as a personal friend.[33]

Of a commencement in 1862 the same diarist gives this account:

The students made their way to the Exhibition Hall . . . soon the entertainment began, a theatrical play in costume, "Isabelle of Castille." (author: Mrs. E. Guthrie) I remember so well the part that Mary McVicker from Chicago played; she was afterwards the wife of Edwin Booth, the famous actor. Sister M. Elizabeth was in charge at Saint Mary's; Mother M. Angela was way down south with her hospital work. We stayed all summer at grandma's cottage (Mrs. Phelan lived in a cottage on the Saint

Mary's campus) and in September, 1862, the first brick building was opened and Agnes and I entered with the other pupils, many more than fifty boarders, at the opening of the school year. Mother (Mrs. Mary Gillespie Ewing) went back to Lancaster. Grandma stayed in her cottage and went with us at the end of the school year in June. For many years she divided her time between her daughter's home in Lancaster in the summer time and her grandchildren at Saint Mary's during the winter time.[34]

Mother M. Angela made contacts both before and after her entrance into Holy Cross with clergy who attained distinction.[35] "Eliza grew up with her cousins, the Ewings, the Shermans, the Blaines, associating with young clergymen, the future bishops Young, Gilmour, Kenrick, and Purcell. Later they in turn drew upon her brilliance and executive skill for Catholic pedagogy."[36] Her one year as teacher at Saint Mary's Seminary, a school founded by the state of Maryland, 1840, had acquainted her with Father Thomas Lilly, pastor of Saint Mary's City, Maryland. The regulations of Saint Mary's Seminary stipulated that its principal must be an Episcopalian, but the faculty members might practice any religion. After one year of teaching, she was invited to accept the principalship of this school, the authorities being willing to waive the religion requirement. This experience was again an entrée to the halls and to the hunts of Washington, Virginia, and Maryland families: the Brents, the Carrolls, the Youngs, and the Lees.

Mother M. Angela was among friends and influential people in ecclesiastical, political, and social circles when she returned to the Washington environs after the Civil War. The growth of the Sisters of the Holy Cross in the nation's capital was rooted and nurtured through these influences. In Mother M. Angela's lifetime eight schools, private and parochial, were opened in Washington, D.C., all eight of them operating today.[37]

There are many manuscripts of abortive efforts to write the life of Mother M. Angela.[38] In each there is the implication that this was no ordinary woman, that she was a woman whose history should be known. In "Angela Gillespie, Family Tree" the author makes reference to the closely knit bond of this family, adding:

The children found companionship with their many cousins who as earliest settlers in the town (Lancaster, Ohio) had amassed wealth and intellectual prominence in what was then considered the best society west of the Alleghenies.[39]

One would not wish to give here the impression that wealth, culture, and education were the only assets which contributed to shaping the early history of the quality of teaching and teaching personnel of the young congregation or the quality of its academies.

The Gillespie family tree included converts to Catholicism whose deep faith influenced the lives of those with whom they came in contact. Moreover, a glance at the family tree will show the strong penchant for service which was to characterize the descendants of the Gillespie clan. Priests, sisters, teachers in public schools, superintendents of public school systems, doctors, lawyers, judges, professional military men, and politicians are everywhere evident.[40]

The sustained leadership for thirty-four years of a woman of this character left its mark on the young Congregation of the Sisters of the Holy Cross and on the academies which it opened from 1855 to 1900.

Archival references show that the term "academy" was used loosely in the midnineteenth and early decades of the twentieth century. Schools were opened and given the title "academy" when in reality they were not. Types of schools bore this misnomer under several conditions: (1) if the school was owned by a religious community and not parish owned,

TABLE No. 1
Academies Patterned on "The Programme of Studies for Academies"

Name	Place	Date
Saint Mary's Academy	Notre Dame, Indiana	(1855–1945)
	South Bend, Indiana	(1945–)
Academy of the Assumption, now Saint Joseph's Elementary School	Lowell, Indiana South Bend, Indiana	(1867–1890)
Saint Patrick's Academy, then Academy of Holy Cross when it merged with the parish school, becoming Saint Patrick's School	Baltimore, Maryland	(1859–1870) (1870–1887)
Saint Rose's Academy became Saint Peter's School	La Porte, Indiana	(1864–1919)
Saint Angela's Academy	Morris, Illinois	(1857–1958)
Saint Vincent's Academy became Holy Angels' Academy	Logansport, Indiana	(1863–1871)
Saint Joseph's Academy became Saint Joseph's High School	South Bend, Indiana	(1865–1952) (1952–)
Academy of Our Lady of the Sacred Heart	Fort Wayne, Indiana	(1866–1934)
Academy of the Holy Cross, now moved to	Washington, D. C. Kensington, Maryland	(1868–1955) (1956–)
Saint Cecilia's Academy	Washington, D. C.	(1868–)
Saint Mary's Academy	Alexandria, Virginia	(1869–)
Sacred Heart Academy	Lancaster, Pennsylvania	(1873–1958)
Saint Mary's Academy	Austin, Texas	(1874–)
Saint Mary's Academy	Salt Lake City, Utah	(1875–)
Saint Mary's Academy, now Saint Joseph's parish school	Marshall, Texas	(1880–1957)
Holy Rosary Academy, now a parochial school	Woodland, California	(1886–1953)
Saint Teresa's Academy, now a diocesan high school	Boise, Idaho	(1889–1964)
Academy of Saint Catherine	Ventura, California	(1925–)
Holy Cross Academy	Brookline, Massachusetts	(1948–)

TABLE No. 2

Private Schools Owned by the Sisters of the Holy Cross: 1964

Midwest Province

* Saint Mary's College, Notre Dame, Indiana

* Saint Mary's Academy, Notre Dame, Twyckenham, South Bend, Indiana

Eastern Province

Dunbarton College of Holy Cross, Washington, D. C.

Cardinal Cushing College, Brookline, Massachusetts

* Academy of the Holy Cross, Kensington, Maryland

* Saint Cecilia's Academy, Washington, D.C.

* Saint Mary's Academy, Alexandria, Virginia

* Saint Mary's Academy, Austin, Texas

Holy Cross Academy, Brookline, Massachusetts

Western Province

* Academy of Saint Mary-of-the-Wasatch, Salt Lake City, Utah

Academy of Saint Catherine, Ventura, California

Saint Catherine's Grade School, Ventura, California

Holy Cross High School, Mountain View, California

Holy Cross Missions Abroad—Community Owned

East Pakistan

Holy Rosary Convent, Tejgaon, Dacca 5, East Pakistan

Holy Cross College, Tejgaon, Dacca 5, East Pakistan

Brazil

Vila Betania, Sao Paulo 18, Brazil, Colegio Santa Maria

Vila Nazare, Sao Paulo 18, Brazil

* Opened by Mother M. Angela.

even though patronized by a parish, it frequently was called an "academy," (2) if private music and/or art was added to the curriculum of a parochial school, (3) if it was a parish school with a more developed and enriched curriculum for students who came from a more privileged socio-economic background.

The community had its share of each type of these "academies." But it is not to schools of this type that the term is to be used in this study. Rather it applies only to those foundations which followed the plan that Father Sorin and Mother M. Angela worked out in detail on their return from France in 1854. The program drew heavily on the works of pedagogy of Father Moreau, the college and university experience of Father Sorin, and the thoroughly American education of Mother Angela in the tradition of the eastern schools of her time.

Eighteen in number, these academies did not all develop to the same degree. Their growth was conditioned by the section of the country in which they were located, socioeconomic changes in a city or in a neighborhood, and the demands of accreditation which favored survival of larger schools. All but six of the academies opened before 1900 have become parochial, diocesan, or coinstitutional high schools.

Table No. 2 contains a list of private schools owned by the Sisters of the Holy Cross, 1964. Four of these are missions abroad.

The academies opened between 1855 and 1889 by the Sisters of the Holy Cross were not institutions of expediency. They were organized, planned centers of learning, all modeled on the same philosophy and objectives of a Catholic school, all with the same type of curriculum. Each grew to its own stature; each had the advantage of union, without the stifling disadvantage of uniformity.

Marion McCandless, 1900, gives a graphic description of life at Saint Mary's Academy in 1896.

My association with Saint Mary's College, Notre Dame, began ten years before I was born. My grandfather James Ritchie, a country doctor of Pinckneyville, Illinois, strangely enough had a warm feeling for the Catholic Church, though he knew little about it, being a non-Catholic of no special religious commitment. But he sensed the modesty, integrity, and goodness of the Catholic women in his country practice. Few of them had had formal education—only the culture of their faith.

Dr. Ritchie was looking for a boarding school for his eldest daughter, Loretta, then sixteen, and his second daughter, Elizabeth, then thirteen. A friend in Saint Louis said to him, "I know just the school for your daughters, Saint Mary's Academy, Notre Dame. You could look the world over and not find a better school."

Dr. Ritchie sent for a catalog. That September (1870) he drove his daughter Loretta and her aunt, Frances Murphy (younger sister of Mrs. Ritchie), and Zoe Osburn ten miles in a wagon with their trunks, to DuQuoin, Illinois on the main line of the Illinois Central Railroad between Chicago and Cairo, Illinois. The girls changed cars in Chicago, came to South Bend, and entered Saint Mary's Academy, Notre Dame, one mile west of the University of Notre Dame. They were all non-Catholics, had never talked to a priest, and had never seen a sister before.

Loretta Ritchie graduated in the class of 1875. Two of her classmates later became the mothers of Eugene O'Neill (Ellen Quinlan) and George Jean Nathan (Ella Niedlinger).

In 1872 Elizabeth Ritchie came here to the academy, graduating in 1877. Both Ritchie girls became Catholics in their senior year. Elizabeth later as Mrs. William L. McCandless, became my mother. She was especially talented in French. She was one of the best artists among the student body of her time, a special pupil of Sister M. Florentine, C.S.C. (Ellen Tong, 1868).

When I came in September 1896 as a freshman, the campus was an ivory tower, whence we departed not, from September until Christmas holidays. If we were ill, the doctor came to see us; if a tooth ached, we either had the dentist come here or we went to his office under heavy chaperoned surveillance.

On Sundays after Mass we wrote in an English copy book our weekly letter home, and to the few others to whom we were permitted to write. The English teacher corrected these. They were returned Wednesday after Mass and then copied them on our stationery. You can imagine how spontaneous those letters were and the paucity of news we had to relate. We rarely saw a newspaper, went nowhere, saw few persons. We just studied, ate, slept, played, had fun and were perhaps as happy as any girl in college in 1964, maybe even more so.

We had collation (bread, butter, jelly, syrup—all homemade) at 10 a.m. and 4 p.m. We had a bag of fresh fruit from a town fruit shop—on Wednesday. But not all could afford this 75¢ each week. I was *not one* who got fruit.

We had simple, well-balanced meals, but nothing like the elaborate ones of today. Ice cream was a rarity and loud screams went up in the refectory when a feast day produced ice cream—and never anything but vanilla.

We did not have daily Communion, nor even urgings to go to daily Mass. We were supposed to go at 6 a.m. on Mondays and Saturdays, but there was no insistence. Wednesday was a free day instead of Saturday (French!). On that day we had Mass at 7 a.m. after breakfast. We went to Holy Communion (1896–1901) every two or three weeks. This was considered very pious.

When my father came to visit me (my mother died when I was six), he hired a horse and buggy in town and drove out here. Then we drove together to town for dinner at the only hotel, the Oliver, and bought some fruit and candy for me and my friends. Then Dr. McCandless took the train back to Chicago in the afternoon, with the night Pullman down to southern Illinois.

I felt it a privilege to come to Saint Mary's. I always felt I got value received for the money my hard-working father was putting in my education. I was at Saint Mary's in 1898 in the physics class when Professor Green made the first "long distance wireless" message from the Notre Dame campus to ours—the first long distance on the western hemisphere. When Roentgen discovered the x-ray in Europe (1895) we had a small machine to make x-rays in our lab., (1896–97). Mother M. Pauline always had Father John Zahm, a great scholar, buy anything in Europe which he thought the school should have . . . no gifts, however.

We took six sciences: mathematics, chemistry, physics (with fine lab.), botany, geology, and astronomy. The only constellations we studied were those visible at 7 p.m. in this latitude and

longitude in October. We were never permitted outside the building at night except when our teacher, Sister M. Eleanore (Sturgis,
1871), took us out to gaze at the stars.

Not one sister on the faculty then had a B.A. degree, yet each
one was a highly educated person. They all attended summer
school lectures in the 1880's and 1890's before they began giving
degrees. Mary O'Callaghan, sister of the famous Peter J. O'Callaghan, was a graduate of Radcliffe (sic), the first postulant to
enter Holy Cross with an A.B. (1897). The new Sister M. Angela
taught Greek to Sister M. Francis Jerome (O'Laughlin). The
latter taught us Latin and Greek in 1900. I also had Latin with
Sister M. Angela (O'Callaghan) ; she was a real eastern scholar.[41]

Mother Kathryn Marie (Gibbons), superior general, knew
from her mother and her mother's three sisters of the early
education at Saint Cecilia's Academy, Washington, D.C., in
the 1870's and 1880's.[42] The course of study was that drawn
up by Mother Angela and entitled "Programme for Academies and Select Schools." The curriculum included logic,
ethics, solid geometry, four years of Latin, and geology. German and French were taught by Sister M. Anita (Even) from
Alsace-Lorraine. Though of French background, she was a
specialist in both tongues.

In my childhood, listening to family narratives, I heard much
about school life at Saint Cecilia's. I saw in my aunts the personi-
fications of those values which were considered a part of total
education—an appreciation for fine arts, particularly music, painting, and needlepoint. My mother's first grade teacher, Sister M.
Baptista (Ring), was my first grade teacher. She impressed me by
her kind recollections of my mother and of my grandmother.
Mother M. Aquina (Kerwin) and Mother M. Perpetua (Wilson)
taught at Saint Cecilia's when they were young sisters.[43]

Mother then referred to the strong French heritage which
was evident in the details of boarding school life at the academy with special reference to the horarium. It closely matched

one found in the council minutes of 1850. The latter is quoted here for its unique manner of expression.

It has been resolved Art. No. 1 that the following regulations should be observed in the Academy (of the House of Bertrand, U.S.A.).

5:25	1st Bell	Rising
5:55		Prayer, Christian Study
7¼		Breakfast, followed by recreation
8		1st English course
		2nd Arithmetic class
9		Preparatory course
		1st Arithmetic class
10		Recreation
10¼		Penmanship; Drawing on Tuesday, Thursday, and Saturday
11¼		French class
12		Dinner followed by recreation
1½ p.m.		Study
2		1st English course
		Preparatory course
3½		Duties redactions for 1st course and Preparatory course cont.
4½		Luncheon; recreation
5		Needlework
6		Study
7		Supper followed by recreation[44]

To these regulations Mother Kathryn Marie adds that French and German were an integral part of the elementary curriculum as well as physical geography. Great emphasis was given to a "family spirit." Sisters ate at the table with the students at all meals and attended recreation with them. The principal presided at oral examinations in all subjects, each semester. She gave the examination grade. Mother concludes:

All that I have mentioned here reflects the prevailing spirit and techniques at young Saint Mary's and at Notre Dame. Both the spirit and the means to achieve it were carried forth to other missions—Saint Joseph's Academy, South Bend, Indiana; Academy of Holy Cross, Dunbarton, and Saint Cecilia's, Washington, D.C.; and to Saint Edward's Preparatory Department, Notre Dame, Indiana.[45]

Saint Mary's Academy, Alexandria, Virginia, was opened in 1869 with Sister M. Ambrose (Corby) as superior and directress of studies. Sister Ambrose had recently opened Saint Cecilia's Academy in the nation's capital, where, the archives read, "She returned as soon as the new school in Alexandria was well established."[46] The statistics for the first year were six sisters, two lay teachers, seven boarders, and eighty-six students. Records show that its superiors were to be found in the ranks of the community leaders: Mother M. Compassion (Gleason), Sister M. Lydia (Clifford), Sister M. Assumption (Boyle), Mother M. Cyriaca (Keating), Mother M. Bethlehem (Desneau), Mother M. Bettina (Reale), Mother M. Vincentia (Fannon), Sister M. Antonine (Farmer), and Sister M. Assumpta (Dougherty).

Father Sorin and Mother M. Angela jointly founded Saint Mary's Academy, Austin, Texas, in 1874. Then a struggling village with natural scenic beauty as its only adornment, Austin would never have attracted administrators of less daring than the pioneers of Bertrand. Mother M. Angela and Sister M. Austin (Barnard) arrived in April to prepare for the opening of the school in September. They both taught the first year with a faculty augmented by nine other sisters. The enrollment at the end of the first year was eighty. The archives report thus on the first year:

It is not fine buildings, excellent instruments, fine art furnishings, apparatus, books, and stationery which constitute an efficient educational institution. It is well-informed, religiously inspired, heartily endowed, dedicated teachers who cooperate with a wise and faithful administration, that vitalize, prosper, exalt, and perpetuate an academy. With such teachers, such an administration, Saint Mary's Austin, is endowed.[47]

As mentioned earlier with reference to Saint Mary's Academy, Alexandria, Virginia, the directresses of studies in Austin included many who later were to serve the community in the capacity of elected administrators.[48]

With the prestige of the first year their reputation for culture spread, and in 1875 there were repeated requests for a school to be established for the education of children of wealthy families.[49] A series of purchases of property matched by bequests of valuable lots in Austin made possible the fulfillment of a dream, a Saint Mary's of the South. A pretentious structure was built. When sold in 1948, to an association of business men, it still was an architecturally imposing building.

In both academies in Texas—Saint Mary's, Marshall, and Saint Mary's, Austin—the typical Holy Cross curriculum prevailed. Although English, mathematics, history, languages, science, and Christian Doctrine were the core subjects, the schools excelled in their departments of music, voice, and dramatics. The commerce department of Saint Mary's, Marshall, had adult night classes available.[50] Non-Catholics patronized both academies in large numbers.

The academies in the West were in the same tradition. Sister M. Rhoda (Hyde) attended Saint Teresa's Academy, Boise, Idaho, in the fifth grade (1886). She returned for four years of high school as a boarder, graduating in 1900. In an interview Sister spoke with accurate recall of life in the mountains of Idaho where she was born and reared:

I am the daughter of a western cattleman, Mr. Michael Hyde, who named the valley where he settled, Oreana, i.e., "lost, strayed, or stolen." As a child I rode on horseback over the mountain trails—side saddle. Although other girls were sometimes permitted, my father would never let me round up cattle.

He sent me to Saint Teresa's even though we were not Catholics because it was the only high school in the area. Sister M. Sienna (Seely) was in school with me at the same time. Yes, I recall the classes we had—a great deal of science: geology, botany, astronomy, physics, chemistry, and mathematics. We used Quackenbos' rhetoric. Sisters M. Remigius (Murphy), M. Columbina (Dempsey), and M. Diego (Roberts) taught me in high school. I took music from Sisters M. Hildetta (Brennan) and M. Alicia (McDonald). Etymology, algebra, geometry, and mental arithmetic were also in the curriculum. We had wonderful art classes. Father Vander Heyden, chaplain of Saint Alphonsus Hospital, Boise, came to the academy to teach us Christian Doctrine, French, Latin, and philosophy. Father Vander Heyden was a Belgian scholar who had held a chair at the University of Louvain. We loved him. He came frequently, taking us for long walks which were a part of each day's recreation. We loved Sister M. Julitta (Mooney); she had charge of the kitchen. She fed us especially well. Our favorite was her Boston brown beans which she baked in an earthen pot all day Saturday. Then we had for Sunday breakfast hard rolls, wieners, and those delicious Boston brown beans.

Father Vander Heyden baptized me and Mother M. Francis Clare (Counihan) was my godmother. After I became a Sister of the Holy Cross, I taught music for sixty-three years. During the summer schools at Saint Mary-of-the-Wasatch, Salt Lake City, we had regular classes. I continued my study of music summer after summer with such professors as Miss Frost, Miss Robyn, and Mr. Bernard Wagness.

We were trained with strict discipline, but I guess everyone was at that time. But we loved the sisters and they loved us, so we were a happy family.[51]

Hence it is clear that it made little difference whether an academy was in the East, West, South, or Midwest. The course of study was basically the same; the spirit was essentially a familial one. The same administrators were found recurring in the annals of each academy, with Mother M. Angela opening every one personally with the exception of Saint Teresa's Academy, Boise, and Holy Rosary Academy, Woodland, California.

Complex factors multiplied Catholic school expansion in the second half of the nineteenth century. Religious teachers were a part of a democratic society where the demand for teachers far exceeded the supply. Quality was sacrificed for quantity. The secularization of the public schools, indirectly the result of efforts to strip them of denominational instruction, influenced the hierarchy in their efforts to establish parochial schools. The First Plenary Council of Baltimore (1852) merely recommended building parish schools; the Third Plenary Council (1884) ordered a school for each parish and a two-year deadline to accomplish this.[52]

Most of the Catholic immigrants were poor; they could contribute little in a financial way to the building and maintenance of schools. Financing Catholic education was prohibitive apart from the services of the religious communities of men and women teachers in the United States.

Despite the demand for more schools and more teachers, there was an effort to restrain expansion in the interests of better qualified teachers. In a letter from Mother M. Angela to Father Sorin, she recognizes his previous directive "not to open any school this year (1862) because of a lack of teachers."[53] In another letter (1869) Mother Angela writes from Washington, D.C., to Father Sorin:

We are following your sage advice to take no new establishments so that we may be able to develop the schools which we now have with greater advantage next year. . . . I am returning home four promising postulants. Three of them will make good English teachers.[54]

The demand and supply have never been balanced. In the first decade of the twentieth century Bishop Alerding spoke appreciatively of the dominant qualities which he thought characterized the teachers of the Holy Cross.

The community in its formative period was stamped with the characteristics held to be its distinguishing marks today—a spirit of progress, common-sense, zeal, devotedness, and self-sacrifice.[55]

But the bishop cannot stop here:

The excellence of the community is recognized . . . but there is a lack of subjects to meet the demands of the times. . . . This brief sketch would have included many more . . . establishments of the order had there been sisters to take charge of the work waiting. They have refused ten openings for want of teachers . . . such is their record in Fort Wayne for the first six months of 1907![56]

What was the source, then, of the personnel who were to staff the Holy Cross schools which by the end of the nineteenth century were to number more than fifty?[57] A new energy pervaded the ranks of the sisters after their return from services in the Civil War.[58] Calls from the Atlantic to the Pacific, from the Northwest to Texas, all asked for more schools to be opened. Mother M. Angela responded with parochial schools, academies, and a normal school—all supervised for excellence. She turned to Catholic countries of Europe, disturbed by internal political turmoil, in quest of personnel.

In 1873 Mother M. Angela and Sister M. Ferdinand (Bruggerman) went to Europe to obtain members, traveling through France, Luxembourg, Belgium, and Ireland. The archives state they recruited not only in quantity but also in quality.[59] The register indicates that these new postulants were a little older than the average aspirant heretofore (late twenties as compared with early twenties).[60]

In March, 1874, forty-four postulants from Ireland received the habit of the Sisters of the Holy Cross. Educated in the convents of their native land, imbued with traditions of constancy and of faith, these young women supplied the community with recruits for the schools which it was opening.

A second group received the habit that same year (1874), bringing the total to ninety-three, the largest number ever to be admitted to the Sisters of the Holy Cross in one year. Of these, fifty-seven had been born in Ireland; six, Luxembourg; two, Belgium; four, France; and the remaining twenty-four in the United States.[61]

The colorful Sister M. Eugenie (D'Orbesson) was a member of this group. She was head of the French Department at Saint Mary's College for thirty years.[62] In this same recruitment the Koppes family (Belgium) was added to the Congregation of the Holy Cross: Sisters M. Wigbert, Bibiana, and Willibrord; their brother, Rev. J. Koppes, was ordained for the Peoria diocese. Again in 1875, accompanied by Sister M. Wigbert (Koppes), Mother M. Angela went to Germany, returning with eight aspirants.[63] These, too, had a high degree of persistency.[64]

Mother M. Angela planned the education of these teachers carefully. She had employed Miss Eliza Allan Starr, artist-in-residence, to teach art in the novitiate and to the pupils at the academy.[65] At the time of Mother Angela's death Miss Starr wrote in the *Freeman's Journal:*

Mother M. Angela committed her postulants to the best teachers of the order, those capable of teaching higher studies, language, music, and art. Nor did she hesitate to call in secular teachers to aid in this program. Far from allowing her religious to feel that it was a discredit to receive instructions from seculars, she put before them the duty of being able to compete, honorably and fairly, with any teachers in the land, and to make themselves thoroughly familiar with the most improved methods in all branches. . . . Nor were studies, music, drawing, and painting her only care. From Ireland and Flanders, she brought lacemakers skilled in the choicest embroideries.[66]

Classes in sewing, embroidery, and lace-making, extracurricular to be sure, were basic requirements of a finished education. These subjects continued in the academy curricula until after World War I.

The aspirant or postulant[67] who became a Sister of the Holy Cross came from a home with a solid training in the qualities which religious life demanded: respect, hard work, service to the Church and to others, reverence for elders, a sense of responsibility, habits of obedience, and devotion to family.[68] It was easy to teach her to supernaturalize these already acquired traits. She found in the classroom the same atmosphere of order and application which had characterized her own early training. In the secular schools, too, prevailed the firmly fixed idea that discipline was identified with education. Textbook, rote teaching, and self-learning were the accepted methods of pedagogy. "Predominantly, it was an epoch when traditions were held in considerable respect, and when individual authority was the chief instrumentality of instructional progress."[69]

Often the prestige of an academy was based on the reputation of one or two members of its faculty whose names for generations became synonymous with culture. The example of these sisters was a stimulus to the less gifted. Private study played an important part in the maintenance of scholastic and teaching ideals. Classed as private study were the lectures given by priests from local colleges.

There was no state law or rule requiring teachers to possess certification (1845–1895). The simple line of conduct was to have sisters study in the after-class hours and during the summer months, coached by one of the older and more experienced teachers.

Catholic education in the United States was from its beginning dependent chiefly upon the teaching activities of religious communities. These, having the spread of the Faith and its conservation as their chief objective, gave to its early days a strong missionary cast. Both European communities and those of American origin adapted their teaching technique and curricula to the conditions that faced them, and dispensed largely with pre-service training of teachers, substituting for it the apprenticeship method of learning while doing.

In the fourfold training of the Sisters, emphasis was placed on the religious and social rather than on the cultural and professional. Since the needs of the time called for services of the Sisters in the social and charitable as well as the educational field, dependence for success in the work assigned was placed on the religious vocation itself.

Beginning with 1840, immigration, church legislation on education, and the definitely secular character of public schools, served to accentuate the need for Catholic schools and teachers. Quantity rather than quality was the demand; the communities were forced to respond by sending professionally untrained workers into the field.

Such professional preparation as the Sisters received prior to the middle 90's consisted of private study, teaching and supervision of the younger nuns by older members of the community, Mother House normals and summer schools conducted by the Sisters themselves.

In the secular field teaching was a poorly paid employment, and had not reached the status of a profession. Little or no preparation was demanded of teachers in the public school system, and although state normals began in 1839, most of the teachers up to 1900 were admitted to the teaching field through county or state examinations in which political influence often counted for more than intellectual endowment.[70]

Elsbree describes the status of the public school as similar.[71]

While it is true that in the teacher education in the Congregation of the Sisters of the Holy Cross there was emphasis on the training of the sisters religiously and socially, nevertheless from the first days of Saint Mary's, Bertrand, there was strong emphasis on the cultural as well. The emphasis was the result of the leadership and vision of Father Moreau, Father Sorin, and Mother M. Angela, complemented by the talents and services of Mother M. Elizabeth, the Redmans, Lillys, and Phelans. If any aspect was neglected, it was the professional. But professional training of the public school teacher of the same period was woefully neglected.[72] Preservice teacher training was inadequate in public and private school systems, but the inservice training of religious communities was better established than that of the teacher in the public school system.

But what was the ordinary means by which the teacher in the era 1855 to 1900 was prepared in Holy Cross? The training ran a gamut of practices: individual instruction; the opening of a scholasticate for formal study; apprenticeship under a master teacher; lecture series on pertinent subjects, emerging in the seventies and eighties into more formalized programs; and by the end of the century the summer school and the institute.

The actual professional preparation of sisters (1855–1900) compared not too unfavorably with public school teachers. But the training was still inadequate for the needs.

The Sisters of the Holy Cross had a teachers' guide from the first days of Bertrand. With the coming of Mother M. Angela there was a course of study, textbooks to implement it, regular class meetings, and academic guidance from the priests, brothers, and professors from Notre Dame.

The members of the August 27, 1868, regular chapter advocated the opening of a "scholasticate where novices and young professed could continue their studies."[73] The entire emphasis was on subject matter. But inexperienced teachers were not turned out in large numbers. Generally but one apprentice was found in each academy, where the directress of studies had the responsibility of a master teacher. The young teacher stayed in the same grade until subject-matter and technique warranted advancement.

Secondary schools suffered less since the more successful elementary teachers of the school passed on to the academy faculty.

Even when professional education was curtailed, the character formation of a canonical novitiate was not. The lessons of the novitiate—self-discipline, responsibility, courage, sympathy, tact, and an apostolic viewpoint for the warp and woof of a novice's life—were not adequate substitutes for practical training in classroom efficiency. But they did contribute to a stronger, spiritual character, even though this left much to be desired as a teacher.

By 1870 higher superiors were sending out directives for study during the summer time.[74] "The whole month of July is to be set aside for the improvement of the sisters. Classes and lectures will be held every morning; the afternoons may be profitably employed in study, sewing, or other light work and recreation."[75]

In an 1877 record of studies followed by postulants and novices Mother M. Angela describes the course of studies which they were to pursue: "After a review of the primary branches, the first class of the novitiate will correspond to the third class of the academic course."[76] The first semester of this course included: Bullion's Grammar (rules and syntactical analyses, finished); Ganot's Philosophy; Davies' University Arithmetic (to alligation); Fredet's Ancient History; Latin, French, or German. The second semester: Quackenbos' Rhetoric; Davies' Arithmetic and Algebra; Ancient History; Philosophy (finished); Languages as above.[77]

Father Sorin suggested that the scholastic year, 1884, close with a chapter, the chief object of which would be to raise the standards of the schools through the development of superior teachers, and this at any cost.[78] After a short novitiate, young sisters were to be trained as teachers under local superiors. This was a threefold training of character formation, intellectual enlightenment, and teaching skill.

"Each superior or head of a house will see that classes be carefully formed and well attended with the view to the benefit of the sisters and the advancement of the children during the coming year."[79]

Letters were sent out from the general house with directives for such inservice practice:

Let me here again remind you of the necessity of study, which next to prayer, is the groundwork of your success. Knowledge of each particular branch taught in your department is absolutely necessary for you; it is the keynote to the proper imparting of any subject to the mind of the child and it can be obtained only by solid study; hence I repeat to each sister what I have so often said before, prepare your class work well, so that you may be in full possession of the subject, and may win the confidence and respect of your pupils. . . .[80]

Mother M. Annunciata (McSheffrey) asked that weekly class-meeting minutes be kept and forwarded to her at the mother house.[81] The minutes of class meetings as far back as 1855 can be found in the archives of Saint Mary's College. They concern externals of discipline, it is true, but there is always reference to the importance of prepared lessons and to teacher mastery of content.[82]

Of each sister Mother further asked a report "concerning the work, time spent in teaching, and time spent in study to prepare to teach the classes, the progress made so far, and the plans for continued study until the end of the school year."[83]

In 1897 Mother Annunciata recommended to teachers:

Carry out the plans given in the "Teachers' Guide" and the practical application of the virtues of a good teacher. I beg the heads of houses to see that time be given and faithfully taken for the conscientious preparation of class duties and all such class work as compositions, rhetorical exercises, letters, etc.; in a word, every branch taught must be prepared. How great will be the results if all our sisters strive to educate in this thoroughly practical manner—the only way for Sisters of the Holy Cross whether in the highest academy or the lowliest parochial school.[84]

Saint Mary's organized summer-school sessions as early as 1870. The program was rich and solid in content. Because of this practice, academies and convents acquired a reputation for excellence and for scholarship. This was especially so of the programs offered at Saint Mary's, Notre Dame.[85]

The program of lectures for teachers, June, 1896, was typical. Father Stanislas Fitte, Father Alexander Kirsch, and Professor Austin O'Malley conducted classes from 8:00 a.m. to 11:30 a.m. The archives state:

The sisters attended lectures in the pupils' study hall commencing on June 30 and continuing through July. Father Fitte presented a series entitled "Law and Liberty" at 8:00 a.m.; Father Kirsch, "Organic Cells, the Basis of Life" at 9:00 a.m.; and Professor O'Malley, "Principles of Poetics" at 10:00 a.m.[86]

In 1899 an interesting program was prepared for "all teachers of intermediate and junior grades." Classes in literature and composition were organized the last week in June with Professor Austin O'Malley as first teacher and Sister M. Rita (Heffernan), the second. Other offerings were listed.

Geography	Sister M. Berenice (Bruneau)
Grammar	Sister M. Teresa (O'Brien)
Arithmetic	Sister M. Berenice
Reading	Sister M. Ignatia (Guthrie)
Pedagogy	Sister M. Dorothea (Bruneau)
French	Sister M. Eugenie (D'Orbesson)
German	Sister M. Boniface (Lauth)
Greek	Sister M. Francis Jerome (O'Laughlin)

Latin	Sister M. Antonine (Farmer), Sister M. Berenice, Sister M. Eutropia (Oakes)
Polish	Rev. Father Smogger
Italian	Prof. (same one as taught Spanish and Greek during the school year.)[87]

The libraries and studios associated with European schools, the lecture halls, and visiting professors were a part of the program of teacher education and pupil enrichment. From the first days at Bertrand the sisters profited by the proximity of Notre Dame and by the counsel and teaching of the early priests and professors of its faculty. Mother M. Compassion, in her voluminous diary, gives the names of those who visited Bertrand either as teachers or examiners. "Reverend Father E. E. Shawe is our Professor of Rhetoric and Literature, Mr. Gardner Jones a noted orator—and has charge of our composition classes. . . . Mr. Denis O'Leary is devoted to mathematics . . . Brother Basil and Professor Druso, to art and music."[88] Again,

The academy offers for young ladies a finished education in literature, art, music, language, and scripture. Professors from the college come regularly to teach the sisters in order to carry on the studies in an academy; it is to these courageous predecessors that we owe our existence as a teaching body.[89]

This kind of educational interest and guidance continued from 1855 to 1917. *The Chimes* issue of July, 1895, the golden jubilee year, names the examining board:

Brother Boniface was president of the examing board; as head of the German department, he also presided over its examinations. Father Stanislas Fitte and L.M. L'Etourneau, the French; Fathers Fitte and Joseph Scherer, moral philosophy; Fathers Thomas Vagnier and Scherer, Latin; Fathers Vagnier and John Cavanaugh, Christian Doctrine, graduates; Father A. Zahm, astronomy; Fathers James French, George O'Connor, John Zahm, James

Scherer and Thomas Corbett, preparatories; Father Patrick Maloney, primaries.[90]

There are sisters and lay alumnae who remember vividly the oral examinations, a practice which prevailed from Bertrand days until World War I. Eliza Allan Starr, resident artist at Saint Mary's Academy from 1870 to 1878, tells in her Victorian style the reaction of Rt. Rev. Patrick Riordan to the Exhibition Day and its awards, a practice found in all the early academies.

His Grace, Archbishop Riordan of San Francisco, still tells with glee how prizes were given on Exhibition Day (commencement) at Notre Dame and Saint Mary's. Only one, two, or three volumes (books are still awarded as top prizes in the school system of France) answered for Notre Dame thus: When the first prize had been given to one class, it was cheerfully surrendered to another class, and so on. When Notre Dame had thus bestowed its true and enduring laurels, the books were taken over to Saint Mary's and given in the same manner, to the best scholars in the academy. When all was over, the first, second, and third prize winners gayly drew lots for the final possession of the books. The cross of emulation was thus eliminated, and like the Greek crown of wild olive awarded to the victor, the honor of merit was esteemed beyond the prize itself.[91]

The teacher-education practices at Saint Mary's Academy were, in general, similar to those that prevailed in the nineteenth century history of academies. But the facilities of studios, music rooms, lecture halls, and the services of professors from Notre Dame were not in the pattern of the times.

In general, upon the local superior devolved the duty to improve and to advance the young teachers sent to her from the novitiate. These teachers served an apprenticeship in academies and parochial schools, where a more formal teacher preparation program was evolving. Not only were the sisters counseled by a master teacher but they also followed organized courses in summer school programs and in institutes. Although historically normal school training prepared teachers for the classrooms, its influence was not widespread. Elsbree points out that Massachusetts ranked highest of all states, but at the turn of the century only 38.5% of its teachers in public schools had received normal instruction and only 33.5% were normal graduates. Before 1900 the preparation of secondary school teachers was confined chiefly to colleges and universities, but little pedagogy was taught.[92]

The Sisters of the Holy Cross experienced a similar evolution in teacher preparation. There were institutes for in-service training conducted by distinguished lecturers. The summer schools developed, until a report of the 1896 session read:

Long before the inauguration in England of the movement known as "University Extension," or the foundation of the famous Chautauqua Summer School in our own country, the teachers at Saint Mary's every year enjoyed the benefits of pedagogical training during the vacation months. . . . This summer we doubt if those who attended schools at Madison, Plattsburg, or Rochester enjoyed greater advantages than those who were instructed by the learned professors in the Academy Hall. . . . (The lecturers included:) Dr. Austin O'Malley: "The Construction of the Highest Forms of Literary Expression," "Illustrations of Literary Forms," "Analyses of Masterpieces in the World of Letters"; Dr. E. A. Pace, Catholic University of America: "Psychology in Its Relations to Pedagogy," "Fundamental Principles in the Science of Mind-Study," "The Two-Fold Tie of Sympathy Between Teacher and Pupil"; Rev. J. Zahm, C.S.C., doctor of philosophy at the University of Notre Dame: "Demonstrations of Physical Apparatus," "The Array of Cells Forming a Battery," "Ruhmkorff's Coil for a Crooke's Tube," "Experiments with Roentgen-Ray."[93]

Significantly enough, the thesis of the first college graduate, Mary Agnes Ewing Brown, was "Quantitative and Qualitative Teaching." The South Bend public school superintendent requested that it be read at the summer school institute for teacher preparation in 1898.[94]

A logical question arises. How could such a program of studies for schools with their varied personnel finance its works and teacher training?

In 1869 the Sisters of the Holy Cross were separated temporally from the priests and brothers. A settlement was made whereby one-third of the assets and liabilities was awarded to the sisters. Father Moreau was insistent that the young community keep archives and fiscal accounts.[95] There are ledgers containing entries of receipts, expenditures, surplus, deficit, creditors, and interest rates on loans and mortgages. Added are two columns marked "Due House" and "House Owes." "Due House" was tuition, music and art lessons, sheet music, or books unpaid. "House Owes" indicated creditors.[96]

There was no sophisticated economy in the nineteenth century fiscal planning, no twentieth century capitalistic procedures. Detailed accounts of receipts and expenditures for each establishment from the date of its opening are now on microfilm. By 1857, after the regular visit of Father Moreau, the forms used were uniform in all houses. The earliest such record is given for Saint Angela's Academy, Morris, Illinois, 1857. Surplus in a given academy was sent to the general house and then used to liquidate debts in other houses and to pay general house expenses. The community had no investments, no endowments. Patrimony of the sisters was invested, but according to canon law it could not be used until after the death of the owner, and then only if the sister had made her will in favor of the congregation.[97] Father Thomas T. McAvoy, C.S.C., in describing the fiscal practices of the community of Priests of Holy Cross over the same period of years

(1855–1910), points up a similar condition at Notre Dame:

Sometimes the community was without money in August and had to borrow until the student payments came in September. A new building would be built on time and paid off from meagre savings of subsequent years. The gains from the farms and the stipends from the missions to neighboring parishes went into the same funds along with occasional gifts and legacies. The most important item in the weekly meeting of the Local Council was the statement of "cash on hand." The financial wisdom was that of the European peasant.[98]

Prosperous Saint Angela's Academy, Morris, Illinois, sent to the general house, July, 1859, its surplus to leave a precarious "cash on hand" and to be presented with the August situation of borrowing described by Father McAvoy.[99] The accounts from 1857 to 1865 are not in the form of Table No. 3; they give scattered information. The accounts were probably kept with the accounts of the University of Notre Dame, destroyed by fire in 1879. Saint Angela's Academy is an example of a school with benefactors from the beginning.

Holy Cross Academy, Washington, D.C.; Saint Mary's Academy, Austin, Texas; and Saint Mary-of-the-Wasatch, Salt Lake City, Utah, are examples of establishments which paid off heavy debt on time from the meager surplus and savings of the subsequent years. The academy reached a peak of receipts in 1887 to 1888 ($27,899.50), but it was never out of debt in the nineteenth century. The school grew under the leadership of its first two directresses of studies, Sister M. Augusta (Anderson), 1875–1878, and Sister M. Charles (Flynn), 1878–1891.

At Saint Cecilia's Academy in Washington, D.C., the sisters began with no debt. After initial years of success the community expanded the private school to meet the demands of increased enrollment. Only women with astute business

TABLE No. 3
Summaries from Annual Report of First Ten Fiscal Years
Saint Angela's Academy, Morris, Illinois[100]

Year	Sisters	Enrollment	Receipts	Expenditures	Surplus	Creditors	Due to House
1865–66	9	140	$5,187.77	$4,470.05	$ 717.72	$ 100.00	$ 600.00
1866–67	9	150			2,335.40		
1867–68	10	144	6,880.50	6,662.75	2,111.73	700.00	1,000.00
1868–69	10	175	5,597.00	5,785.00	704.10	150.00	600.00
1869–70	10	175			205.00		
1870–71	10	155	6,394.00	5,196.44	1,197.59	1,100.00	1,000.00
1871–72	9	87	4,750.00	2,409.28	2,340.72		2,000.00
1872–73	9	110	5,573.00	4,315.26	1,257.74		
1873–74	9	110					
1874–75	9	140	8,004.00	5,210.00	2,794.00	250.00	2,400.00

TABLE No. 4
Summaries from Annual Report of First Five Fiscal Years
Saint Mary's Academy, Salt Lake City, Utah[101]

Year	Sisters	Enrollment	Receipts	Expenditures	Surplus	Creditors	Due to House
1875–76	13	184	$17,014.92	$43,530.27		$19,655.35	$1,087.00
1876–77	14	118	8,854.67	7,334.54	$1,520.13	16,644.43	1,329.75
1877–78	12	142	8,725.02	7,622.08	1,102.94	13,001.60	1,994.70
1878–79	16	175	11,446.55	8,555.94	3,015.61	10,845.76	1,280.00
1879–80	17	252	14,141.55	14,265.08	(123.53)	12,580.59	1,975.00

acumen could have built in kind and borrowed to the extent indicated in the record of 1874 to 1875. See Table No. 5.

Parochial schools were often staffed by teachers in residence at community-owned academies. It was the exception for a parish to support adequately a teaching faculty. Contracts indicate[103] that salaries were as low at $200 per annum. When the pastor of Immaculate Conception Parish, Morris, Illinois, (1858) charged fifty cents per pupil per month to finance teacher salaries in his parochial school, the parents sent their children to public schools. The sisters added to Saint Angela's faculty, leaving but one teacher to give religious instruction to the remaining students of the parish school.[104]

Father Sorin reminded an applicant for Holy Cross teachers in a school in Bourbonnais (1858) that he could not accept a contract for a twelve dollar salary per month, especially since no board was included in the proposal. Experience, he added, had told him that houses opened with low salary arrangements ultimately lead to failure.[105]

Community-owned schools prospered during the period from 1855 to 1900 when forty-four parochial schools in which the Sisters of the Holy Cross taught were closed because of isolation, economic decline of an area, ecclesiastical differences, or indebtedness. Poverty characterized most parochial beginnings. Had it not been for the academies of this period many of the parochial schools could not have remained open. Also, a living, productive endowment in the teaching services of the sisters gave a stability to community finances. A faculty for a nearby parochial school lived at every academy; parishes without a school were taught religion on Saturdays by sisters from the academy.

Mother M. Angela was a woman of business acumen with experience in handling large sums of investments for her stepfather, Mr. William Phelan. Mother M. Augusta, too, demonstrated fiscal skill in financing building projects of

TABLE No. 5

Summaries from Annual Report of First Ten Fiscal Years

Saint Cecilia's Academy, Washington, D. C.[102]

Year	Sisters	Enrollment	Receipts	Expenditures	Surplus	Creditors	Due to House
1868–69	7	302	$1,853.23	$ 2,099.22	$(245.99)	$ 331.41	$ 857.37
1869–70	7	340	3,729.79	2,015.35	1,714.54		630.48
1870–71	9	293	3,705.15	1,632.53	2,072.62		744.38
1871–72							
1872–73	11	327	6,684.31	4,023.54	2,660.77	4,936.83	549.40
1873–74	11	340	6,374.28	1,665.07	4,709.21		
1874–75*	13	433	5,687.51	21,200.52	(15,513.00)	15,522.46	878.00
1875–76	16	667	8,657.19	5,281.00	3,345.86	12,136.13	1,738.38
1876–77	15	408	7,503.14	4,876.44	2,626.70	9,829.21	1,110.16
1877–78	15	452	6,248.83	4,537.75	1,711.08	8,546.52	1,913.53

* New building erected.

five-digit numbers. Possessed of a keen sense of justice, she returned to individual establishments (1887) the endowments which had been forwarded to the general house during times of financial crises.[106]

In summary, although there are accounts for each house from the time of its opening, the accounting was done on a strictly "cash in" (income as earned) and "cash out" (expenses incurred) basis.[107]

Most of the early preservice and inservice teacher education was done at Saint Mary's Academy, Notre Dame, Indiana. There was no cash exchange for such education; hence, the absence of cash expenditures for education on early account forms. There are, however, entries for teachers' salaries for those sisters who took art, piano, harp, or voice from a distinguished master.[108]

Visitors to the Saint Mary's, Notre Dame, campus in the latter half of the nineteenth century included distinguished men of arts, letters, and science as previously mentioned: Henry Van Dyke, Hamilton Wright Mabie, Eliza Allan Starr, Henry James, Dr. Thomas Shahan, Dr. Edward Pace, Maurice Francis Egan, Marion Crawford, Rev. Fidelis Stone, Elizabeth Jordan, William Butler Yeats, Seumas McManus, Colonel Charles Bonaparte, Rev. T. E. Judge, and Dom Gasquet. Among the visiting musicians who had given recitals and lectures on music masters were Prof. N. Ledochowski, Prof. S. Moskzkowski, Fannie Bloomfield Zeisler, Madame Elye, Msgr. E. Remenyi, Prof. Richard Seidel, Frederick Boscovitz, Harrison Wilde, and others.[109] Accounts listed the honoraria given to these lecturers and artists. To these might be added Rt. Rev. J. L. Spalding, bishop of Peoria; His Excellency Monsignor Satolli, papal delegate; Prof. E. Schuecker; Rt. Rev. J. A. Watterson; Rt. Rev. John Ireland; Dr. Austin O'Malley; Prof F. H. Clark; Max Bendix with the Sherwood Quartette; and Signor Luigi Gregori of Rome, Italy. The latter painted the murals in the Church of the Sacred Heart, Notre Dame, and in the administration building. He taught art two afternoons a week at Saint Mary's. Both sisters and students took lessons from him.[110]

In the same period, high dignitaries of church and state visited the campus: James G. Blaine, democratic candidate for the presidency (1876, 1880, 1884), cousin of Mother M. Angela; Thomas A. Hendricks; Oliver P. Morton; Carl Schurz; General Lew Wallace; Schuyler Colfax; Orestes Brownson; Edwin Booth; General W. T. Sherman; Sebastian Cardinal Martinelli; James Cardinal Gibbons; Archbishop James Ryan; Archbishop James Keane; Archbishop Patrick Riordan; and Archbishop James Glennon. Many dignitaries visited the Saint Mary's campus as guests, many as guest lecturers gratis. This much is certain: no fee entered as "lectures" could pay in value for the quantity and quality of the visiting lecturers and artists.

Historically the academies were the training schools for teachers, the forerunner of the normal schools. The Sisters of the Holy Cross opened the first Catholic normal school in the United States, Saint Catherine's Normal Institute, Baltimore, Maryland, in 1875. It is unique in that it is the only school of the congregation that overtly expressed this purpose:

The original and main objective of the institution is to train young ladies in the all-important art of teaching. Nothing is omitted which will give them a thorough knowledge of the various branches required in that profession and the best methods of instruction, thus qualifying them to fill a position in either the Catholic or the public schools, . . . The Normal Course includes all those branches in which a candidate for a teacher's certificate of the highest grade, must undergo an examination.[111]

Most Reverend Archbishop Roosevelt Bayley persuaded Mother M. Angela that Baltimore, the oldest diocese in the United States, was the proper setting for such an undertaking.

Mother Angela had favored Washington, D.C., because it was the nation's capital. The archbishop purchased the property and then transferred the deed to the Sisters of the Holy Cross, who, because they were not property owners in Maryland, could not borrow money to make the purchase.[112]

Saint Catherine's had the traditional "programme of studies" which Mother Angela used at Saint Mary's Academy, Notre Dame, Indiana, to which was added a normal course including student teaching. Many of the personnel who had opened the other academies of Holy Cross initiated the normal school academically. Among its early teachers were Sister M. Eleanor (Kelly), Sister M. Liguori (Dillon), Sister M. Loyola (McMahon), Sister M. Incarnation (Cullen), Sister M. Annunciad (Sargent), and Sister M. Andrew (Pigeon).

An imposing building was built on the corner of Harlem and Arlington Avenues, where teachers were educated in a two-year normal course from 1875 to 1929. The subjects offered as part of the normal training were psychology, theory of teaching, and practice teaching.[113] The practice teaching was done in the elementary department of the same school as well as at Saint Pius Elementary School. Like Saint Mary's Academy, Notre Dame, upon which it had been modeled, the music department was one of its strongest features. Historically, though, the death knell of the normal school had sounded at the turn of the century. When the neighborhood of Saint Catherine's became a depressed area economically, the school was closed because its enrollment no longer warranted its functioning.

Much could be said about Saint Catherine's Normal Institute, not relevant here. Alumnae today, approximately forty in number, meet semiannually; they are active members of the International Federation of Catholic Alumnae. A Sister Ferdinand Scholarship Fund Award, given annually, keeps alive the memory of the superior and directress of studies who served from 1875 to 1916. The long tenure of Sister M. Ferdinand (Bruggerman), the episcopal favor of James Cardinal Gibbons, and the civic recognition given its graduates who taught in the public school system are factors in the spirit which characterized this institute and which still prevails among its alumnae.

In 1925 the Reverend John I. Barret, archdiocesan superintendent of education, praised Saint Catherine's as a training school for teachers, enumerating that, in fifty years, seventy-six students had entered religious life. Of that number fifty-four had become Sisters of the Holy Cross.[114]

Because Saint Catherine's Institute was kept open throughout the year and regular summer classes were scheduled for those teachers who could not return to Saint Mary's, Notre Dame, it is important in the history of teacher education of the Sisters of the Holy Cross, especially for those who taught in the parochial schools. Sisters teaching in secondary schools resided there also and attended summer classes at Johns Hopkins University.[115]

The history of the academies of the Congregation of the Sisters of the Holy Cross closely parallels developments in the history of the academy as an educational institution. Because of the character of its leadership and the directed purpose of its membership, the community developed a pattern for academies that was marked with a degree of scholastic excellence and a familial spirit. Its teacher preparation was similar in a measure to that found in other religious communities and in teacher education generally. Saint Catherine's Normal Institute was a natural outgrowth of the academy as a training school for teachers.

The community teacher education at St. Mary's differed somewhat because its leader was a distinguished, recognized educator; it differed because of its proximity to the University of Notre Dame and to the Priests of Holy Cross, who manifested an interest in its growth and development. Financing such a program of teacher preparation can only be understood as it relates to the factors of leadership, personnel, and accessibility to a higher institution of learning.

Elsbree makes a comparable summary of the state of teacher training in the United States (1839–1900):

As one reviews the history of teacher training in the United States, he can scarcely avoid the conclusion that in our efforts to supply enough teachers for the public schools we have sacrificed quality for quantity. No other alternative seemed consistent with a democratic school system. If every pupil were entitled to be educated at public expense, then teachers must be trained in sufficient numbers to make public education a reality. Training standards could be raised only as the supply of teachers approached or exceeded the demand. The American policy of attempting to educate everybody has, until recently, thrown a terrific burden upon teacher-preparatory institutions, with the result that, on the average, teachers in the United States have not attained a high academic status. Educators are prone to classify teaching with the professions of medicine and law when, in reality, the latter groups have advanced their training standards at least three years beyond those commonly required of teachers.

A second observation, which is not altogether related to the previous discussion, is that the training of teachers is a relatively young movement in America. In fact, it is only one hundred years old, which is a brief period of time in institutional history. It has been a century of exploration, experimentation, and change in teacher training. Institutes came and went; the reading circle flourished and died; the normal school was transformed into the teachers' college. . . . the whole period was one of change. No clearly conceived pattern of teacher training has yet evolved in America. We have not had long enough experience with any single institution to get a true measure of its worth.[116]

References

[1] Ellwood P. Cubberley, *Public Education in the United States* (Boston, 1934), p. 113.

[2] *Ibid.*, pp. 246ff.

[3] Isaac L. Kandel, *History of Secondary Education* (Boston, 1930), p. 168.

[4] Cubberley, *op. cit.*, p. 250.

[5] Kandel believes the Franklin Academy in Philadelphia was first (1751); Cubberley claims that South Carolina had a school designated as academy in 1712. Most writers, however, agree that Franklin Academy, founded in 1749 and chartered in 1753, was the first true academy as we understand the term today.

[6] Kandel, *op. cit.*, pp. 171–172.

[7] Elmer Brown, *The Making of Our Secondary Schools* (New York, 1907), p. 192.

[8] B. A. Hinsdale, "Early Views and Plans Relating to a National University," *Report of the United States Commissioner of Education*, II, 1893, 1293ff.

[9] A. J. Inglis, *Principles of Secondary Education* (Boston, 1918), pp. 161ff.

[10] *Catalogue*, 1863, p. 7.

[11] *Circular Letters of the Very Rev. Edward Sorin* (Notre Dame, Indiana, 1894), II, 261.

[12] Cubberley, *op. cit.*, p. 184.

[13] R. G. Boone, *History of Education in Indiana* (New York, 1892), pp. 128ff.

[14] Kandel, *op. cit.*, p. 411.

[15] Cubberley, *op. cit.*, p. 248.

[16] Articles of Incorporation, 1855, AGH. The charter specified that fifty thousand dollars had been divided into shares that were assignable if the holder was not in debt to the corporation. Further, until some plan for fund raising was adopted, the institution would be maintained by such compensation as capable and efficient teachers could command. Filed in the Clerk's Office, Saint Joseph Circuit Court, South Bend, Indiana, July 24, 1855. S. M. Chord, Clerk.

[17] Msgr. Francis J. Macelwane, "The Superintendent's Responsibility for the Professional Advancement of His Teachers," *NCEA Bulletin*, XXVIII (November, 1931), 573.

[18] Many students came from the South during the Civil War years. The spirit of patriotism stirred the quiet of the convent halls when the North and the South met in quick give and take of charge and retort. Minnie Sherman, daughter of General W. T. Sherman, was the leader of the Union party. At times even the presence of Mother M. Angela

was not enough to prevent "civil war" with the loyal daughters from the South.

[19] Saint Mary's School (South Bend, Indiana) and Saint Joseph's School (North Chicago, Illinois), German; Saint Hedwige School (South Bend) and Saint Stanislaus School (Michigan City, Indiana), Polish; Sacred Heart School (South Bend), Belgian.

[20] Sister M. Elizabeth (Lilly), Memoirs of Mother M. Angela, pp. 20–30, AGH.

[21] Ibid., p. 20.

[22] Ibid., p. 27.

[23] G-II, 37 AGH.

[24] Sister M. Euphrosine (Pepin), Diary, p. 137, AGH. Sister M. Euphrosine kept a remarkable diary. She knew no English when she came to America in 1852. The quality of her English composition is a tribute to her industry and to the teachers who taught her, American-born sisters, priests, and professors from Notre Dame. Cf. Rose Lathrop Hawthorne, The Story of Courage.

[25] The Boston Pilot, July 21, 1855.

[26] Ibid.

[27] G-II, 133, AGH.

[28] Sister M. Euphrosine, op. cit., p. 140, AGH.

[29] G-II, 127, AGH.

[30] Sister M. Carol (Schroeder), O.S.F., The Catholic Church in the Diocese of Vincennes, 1847–1877 (Washington, D.C., 1946), pp. 37–38.

[31] Rt. Rev. H. J. Alerding, The Diocese of Fort Wayne: a Book of Historical Reference, 1669–1907 (Fort Wayne, Indiana, 1907). p. 448.

[32] Ibid., p. 447.

[33] Ella Ewing Brown, Memoirs of Eliza Gillespie: Mother Mary Angela, p. 25, AGH.

[34] Sister M. Elizabeth, op. cit., p. 32.

[35] Ibid., p. 48.

[36] Ibid., p. 50.

[37] Residence Directory of the Sisters of the Holy Cross (Notre Dame, Indiana, 1963), AGH.

[38] AGH.

[39] Sister M. Elizabeth, op. cit., p. 22.

[40] Family Tree of Neal Gillespie, Sr., Ewing Papers, AUND; Ewing File, AGH.

[41] Interview with Miss Marion McCandless, '00, Saint Mary's College, Notre Dame, Indiana, March 10, 1964.

[42] The original academy was on C Street, S.E., opposite the Blaine residence.

[43] Interview with Mother Kathryn Marie, superior general, Saint Mary's Convent, Notre Dame, Indiana, February 17, 1964.

[44] Council Minutes, April 4, 1850, Bertrand, AGH.

[45] Mother Kathryn Marie, *loc. cit.*

[46] Saint Mary's Academy, Alexandria, Virginia, I, 1869, 24, AGH.

[47] Saint Mary's Academy, Austin, Texas, I, 1875, 18, AGH.

[48] *Ibid.* Mother M. Perpetua (Wilson), Mother M. Pauline (O'Neill), Mother M. Cecily (O'Riordan), Mother M. Francis Clare (Counihan), Mother M. Remigius (Murphy), Mother M. Vincentia (Fannon).

[49] *Ibid.,* I, 1875, 22.

[50] Saint Mary's Academy, Marshall, Texas, I, 1880, 355, AGH. The commerce department of the academy later provided adult education under the GI bill of rights for men and women of Marshall and its environs.

[51] Interview with Sister M. Rhoda (Hyde). Facts of family life in "Michael Hyde—Early-Day King of Owyhee Cattle Empire," *Scenic Idaho,* XII (1939), 31–32.

[52] James A. Burns, C.S.C., and Bernard J. Kohlbrenner, *History of Catholic Education in the United States* (New York, 1937), p. 110.

[53] Correspondence, Mother M. Angela to Sorin, 1862.

[54] Correspondence, Mother M. Angela to Sorin, 1869.

[55] Alerding, *op. cit.,* p. 449.

[56] *Ibid.,* p. 454.

[57] See graph "Comparative Rise of Parochial Schools and Decline of the Academy (Community Owned)," Appendix, p. 191.

[58] See graph "Persistency of Sisters of the Holy Cross," Appendix, p. 192.

[59] G-II, 325, AGH.

[60] Community Register, 1874, AGH.

[61] *Ibid.* Persistency in this group was eighty-six percent, slightly higher than the over-all persistency of eighty-three percent of the total membership as is shown in the Persistency Graph of Sisters of the Holy Cross.

[62] Sister M. Eugenie received from the French government the title and ribbon of Officer d'Academie in recognition of her rich service in making France known and loved. It was conferred by the American Consul of France, A. Barthalemy, and presented by the Militaire Attache in Washington, G. E. Bubernil (Microfilm, Reel 13B, Personal file, AGH). In this day of the enigma of Charles DeGaulle, her story of the indomitable spirit of the French, told by a former pupil, is more meaningful. The students were discussing the word "surrender" as used by different nations. Someone asked, "Sister Eugenie, what do the French say for 'surrender'?" "They do not say it," was her prompt reply.

[63] Community Register, 1875, AGH.

[64] See "Persistency of Sisters of the Holy Cross," p. 192.

[65] Eliza Allan Starr was a distinguished artist and lecturer whose home and studio were destroyed in the great Chicago fire. Mother M. Angela invited her to take up her residence at Saint Mary's until 1878 when

she once more moved to Chicago and reopened a studio. She received the Laetare Medal in 1885 in recognition of her contribution to religious art and to humanity. *New World,* September 14, 1901, p. 44; G-II, 314, AGH.

[66] Eliza Allan Starr, "Mother M. Angela of Holy Cross," *New York Freeman's Journal,* March 26, 1887, AGH.

[67] The postulancy is a time of probation, the purpose of which is to initiate the candidate into religious life and to test her vocation (Constitution 9:41). The time varies in different religious communities. In the Congregation of the Sisters of the Holy Cross the period is six to twelve months. After investiture in the religious habit, a novice commences her canonical year under the direction of the mistress of novices. The object of the novitiate is the spiritual formation of the mind and soul of the novice (Constitution 10:52) . In a post-canonical year, second-year novices under the direction of the mistress of novices devote themselves to the study of the vows in preparation for first profession. During this year they may take courses ordered to the apostolic works of the congregation (Constitution 10:66). After the two-year novitiate, sisters may make simple vows of poverty, chastity, and obedience. These vows are temporary for five years and then perpetual (Constitution 11:67).

[68] Personnel files, letters of recommendation, questionnaires, AGH.

[69] Benjamin W. Frazier *et al. Special Survey in Nine Parts: National Survey of the Education of Teachers,* Vol. V, United States Office of Education Bulletin No. 10 (Washington, 1933), p. 17.

[70] Sister Bertrande Meyers, *The Education of Sisters* (New York, 1941), pp. 20–21.

[71] Willard S. Elsbree, *The American Teacher* (New York, 1939), pp. 35–37.

[72] Edward S. Evenden, Guy C. Gamble, and Harold G. Blue, *Teacher Personnel in the United States: National Survey of the Education of Teachers,* Vol. II, United States Office of Education Bulletin (1933) No. 10 (Washington, 1935), p. 74.

[73] G-II, 309, AGH.

[74] Correspondence, Mother M. Angela to the sisters, 1870, AGH.

[75] G-II, 54, AGH.

[76] Novitiate Record Book, 1877–1893, introduction, AGH.

[77] *Catalogue,* 1877, p. 14, ASMC.

[78] G-I, p. 402, AGH.

[79] Circular Letter of Mother M. Annunciata, April 25, 1896, AGH.

[80] Mother M. Annunciata, *op. cit.,* September 24, 1897, AGH.

[81] *Ibid.,* December 18, 1897, AGH.

[82] Class Meeting Minutes, 1855–1860; 1861–1865; 1866–1870; 1871–1875; 1876–1880, ASMC.

[83] Mother M. Annunciata, *op. cit.,* September 24, 1897, AGH.

[84] *Ibid.*

[85] "History of Saint Mary's Academy," *An Illustrated Historical Atlas of St. Joseph's Co., Indiana* (Chicago, 1875), pp. 38ff. In 1903 a Committee on Accredited Schools from the North Central Association visited Saint Mary's Academy and advised that the title be changed to Saint Mary's College because of the character of curriculum which it offered. The title Saint Mary's Academy was to be used for the academic curriculum. From 1903 to 1905 the name Saint Mary's was used in the yearly catalogs. Saint Mary's College and Academy appeared for the first time in the catalog of 1905–1906. Saint Mary's Academy was moved from Saint Mary's, Notre Dame, Indiana, to Twyckenham, South Bend, Indiana in 1945.

[86] G-2, 67, AGH.

[87] G-2. 3. AGH. It is the first time that a class in pedagogy was specifically mentioned.

[88] Mother M. Compassion, "Life of Mother M. Angela," III, 399, AGH.

[89] *Ibid.*, II, 209. Although Mother M. Compassion does not mention it herself, she walked three times a week from Bertrand to Notre Dame for a two-hour lesson in mathematics with Professor O'Leary (Council Meeting Minutes, 1850, AGH).

[90] *The Chimes*, July, 1895.

[91] Eliza Allan Starr, *op. cit.*

[92] Elsbree, *op. cit.*, pp. 321–331.

[93] G-2, 69, AGH.

[94] G-3, 8, AGH.

[95] *Circular Letters.* (Concluding paragraphs of many of these letters.)

[96] Record of Annual Statistics, 1844–1895, AGH.

[97] *Constitutions of the Congregation of the Sisters of the Holy Cross* (Notre Dame, Indiana, 1962), Constitution 14, a, 105.

[98] Thomas T. McAvoy, C.S.C., "Notre Dame, 1919–1922; The Burns Revolution," *Review of Politics*, XXV, 433–434. In an interview Father McAvoy, University of Notre Dame archivist, explained the dearth of early university records, including accounts, to the heavy archival loss in the fire of 1879 which destroyed the administration building. At this time the early communal fiscal records of the sisters, kept jointly by Father Sorin, were lost.

[99] *Ibid.*

[100] Microfilm, Reel 1, Microdex 2, AGH.

[101] *Ibid.*, Reel 4, Microdex 2, AGH.

[102] *Ibid.*, Reel 1, Microdex 2, AGH.

[103] Documents, 1850–1860, AGH.

[104] Saint Mary's Academy, Morris, Illinois, I, 1855–1860, AGH.

[105] Correspondence, Father Sorin to pastor of St. Philomena Parish, Bourbonnais, Illinois, 1858, AGH.

[106] Ella Ewing Brown, Memoirs of Sister M. Elizabeth Lilly, n.p., AGH.
[107] The quinquennial reports to Rome must still be made on a cash basis, with a summary showing actual cash income and cash disbursements.
[108] Eliza Allan Starr, art; Richard Seidel, violin; Carlos Salzedo, harp and piano; Alberto Solvi, harp; Fanny Bloomfield Zeisler, piano master classes. G-I, G-II, G-1, G-2, Indices, AGH.
[109] G-I, G-II, G-2, Indices: Lecturers, AGH.
[110] G-II, Index: Lecturers, 1883, AGH.
[111] Twelfth Annual Catalogue of Saint Catherine's Normal Institute, Baltimore, Maryland, June, 1887 (Baltimore, 1887), p. 18.
[112] Saint Catherine's Normal Institute, Baltimore, Maryland, 1875, p. 18.
[113] Twelfth Annual Catalogue of Saint Catherine's Normal Institute, p. 16.
[114] Baltimore Sun, June 13, 1925. Seven others became Sisters of the Holy Cross after 1925, bringing the total to sixty-one.
[115] Saint Catherine's Normal Institute, op. cit., p. 114.
[116] Elsbree, op. cit., p. 334.

CHAPTER IV

CERTIFICATION AND
ACCREDITATION: 1900-1964

THE AGE of the academies of the Sisters of the Holy Cross is identified with the educational leadership of Mother M. Angela; the period of accreditation, with the tenure of office of Mother M. Pauline (O'Neill), the first president of Saint Mary's College. Briefly, Mother M. Pauline was born in Peoria, Illinois, in 1854 into a moderately wealthy family. She had graduated from Saint Mary's in the class of 1871, returning to enter the Congregation of the Sisters of the Holy Cross in 1879. Like many of the early leaders in the congregation, Sister M. Pauline was given administrative responsibility as soon as she was a professed member: prefect at Sacred Heart Academy, Fort Wayne, Indiana, 1882; superior at Saint Mary's Academy, Austin, Texas, 1885. For six years as superior at Sacred Heart Academy, Ogden, Utah, Sister M. Pauline built the "educational mecca in the West," which an archivist in her pride wrote "excels the mother house in magnificence and beauty."[1] It was with regret that the sisters of the West saw Sister M. Pauline leave in 1895 for the general house, where as an elected assistant to the mother general she became the directress of Saint Mary's Academy.

Mother Pauline had no illusions as to the scope of her responsibilities. Saint Mary's was the first in importance of the schools belonging to the congregation; besides, it was her Alma Mater and as such she idealized it and its faculty. The years had made no change, unless to render it a more perfect instrument. Again we must bear in mind that Saint Mary's was always more than a high school or an ordinary academy.[2]

Spanned over a period of thirty-six years of presidency, the tenure of Mother M. Pauline was characterized by a period of academic and physical expansion. Holy Cross Hall was erected in 1904, and LeMans Hall in 1925;[3] today both halls accommodate a resident student body of approximately 800.

During the same period Saint Mary's Academy was to change its title to Saint Mary's College, a recommendation of the first visiting team from the young regional accrediting association, North Central Association of Colleges and Secondary Schools. The state of Indiana granted approval to Saint Mary's College.

Mother M. Angela had brought through her personal contacts a rostrum of distinguished artists, musicians, and lecturers. Mother M. Pauline was to continue in the same tradition. Among her close friends was Rt. Rev. John L. Spalding, bishop of Peoria, a family friend whom she had known from childhood. He was a frequent visitor at Saint Mary's College, often addressing the faculty and the student body.

Mother M. Pauline was keenly interested in the continued education of the sisters as teachers. Her first summer school in 1896 included courses in moral theology, the phenomena of cell life, English literature, science, painting, and music.[4] When through premature deaths the faculty lost the intellectual leadership of Sister M. Rita (Heffernan) and Sister

M. Eleanor (Sturgis), she turned to Notre Dame. They befriended the third group of the family of Holy Cross by sharing priests and lay members of their faculty.

Mother M. Pauline sent Sister M. Irma (Burns) and Sister M. Rita (Heffernan) to study at Harvard University in 1898, and supplemented their formal education by travel abroad in 1901. To prepare adequate college faculty, Sister M. Agnes (Mahoney) and Sister Francis Jerome (O'Laughlin) studied for doctorates at Fordham University and then Columbia University. When the University of Notre Dame opened its first summer session to women in 1918, the Sisters of the Holy Cross attended in large numbers.[5]

At the reunion of The Holy Cross Alumnae Association of Saint Mary's College, Notre Dame, Indiana, June 9, 1962, Sister M. Benedictus (Kern) spoke for her class on the occasion of its golden jubilee. Excerpts from her address give us an insight into Mother M. Pauline as an educator. She spoke thus of Saint Mary's College of the early twentieth century:

I shall spend these five minutes answering questions often asked about a jubilarian's college program:

What kind of college was Saint Mary's in 1912?

Was it liberal arts?

What courses did you study?

Who were your teachers?

What was the college endowment?

Did you have Christian Culture?

In 1912 Saint Mary's was a liberal arts college, essentially the same in academic status as it is today. There were departments in the classics, modern languages, English, history, and political science. In science, biology, general science, pharmacy. In fine arts, music, speech, and painting.

Each was a distinct department and they were all well established when our class entered Saint Mary's in the freshman year (1908). There were also other beginnings. A three years curriculum in domestic science, first year curriculum in education with the promise of a major program for the future. There was the course in Scripture and a one-year course in journalism.

The liberal arts program was, as we know, the result of a definite plan. The plan appeared as a statement on the aim and end of education in the college bulletin of 1910–1911 over the signature of Mother Pauline, and under the title: TO PARENTS SEEKING AN IDEAL SCHOOL FOR THEIR DAUGHTERS. I quote: "Saint Mary's stands for the development of the mind and heart; it aims to make its students women of ideas rather than women of accomplishments; to bring them into personal relation with wider worlds by placing before them Truth in all its aspects —literature, history, science, and art." This is Mother Pauline's statement on Education for Truth. A half century ago it laid the foundation of our liberal arts studies.

Most of the teachers were Sisters. Some of them had done graduate work—two of them at Harvard. In those days students did not evaluate their teachers in terms of academic degrees; rather in terms of excellence. They did esteem the well-prepared, well-ordered, and devoted teacher. By the time we were seniors, the faculty was supplemented by distinguished professors, clerical and lay, from the University of Notre Dame,—among them were Fathers Nieuwland, Charles O'Donnell, Leonard Carrico, William Bolger, Cornelius Hagerty. Miss Katherine Conroy was in residence at the college.

What was the college endowment? In the same bulletin, 1910–1911, Mother Pauline made these remarks upon the subject of the College Endowment: "Saint Mary's endowment consists in her boundless reverence for the students; the students' love and respect for their school; the devotion of the alumnae; the consecrated lives of its teachers; the encouragement of the Church, and the blessing of God." This is our most precious endowment—even to this day. . . .[6]

But to understand the educational ferment of the period in which Mother M. Pauline was president of Saint Mary's College, a consideration of the development of education in its proper historical context is necessary.

In the United States, from earliest colonial times, some committee or other examined the moral and scholastic qualifications of all prospective teachers. Every state provided at some time for certification by examination.

In more than half the states it was possible to secure a teacher's certificate and become a teacher with no other educational equipment than a knowledge of the common school subjects—the merest rudiments of an education.[7] To obtain a high-school teacher certificate of the first grade in one-third of the states one was not examined on any subject; in two-thirds of the states only the knowledge of algebra was tested.

TABLE No. 6

Examination Requirements for the First Three Grades
of County Certificates: 1899[8]

High-School Subjects	First Grade	Second Grade	Third Grade
Algebra	23 states	5	1
Physics	16	1	1
Geometry	11	1	0
Physical geography	10	5	0
Literature	9	1	1
Rhetoric	3	0	0
General history	4	0	0
Economics	3	0	0
English history	1	1	0
Natural sciences	2	0	0
Botany	1	0	0
Chemistry	1	1	1

In some states these examinations were taken on the county level, and the certificates were good only in that county.[9] In others the states were supreme, granting professional certificates and life diplomas to experienced teachers who had previously earned two or three county certificates.[10]

Another class of certification was the city certificate. The city certificate evolved from the effort to raise educational standards as well as from an urban spirit found in large cities like Chicago, New York, and San Francisco. The state requirements were minimal. The general trend of city certification was to improve state certification.[11]

The pedagogical subjects offered in teacher-training schools were few: theory and art of teaching, school law, psychology, and history of education.

TABLE No. 7

Examination Requirements for the First Three Grades
of County Certificates: 1913[12]

Pedagogical Subjects	First Grade	Second Grade	Third Grade
Theory and art of teaching	28 states	25	20
School law	10	7	3
Psychology	1	0	0
History of education	1	0	0

So great was the diversity of requirements for certification that it was difficult for a teacher to transfer from one state to another or even from one county to another. Some of these restrictions were narrow and unwarranted; from an educational point of view many of the restrictions were indefensible.[13]

The education of future teachers was the task of the normal schools, state and private, city training schools for teachers, colleges, and universities that offered a special course for teachers. In the year 1903 to 1904, 499 private high schools and 272 public high schools offered some course of instruction intended for future teachers.[14] Actually the number of trained teachers in the states was very small because it was easy to enter teaching, and in most states to do so without the necessity of any training. If we average all the states of the union, we find 15 to 20% of teachers in the public school had received some training. The remaining 80 to 85% had been prepared by private study, tested wholly by examination and experience, and had had no professional preparation at that time.[15]

Two methods were common to determine whether an individual possessed the education prerequisites necessary for admission to teaching: (1) examination, oral and written, by a member of a school committee or by a professional examining body; (2) satisfactory evidence of proper education and professional training, that is, a college or normal school diploma, or certificates of qualification issued elsewhere. The latter method, although obviously the better, was difficult to use. For some time to come both methods existed side by side.[16]

In Indiana in 1899 an applicant for a teacher's license could request that the county examination be forwarded to the state superintendent of public instruction for a license which would enable him to teach anywhere in the state.[17]

Renewals of certification often resulted in life certification. This was true in Indiana where the law provided in 1903 that any person who taught six consecutive years could obtain a first-grade license without re-examination provided he continued to teach the same subject.[18]

The use in Indiana of uniform examination questions early evolved into a state certification.[19] Even by the provision of the revised school law of Indiana in 1903, all certification was based on a written examination without any requirement of definite educational preparation. Indiana was, however, the first state to make high-school graduation a prerequisite for certification (1907), although California led in the quality of the standards which it established.[20]

In Indiana the state department of education continued to be responsible for teacher education and certification. Control was effected through the establishment of basic criteria, an approval of the curriculum of the education department of the normal school or college, an inspection of the institution, the publication of lists of approved institutions, and a periodic review.[21] Saint Mary's Academy and Saint Mary's College have met these changes in certification in keeping with the state requirements. The survey of the educational background of the Sisters of the Holy Cross shows that between 1900 and 1920 sisters were certified by examination.[22] This certification became a life certification with experience.

By 1923 Indiana certified prospective high-school teachers in five different ways: (1) college graduate; (2) partial college course; (3) normal-school graduation (two-year course); (4) partial normal course; and (5) examination only. The actual statisics for Indiana are indicated in Table No. 8.

TABLE No. 8
Variation in Training of Regular Senior High-School
Teachers in Indiana: 1923[23]

Training	Number of Teachers	Percent
Elementary school only	3	0.1
Less than full high school	28	1.0
Full high school	27	0.9
Above high school: one year	218	7.6
two years	439	15.3
three years	333	11.6
four years	1781	62.2
Training not stated	37	1.3
Total	2866	100.0

In the same year the Sisters of the Holy Cross taught in four secondary schools in Indiana: Saint Mary's Academy, Notre Dame; Saint Joseph's Academy, South Bend; Saint Hedwige's High School, South Bend; and Holy Angel's Academy, Logansport. Twenty-two teachers taught in these schools in 1923. Their qualifications broken down into a table comparable to the table for the senior high-school teachers for the entire state of Indiana are given in Table No. 9.

TABLE NO. 9

Variation in Training of Sisters of the Holy Cross
Teaching in Secondary Schools in Indiana: 1923[24]

Training	Number of Teachers	Percent
Elementary school only	0	0.0
Less than full high school	0	0.0
Full high school	0	0.0
Above high school: one year	1	4.9
two years	4	18.0
three years	4	18.0
four years	13	59.1
Training not stated	0	0.0
Total	22	100.0

The Sisters of the Holy Cross closed seven high schools during the years from 1920 to 1940.[25] Four of these were parochial high schools; three, community-owned. Accreditation became necessary for secondary graduates to attend college. Small parishes could no longer support a high school whose physical equipment of a library and of a science laboratory would meet state requirements. The teaching personnel, too, had to meet the increasing demands for certification.

The state of Indiana issued its revised manual of laws and regulations for teacher training in 1937. At the same time, the state gave notice that no certification under the former regulations would be permitted after 1940. All programs begun after 1940 were to include a four-year college course. However, the grandfather clause[26] was retained to make possible the completion of programs begun under previous requirements as well as the issuing of life certification to normal certificates when the teacher had residence and teaching experience in Indiana.[27]

Saint Mary's College offered double summer sessions and

extension courses in order to meet the new regulations for certification. Sister M. Hildegardis (Gettier), supervisor of education in the midwest province, and Sister M. Frederick (Eggleston), academic dean of Saint Mary's College, evaluated the credits of each sister and set up the sessions for the summer of 1938 and 1939. The enrollment for the sessions was 200 and 238, respectively. Twenty-eight licenses were received at the end of the double session of 1938; twenty-five in 1939; and fifty-seven in 1940.[28] Those certified, as a result of this stepped-up program, then continued to study to earn a degree.

Educational statistics of the sisters who taught in the decades affected by certification changes are shown in Table No. 10.

TABLE No. 10

Educational Status of Teachers of the Congregation of the Sisters of the Holy Cross

Status at time of entrance		*Status in 1964*				
1910–1920		*Ph.D.*	*M.A.*	*B.A.*	*Total*	*Percent*
College[29]	12	5	39	42	86	82%
High School	58					
High School (2 years +)	20					
Elementary	15					
Total	105					

1920–1930		*Ph.D.*	*M.A.*	*B.A.*	*Total*	*Percent*
College	20	16	90	125	231	87%
High School	154					
High School (2 years +)	71					
Elementary	20					
Total	265					

Status at time of entrance		Status in 1964				
1930–1940		Ph.D.	M.A.	B.A.	Total	Percent
College	15	10	71	91	171	89%
High School	15					
High School (2 years +)	25					
Elementary	1					
Total	192					

1940–1950		Ph.D.	M.A.	B.A.	Total	Percent
College	34	10	64	151	225	82%
High School	235					
High School (2 years +)	4					
Elementary	0					
Total	273					

* 1950–1960[30]		Ph.D.	M.A.	B.A.	Total	Percent
College	48	5	34	88	127	41%
High School	248					
High School (2 years +)	4					
Elementary	0					
Total	300					

1960 Band of September, 1964 Teachers		Ph.D.	M.A.	B.A.	Total	Percent
College	6		9	24	33	97%
High School	28					
High School (2 years +)	0					
Elementary	0					
Total	34					

* A projected program to facilitate completion of degrees of this group is under way.

The development of professional requirements for certification in secondary schools in Indiana from 1895 to 1954 is outlined in Table No. 11.

TABLE No. 11
Professional Requirements for Licenses for
Secondary Schools in Indiana: 1895–1954[31]

Pedagogical Subjects Prescribed

1895	1911	1921	1927
Science of Education (Pedagogy)	Science of Education	Science of Education	Principles of Teaching
	School Laws of Indiana	School Laws of Indiana	Psychology and Its Application to Education
	Educational Psychology and Child Care		Secondary Education
	History of Education		Principles of Teaching
	School Systems of Europe and America		Supervised Teaching
	Principles of Education		Junior High School

1937	1949 (Revised 1954)
Psychology and Its Application to Education	Educational Psychology*
Secondary Education	General Methods*
Principles of Teaching	Principles of Secondary Education*
Supervised Teaching	Guidance*
Methods in Teaching of Each of Two Subject Groups Elected	Special Methods in the Comprehensive Area*
	Tests and Measurements
	Mental Hygiene
	Psychology of Adolescence
	Extra-curricular Activities
	History of Education
*Required; other subjects elective; total of 18 hours of professional education.	Philosophy of Education
	Student Teaching*

For the development effected by the 1962 Indiana education legislation see Table No. 13, page 150.

In the struggle for higher standards of teacher education, certification and accreditation became synonymous. The history of formal teacher certification in the Congregation of the Sisters of the Holy Cross and the formal accreditation of Saint Mary's College have a parallel development with both these movements in the United States.

The normal schools and academies had concerned themselves primarily with elementary teacher education. When they transformed themselves into degree-granting colleges, the colleges of liberal arts and the universities grew alarmed at what they considered a threat to their domain, i.e., the preparation of the high-school teachers.[32] The tension grew between liberal arts colleges and teachers' colleges, between private institutions and public institutions, and between academic professors and education professors.

The National Education Association sought to investigate and to alleviate the cause. To this end, a committee of B. A. Hinsdale, Charles De Garmo, and Elmer E. Brown sent a questionnaire to all state departments of instruction inquiring into the practice of teacher certification of college and university graduates.[33] In 1899 the committee made the following recommendations: (1) a college course is basic, with the candidates free from examination; (2) a teacher candidate should study intensively two or three subjects; (3) the certificate to teach should be limited exclusively to the subjects studied specially; (4) twelve hours of study of education as a discipline should be included in the elective subjects of the teacher candidates; (5) the student should take one or more teacher's courses, e.g., methodology; (6) the candidate should have both teacher observation and practice; (7) persons meeting the above requirements should be certified to teach for three years; if successful, then a life certificate without examination should be issued; (8) the student should do his study of education in a college or university or an affiliated school of the same rank.[34] It was to take the traditional lag of a generation to implement this plan.

Meanwhile the colleges continued to find themselves faced with a bewildering array of secondary school graduates who were applying for admission to higher education. The North Central Association of Colleges and Secondary Schools was established to correct this situation by defining the secondary school and by setting up standards for it. Representatives from six universities—Northwestern University, University of Chicago, University of Michigan, State University of Iowa, Indiana University, and the University of Missouri—met at Evanston, Illinois, March 29, 1895. Their aim was to establish closer relations between the colleges and secondary schools of the North Central States.[35]

By 1901 the Association appointed a Committee on Accredited Schools. The Committee made progress in defining the secondary school and in determining the accurate titles of the educational institutions. Mother Pauline invited the committee to visit Saint Mary's Academy. At their recommendation the name of Saint Mary's Academy was changed in 1903, by state charter, to Saint Mary's College for the four-year curriculum leading to the granting of degrees; the title, Saint Mary's Academy, was retained for the four-year secondary curriculum.[36] Next the committee drew up a set of standards for accrediting high schools; by 1905 secondary school accreditation by the North Central Accrediting Agency was under way.[37]

Two examiners from the University of Michigan and the University of Chicago came to Saint Mary's College and Academy, May 28, 1906, for the purpose of accrediting it with the newly formed association.[38] "Formal papers of accreditation followed."[39]

The constitution of the North Central Association, adopted in 1916, recognized that the Association had accepted accreditation as its basis. Three commissions, instead of the single Commission on Accredited Schools and Colleges, were formed: The Commission on Institutions of Higher Education, the Commission on Secondary Schools, and the Commission on Unit Courses and Curricula. By 1922 the Commission on Higher Education had created a board of review and had delegated to it the work of passing on individual cases of accreditation.[40]

A visiting team from the North Central Association of Colleges and Secondary Schools accredited Saint Mary's College as a standard institution of higher education May 13, 1922.[41] The accreditation has been renewed each year since, the last official revisitation having been made in 1961.[42]

Saint Mary's Academy had obtained Indiana state recognition by reason of its charter first granted in 1855.[43] State approval[44] as such resulted from the concern of the state for the power and control that regional accrediting agencies were acquiring. Hence the visitation of a committee from Indianapolis to Saint Mary's College did not come until 1915.

Charles A. Greathouse, superintendent of public instruction in the State of Indiana, reported to Mother M. Pauline that the committee sent to approve Saint Mary's College had rated it a standard college, to be recognized as such by the state board of education.[45]

In 1920 Oscar H. Williams, state supervisor of teacher training, had visited the work of the summer session, whose normal department he highly recommended and accredited for the two-year course leading to an elementary certificate.

The spirit and general attitude of the novitiate in training for teacher service are superior in every way. The visitors (J. N. Study and J. H. Tomlin) saw some excellent teaching, especially in the class "Principles (of Education)" taught by Sister Margaret Marie (Doyle).[46]

Within another year, the state visitor, after observing classes in both the academy and the college, recommended the academy as a training school for the college students to do both observation and practice teaching. He reported thus to Mother M. Pauline, president,

As director of teacher training, the writer especially commends the general plan and organization, as well as the excellence of the teaching in all of the courses bearing definitely on the preparation of teachers. This applies to the collegiate or academic courses as well as those of strictly professional grade. While academies or preparatory departments, for very good reasons, are excluded by the rules of the training board as schools of observation and supervised teaching, the Saint Mary's Academy possesses none of the objectionable features and can be approved as such a training school for the college. . . . The academy, as well as the college, keeps careful and accurate records of all grades earned in courses and maintains high standards of scholarship and strict attendance upon courses. These things justify this department in recommending the academy for use as a training school. . . .[47]

Then Oscar H. Williams made the further recommendation that as a standard four-year college Saint Mary's prepare to offer three- and four-year courses, as well as a two-year course, for teachers' certificates in high schools. The new certificates would be restricted to departments which were prepared to offer majors and minors in their respective fields.[48]

Saint Mary's College and Saint Mary's Academy were accredited separately for the first time in 1922 by the state of Indiana. "Today the state board of education formally accredited Saint Mary's College for the four-year courses in the collegiate department offering majors," wrote the supervisor of teacher training. "I am writing the Washington state department of education of this recognition."[49]

With the introduction of the four-year teacher-training program, the state not only reaffirmed its previous permission to Saint Mary's Academy as a demonstration school for supervised teaching but further recommended that the neighboring city public high schools be utilized as supplementary experience.[50]

The letter was accompanied with a complete explanation of the accreditation for teachers' certificates. Saint Mary's College was qualified to Class A, B, and C certificates, provisional certificates without an examination to those completing the two-year normal course as well as the four-year course, with life certification for all holders after two years of successful teaching. The following instruction makes clear the policy of the state of Indiana in 1922.

ACCREDITATION FOR TEACHERS' CERTIFICATES

St. Mary's College, of Notre Dame, Indiana, is accredited by the State Teachers' Board for Classes A, B, and C certificates of professional training, and for provisional and life certificates for teaching in elementary and high schools without examination.

Class A certificate of training is issued by the college to students who have completed one year (30 semester hours) of college work in academic subjects, or 12 weeks' required work in the summer session.

Class B certificate of training is issued by the college to students who have completed at least two years (60 semester hours) of college work with ten semester hours' credit in approved professional subjects, or a second twelve weeks' required work in the summer session.

Class C certificate of training is issued by the college to graduates who have completed twenty semester hours' credit in professional subjects, which must include a minimum of supervised teaching and observation.

The four-year provisional certificate for teaching in elementary schools without examination is issued by the State Teachers' Training Board to graduates of the approved two-year normal course, with 12 semester hours in education; the provisional certificate for teaching in high schools is issued to graduates of a four-year college course with 24 semester hours in education. Supervised teaching and observation are required in both cases.

After teaching successfully for two years under the provisional certificate, the holder receives from the state teachers' training board a life certificate, without examination, of like force and effect. The two years of successful teaching must be done within the four-year period of the provisional certificate and must be done in Indiana high schools.

The four-year provisional and the life certificate are valid for teaching both in junior and senior high schools.[51]

The Sisters of the Holy Cross were trained and certified at Saint Mary's College, Notre Dame, Indiana, according to these specifications.

The entire post-World War I period was characterized by study and change in teaching training, a period almost as much in a state of flux as the present. Fortunately, Mother M. Pauline was still the president of Saint Mary's College. She set about to meet the change with courage and with vision. She invited the state inspector again, as in the previous year, as a consultant to aid in the strengthening of the department of education. By the opening of the scholastic year of 1923, Mother received the following counsel concerning further policies to strengthen teacher education.

Approval of the two-year elementary courses offered by Saint Mary's College at Notre Dame, for intermediate and grammar grade teachers and for teachers of art and music (continues) to be recommended; the four-year courses for regular high school teachers in the following subjects English, Latin, French, social sciences, sciences (all options) . . . home economics (non-vocational), music, art, and music and art (combined). . . . You will kindly follow literally the specification in Chapters VI and IX of Bulletin No. 64 . . . keep this communication as the official notice of accreditment (sic).[52]

This accreditation was to be considered valid until April, 1935.[53] Between 1927 and 1935 correspondence between Mr. H. M. Whisler, director of teacher training, Indianapolis, and Mother M. Pauline shows that teachers' certification areas were enlarged to include mathematics, Spanish, commerce, speech, and primary specialization.[54]

Sister M. Madeleva became president of Saint Mary's College in 1934, replacing Sister M. Irma (Burns). Her appointment coincided with an intensification on the part of the Teacher Training and Licensing Committee of the State Board of Education.

Sister M. Madeleva invited Rev. William Cunningham, C.S.C., of the University of Notre Dame to Monday evening meetings where the faculty studied and analyzed the curriculum. These discussions found expression in the new catalog outlining the revised liberal arts curriculum and introducing the upper and lower divisions.[55]

A graduate program had been added in 1930 for high-school principals' licenses, first and second grade, and elementary principals' licenses, first and second grade,[56] but was discontinued in 1935.[57] Saint Mary's College requested then and received permission for two years of practice teaching in nonaccredited parochial schools on the condition that the teacher submit elective education courses for those in supervised teaching.

From 1935 to 1948 a continuous study and extension of the major and minor courses for teacher education resulted in the yearly renewal of accreditation. In a report of May

15, 1948, standard accreditation for licenses in the elementary department was reaffirmed. The types of certification in the secondary education included (*comprehensive licenses*) language arts, English, Latin, German, French, Spanish, social studies, biological studies, physical science, and mathematics, business education, arts and crafts, music, and home economics; (*conditional and restricted licenses*) history, journalism, and speech; (*special licenses*) music and home economics.[58]

In August, 1956, H. M. Whisler wrote to Saint Mary's College that no inspection would be made for elementary teacher training according to new standards, published in Bulletin No. 192. "So far as I know, no question has been raised concerning your accreditation."[59]

The question of student teaching has not recurred until recent years when Saint Joseph's High School, South Bend, Indiana, was approved by the Teacher Training and Licensing Commission with the condition that the student teaching would have critic-teacher approval from the state of Indiana for the supervising teachers.[60] All critic-teacher licenses are now invalidated under the 1962 law which provides that colleges themselves shall be responsible for the quality of the supervising teacher.[61]

In May, 1959, almost four hundred persons including representatives of classrooms, of school administrators, of liberal arts colleges, and of teacher-training institutions volunteered their time and experience in a study and revision of the curriculum of teacher education and the rules governing its implementation.[62] The 1962 *Manual, The Education of Indiana Teachers,* is the result of the study. It becomes effective September, 1967, when all previous programs not meeting the requirements are considered "dead." This is the first time that the grandfather clause has not been retained in teacher-education legislation in Indiana. The new program appears in Table 12.

TABLE No. 12
State of Indiana: Rules 44 and 45 of the
Teacher Training and Licensing Commission, Effective 1967

Secondary Schools

A. Secondary *LIMITED* certification requirements

1. Bachelor's degree from an accredited institution.
2. Minimum of 15 semester hours in area of endorsement.
3. Planned program for completing requirements for a provisional certificate.
4. Must earn a minimum of seven and one-half semester hours each year for annual validation.
5. Must complete the program within five years from the date of original issuance.
6. Must be recommended by the institution which set up the planned program and in which it was completed.

B. Secondary *PROVISIONAL* certificate requirements

1. Bachelor's degree from an institution accredited to offer a secondary teacher education program.
2. Recommendation by the institution granting the degree.
3. Must have 50 semester hours of general education according to a set plan.
4. Must have 18 semester hours of professional education including 6 semester hours of student teaching.
5. Must have 40 semester hours of a teaching major with certain subjects specified.
6. Certificate valid for five years. Then it is not renewable.

C. Secondary *PROFESSIONAL* certificate requirements

1. Three years of teaching experience.
2. Master's degree from an accredited institution in which each candidate's graduate program is adapted to his needs.
3. Content of the undergraduate program must be studied as far as general education, professional education, and subject matter concentration are concerned. The graduate program should be structured to strengthen weak areas.
4. The teaching major must be brought up to a minimum of 48 semester hours.
5. Certificate is valid for life unless revoked for cause.[63]

The program began with the freshman class of 1963 at Saint Mary's College. All sisters presently in the formation program will therefore be able to meet the enforcement of the 1962 rules for certification.

A comparison of the requirements for secondary teachers with those required of elementary teachers shows that education for the elementary teacher has been strengthened in content. Professional requirements for both levels have been intensified. The secondary school teachers no longer can certify under the 18—30 semester-hour conversion plan; their teaching major must be strengthened to a minimum of 48 semester hours. For those high-school teachers with a master's degree and a life certificate to teach in Indiana none of the above requirements is retroactive.

TABLE No. 13

State of Indiana: Rules 44 and 45 of the Teacher Training and Licensing Commission, Effective 1967

Elementary Schools

A. Elementary *LIMITED* certificate requirements

   1. Bachelor's degree from an accredited institution.
   2. Planned program for completing requirements for a provisional certificate.
   3. This program must include a minimum of eight semester hours of supervised teaching.
   4. The program must be completed within five years from the date of the issuance of the limited certificate.
   5. A minimum of seven and one-half semester hours of credit shall be taken each year for annual validation.
   6. Must be recommended by the institution which set up the planned program and in which it was completed.

B. Elementary *PROVISIONAL* certificate requirements

   1. Bachelor's degree from an institution accredited to offer elementary teacher education.
   2. Recommended by the institution granting the degree.

3. Must have 73 hours of general education according to a set plan and subject-matter concentration.
4. Must have 27 semester hours of professional education including 8 hours of student teaching.
5. Must have 24 semester hours of electives.
6. Certificate valid for five years. Then it is not renewable.

C. Elementary *PROFESSIONAL* certificate requirements
1. Three years of teaching experience.
2. Master's degree in elementary education from an accredited institution in which each candidate's graduate program is adapted to his needs.
3. Recommendation of the institutions of higher education granting the master's degree.
4. The certificate is valid for life unless revoked for cause.

Saint Mary's College opened a graduate department in elementary education and in specialized education with an Institute, June 14, 1965. Its first graduates will meet the Indiana requirements of a master's degree. The graduate department will be an aid to professional certification of the Saint Mary's College graduate teachers in the Congregation of the Sisters of Holy Cross, the sisters in the five-year Formation Program, and the public school teachers in South Bend and the environs. These teachers must meet the requirements of Indiana, effective April, 1967.

A tentative curricula for elementary education and special education were submitted and approved October 2, 1964. The same tentative program was submitted to North Central Association of Colleges and Secondary Schools. They appointed a consultant with whom the administrators of Saint Mary's College are now working. Provisional accreditation will follow.[64] During the 1964–1965 scholastic year, the Committee on Graduate Studies and the Committee on Teacher Education studied curricula and interdepartmental cooperation.

Members of the Board of Religious Trustees of Saint Mary's College and the Board of Lay Trustees are working closely with Dr. Alex Jardine, Superintendent of Schools in South Bend. Mr. Nelson Mosher, Mr. Richard Rembold, and Mr. Donald Hippensteel, administrators in areas of specialized education, have offered the facilities of School City, South Bend, for the student teaching of those enrolled in specialized education. With the introduction of a graduate program in elementary and specialized education, teachers in the South Bend environs will have accessible graduate work on both the elementary and secondary level, since the University of Notre Dame has an MAT secondary program.

Because the teachers of the Congregation of Sisters of Holy Cross have schools in twenty states of the union, and because there is a centralized program of preservice teacher education, the certification for states with varying requirements has caused problems. For this reason, when the National Commission of Accrediting recognized some twenty accrediting agencies, March 2, 1957,[65] and set up criteria for such recognition, Saint Mary's College was eager to avail itself of national accreditation with the attending reciprocity. This would enable teachers educated at the general house to enjoy reciprocity in 11 of the 20 states where schools of the Sisters of Holy Cross are located.[66] Saint Mary's College spent a year in self-study and in answering a written report to the National Council of Accreditation of Teacher Education (NCATE) before a visiting dean came in April, 1960. The college was accredited by NCATE the same year.[67]

References

[1] Sacred Heart Academy, Ogden, Utah, 1895, AGH.
[2] Sister Francis Jerome (O'Laughlin), *This is Mother Pauline* (St. Anthony Guild, 1945), p. 67.
[3] The ground was broken in 1902. AGH.

[4] *The Chimes,* July, 1895.

[5] Interview with Sister M. Benedictus (Kern), December 20, 1964.

[6] Sister M. Benedictus (Kern), Reunion, The Holy Cross Alumnae Association of Saint Mary's College, Notre Dame, Indiana, June 9, 1962.

[7] Cubberley, Ellwood P., *The Certification of Teachers,* Fifth Yearbook of the National Society for the Scientific Study of Education, Part II (Chicago, 1906), p. 29. In a number of states the law specifically states that the grades of certificates shall be "examined only in the common-school branches" or "in the branches of study taught in the common schools" or "subjects for the examination as enumerated in the law are merely 'the common school branches,' plus perhaps a little 'theory and practice of teaching.'" See, for example, *Arkansas Statutes,* sec. 7577; *Illinois School Law,* Art. VII, sec. 3; *Indiana School Law,* 1903 Revision, sec. 81, p. 75; *Iowa Code,* sec. 2736; *Kentucky Common School Laws,* Art. XI, sec. 133; *New Hampshire Session Laws of 1895,* chap. 49, sec. 3; *Maine Statutes,* sec. 105.

[8] *Ibid.,* p. 28, Table III, part 3.

[9] *School Laws of Oklahoma,* Art. xii, sec. 9, *Oklahoma Code,* sec. 5822. *Ibid.,* p. 10.

[10] State of Alabama: "An Act to establish a uniform system for the examination and licensing of teachers for the public schools," February 10, 1899. *Ibid.,* p. 10.

[11] The California School Law, *Political Code,* secs. 1787–93.

[12] *Ibid.,* p. 28, Table III, part 4.

[13] *Ibid.,* part 3. Many states today retain indefensible restrictions. The State Department of Education, Springfield, Illinois, refuses certification to teachers, certified in Indiana, with twenty or more years of experience, unless the requirement of physical education is met. They recommend that the course be taken by correspondence! (Correspondence in file of author.)

[14] *Ibid.,* p. 7.

[15] *Ibid.,* p. 8.

[16] *Ibid.,* p. 8.

[17] *Indiana Session Laws of 1899,* sec. 1, p. 488. *Ibid.,* p. 21.

[18] *Indiana Session Laws of 1903,* sec. 2, p. 291. *Ibid.,* p. 44.

[19] *Indiana Session Laws of 1899,* sec. 1, p. 488. *Ibid.,* p. 21.

[20] Willard S. Elsbree, *The American Teacher* (New York, 1939), p. 351.

[21] Lloyd E. Blauch, ed. *Accreditation in Higher Education* (Washington, 1959), Table 2, p. 33.

[22] Survey of the Educational Status of the Sisters of the Congregation of the Holy Cross (1844–1964), AGH. Hereafter cited as Survey. At present there are eight teachers in the midwest province who have life certification under this program. The tests were administered.

[23] *Public Education in Indiana* (New York, 1923), p. 279.

[24] Survey, AGH.

[25] See list of Schools and Orphanages of the Sisters of the Holy Cross, Appendix, p. 203.

[26] The "grandfather clause" was a benign or indulgent clause that provided for exceptions, especially for those who had been certified with substandard requirements.

[27] Indiana, Department of Public Instruction, *Laws, Rules, Regulations, and General Information Governing Teacher Training & Licensing,* Educational Bulletin No. 94 (Indianapolis, 1937), 35.

[28] Annual Report to State of Indiana, Department of Public Instruction, 1938–1940. Office of the Academic Dean, Saint Mary's College, Notre Dame, Indiana. Office hereafter cited as OAD.

[29] All twelve of these sisters held administrative positions in the Congregation of the Sisters of the Holy Cross as mother general, general councilors, mothers provincial, superiors, or heads of departments.

[30] A projected program to facilitate completion of degrees of this group is under way. Certification in some regional accrediting agencies comes automatically with a master's degree. This is true of the high schools in the District of Columbia where there is no certification as such for private schools but where schools must be accredited by the Middle States Region.

[31] Elsbree, *op. cit.,* p. 353, for period 1895–1927; Indiana, Department of Public Instruction, *Handbook on Teacher Education in Indiana,* State of Indiana Department of Public Instruction, Division of Teacher Training and Licensing Bulletin 192, 2nd rev. ed. (Indianapolis, 1954), p. 16, for period 1937–1954.

[32] G. K. Hodenfield and T. M. Stinnett, *The Education of Teachers: Conflict and Consensus* (Englewood Cliffs, New Jersey, 1961), p. ix.

[33] Burke A. Hinsdale, Charles De Garmo, and Elmer E. Brown, "The Certification of College and University Graduates as Teachers of the Common Schools," *The School Review,* June, 1899, p. 4.

[34] *Ibid.,* p. 367.

[35] Allan O. Pfnister, "Accreditation in the North Central Region," *Accreditation in Higher Education,* ed. Lloyd E. Blauch (Washington, 1959), p. 52.

[36] Articles of Incorporation, 1903, AGH.

[37] *Ibid.* Pfnister, *loc. cit.* Agency later renamed.

[38] G-7, 178, AGH.

[39] "Important Events in the Annals of the Congregation of the Sisters of the Holy Cross," p. 41.

[40] Pfnister, *op. cit.,* p. 53.

[41] Harry Morehouse Gage to Mother M. Pauline, May 13, 1922. OAD.

[42] Report of the Visiting Team of the North Central Association to Sister M. Alma, June, 1961, OAD.

[43] Articles of Incorporation, 1855, AGH.
[44] State departments of education use different terms for the word accreditation. Indiana uses officially the word "approval."
[45] Charles A. Greathouse to Mother M. Pauline, May 8, 1915, OAD.
[46] Ibid.
[47] Oscar H. Williams to the President of the Normal Department, July 27, 1920, OAD.
[48] Oscar H. Williams to Mother M. Pauline, December 16, 1921, OAD.
[49] Ibid.
[50] Ibid., March 8, 1922, OAD.
[51] Ibid., March 15, 1922, OAD.
[52] Ibid., September 8, 1923, OAD.
[53] Ibid.
[54] H. M. Whisler to Mother M. Pauline, June 14, 1927; November 30, 1927; August 30, 1930; September 6, 1935, OAD.
[55] Archives, Saint Mary's College and Academy, 1934–1935, ASMC.
[56] C. L. Murray to Sister M. Frederick, February 18, 1935, OAD.
[57] Dorothy Hodges to Sister M. Frederick, September 1, 1937, OAD.
[58] State Department of Instruction to Saint Mary's College, May 15, 1948, OAD. Previous accreditation continued in accordance with the pattern of Bulletin 192.
[59] H. M. Whisler to Sister Mary Alma, April 28, 1958, OAD.
[60] Robert L. Pabst to Sister Mary Alma, April 28, 1958, OAD.
[61] Indiana, Department of Public Instruction, The Education of Indiana Teachers, State of Indiana Division of Teacher Education and Certification Bulletin 400 (Indianapolis, 1963), p. 62.
[62] Ibid., p. 6.
[63] Indiana, op. cit., pp. 23–24.
[64] John E. Reisert to Sister Mary Alma, June 21, 1963, OAD.
[65] Blauch, op. cit., p. 22.
[66] See map, Appendix, p. 197.
[67] W. Earl Armstrong to Sister M. Madeleva, May 12, 1960, OAD.

CHAPTER V

TEACHER EDUCATION IN THE CONGREGATION OF THE SISTERS OF THE HOLY CROSS: 1944-1964

THE CONGREGATION of the Sisters of the Holy Cross had prepared its teachers in elementary and secondary schools, during the period of 1900–1940, under the pressures of expediency. Movements in the history of secular training have all made their impact upon Holy Cross. Sisters had studied as postulants and scholastics to acquire licenses through examination or certification in normal school. Once certified, the next step had been the long summer school road to a degree in education.

Saint Mary's College from its inception had had a liberal arts curriculum. It moved slowly in its adoption of courses of a normal school or of a teachers' college. Eliza Allan Starr had written of the 1897 summer school session,

Before the inauguration of the famous Chautauqua Summer Session, the teachers at Saint Mary's enjoyed the benefits of a normal-school training during the vacation months . . . the courses of lectures were comparable in interest and value to those offered at Madison, Plattsburg, or Rochester.[1]

The first "methods" course in the curriculum was one enti-

tled "Methods in Studying Psychology" by Rev. Edward Pace,
1895. Three years later "Methods in Teaching Music" was
added. Saint Mary's College introduced the first classes in
pedagogy in 1899.[2] A department of education was not set up
until 1912–1913,[3] when the first degree of bachelor of pedagogy (Ph.B) was granted by Saint Mary's College to Sister
M. Benedictus (Kern), who had graduated the previous year
with a major in the classics. But the forces behind this slow
emergence of a formal program in teacher education were
the external forces of history. The Sister Formation Program,
which was to begin to grow painfully and to emerge into a
full-fledged program in the decades of 1940 to 1960, was to be
the result of an internal force within the sisterhoods themselves.

Previously religious communities had plans already par-
tially implemented to educate integrally the religious, intellectual, and cultural teacher. But if the ideal was to be a fait
accompli, the movement needed concerted cooperation. Every
religious community has had its difficulties in realizing this
program; the Congregation of the Sisters of the Holy Cross
is no exception.

No one can actually say, "This was the beginning of the
Sister Formation Program." Its beginnings were incipient
efforts in many communities to achieve the ideal of the Sister Formation Program which met with varying degrees of
success and failure. Before the publication of *The Education
of Sister Lucy,* a brochure reprinting a series of talks on sister
formation given at a National Catholic Education Association convention in 1949, there had been multiple but sporadic
efforts to lengthen the formation period within the Congregation of the Sisters of the Holy Cross. As far back as 1932,
Sister M. Lauretanna (Unrich), supervisor of schools in the
western province, submitted to Mother M. Vincentia (Fannon), superior general, a plan for teacher preparation in the

western province. In a letter of reply, Mother Vincentia approved of the plan, adding:

I agree that we should train four groups and strive to perfect everyone in the group which she is best qualified by nature to adorn. Some are naturally fitted to the first group, primary teachers. . . . Why run the risk of spoiling such fine teachers by shifting them into schools to go up higher? Add training, experience, and pedagogy. These (teachers) are invaluable. The second class of teachers is the grammar grade teacher. At present, many of our students in public and parochial schools go no higher than the eighth grade. It is important that we (certify) these teachers properly. Still other sisters have a natural aptitude for older boys and girls. They have found their level. Even with all their ability they would probably be lost if transferred to a freshman class in college. . . . Of course we need doctors' (degrees) and we will continue to train them. But let all first be certified by the state; let her meet all the requirements of diocesan and educational boards. I am glad to see that you have set forth this idea in your plan.[4]

Sister M. David (Hopfinger) with Sister M. Lauretanna prepared a report for the general chapter of 1937, showing how the initial educational and professional training of the young religious teacher could be met.[5]

In August, 1943, Mother M. Rose Elizabeth (Havican), superior general, lengthened the training of sisters who were finishing their scholasticate[6] and retained four of them at the general house in August of 1943.[7] Four to six remained from both bands whose canonical formation was terminated during the years 1943 to 1946.[8] They continued their studies at Saint Mary's College and continued their religious formation at the nearby scholasticate. Again it was an attempt, but it was not a formalized program. More than that, pressures of increased enrollment in parochial schools, and the reluctance, and at times the inability, of bishops and pastors to meet the financial outlay required to employ lay teachers made it difficult for provincial superiors in their respective provinces to support the program.[9]

In the "Educational Report: Sisters of the Holy Cross, 1943 to 1949," a plan for the education of our sisters was presented whereby a bachelor's degree and teacher's license, elementary or secondary, was made possible in four and one-half years of formation to "acquire the essential intellectual, cultural, and religious disciplines."[10] The importance of this professional preparation for sisters still in their years of formation was stressed. They would have the advantages offered by Saint Mary's College. This decision hinged on the opportunity to develop as a family of Holy Cross. The facilities at Saint Mary's College permitted the young sisters to attend musicals, lectures, and other cultural and religious activities. The program definitely referred to the types of courses suggested in *The Education of Sister Lucy*, page 12.[11]

But by August, 1947, the school population had greatly increased;[12] the number of religious vocations had not kept pace;[13] and pastors had not reconciled themselves to the place of the lay teacher in the Catholic school system. The problems which confronted every major superior in carrying through the program made her daily correspondence a Pandora's box. Under these pressures the sisters were once more sent out to teach following a three-year period of formation. But one problem, the proper education of teachers of religion, was rightly to be met first.

Sister M. Madeleva, president of Saint Mary's College, had taken an active part in the work of the Problems Committee of the College and University Department of the National Catholic Educational Association. Teacher education, especially education of teachers of religion, posed the most acute situation facing wartime adjustments in 1943. A pioneer in sister education reform, Sister M. Madeleva describes the sequence of events as follows:

During the late 1930's and well into the 1940's of our present century, the Midwest region of the National Catholic Educational Association maintained—for purposes of expedition and clarification—a Problems Committee. This committee ordinarily met the day before the regular annual regional or national meeting of the NCEA. There were always acute problems to be considered. The year 1943 was true to form.

On March 23, 1943, the committee reported the problem of the teaching and teachers of religion in college as, by all means, the most important problem, this in the face of wartime adjustments. The committee presented the fact that, "Nowhere," quoting Frank Sheed, "is there a school in the United States where a layman can study theology." The flagrancy of this situation was immediately recognized. A committee was appointed to investigate the possibilities of remedying this situation and of organizing what would ultimately be a graduate school of sacred theology. I, Sister M. Madeleva, C.S.C., was appointed chairman of a committee to make this preliminary investigation.

All of the procedures following were authorized by Most Reverend Edwin V. O'Hara, D.D., Chairman of the Episcopal Commission on the Confraternity of Christian Doctrine, and with the approval of Most Reverend John Francis Noll, D.D., of the Diocese of Fort Wayne.

To begin with, I contacted the graduate schools in the Midwest region: the universities of Notre Dame, Saint Louis, Marquette, Loyola, De Paul, with no success. They were all too deeply involved with programs of GI's and other wartime emergencies. I was directed to write to the Catholic University and ask whether religious and other women could be admitted to the school of Sacred Theology. This request was also refused. Reporting my complete failure to Bishop O'Hara, I received this recommendation: "Why don't you begin the school here?" I protested our lack of qualifications and the possible presumption in such an undertaking. Citing his chairmanship of the Episcopal Commission on the Confraternity of Christian Doctrine, the bishop directed me to organize and open such a graduate school at Saint Mary's College, Notre Dame, Indiana.

There was no time to be lost. By late May, we had assembled a faculty consisting of Reverend Matthew Schumacher, Reverend Michael J. Gruenthaner, S.J., Reverend Gerald Ellard, S.J., and Right Reverend Msgr. William L. Newton. We offered the course to sisters and other laywomen, without credit and without tuition, as our preliminary graduate program in Sacred Theology. Classes opened in June, 1943.

The response was so immediate and the enthusiasm so spontaneous and pentecostal that we were left in no doubt as to the future of the school. The first regular session opened on June 19, 1944, and has continued without interruption for these twenty years—a two-semester regular session and a six weeks summer session yearly.

The school functions academically under the charter granted by the state of Indiana in 1855. It enjoys the papal approbation of His Holiness, Pope Pius XII, as well as the commendations from His Eminence Cardinal Pizzardo, and Excellencies Charles P. Greco and Leo A. Pursley.

There were, when we set up our program, no Sacred Theology graduate schools in the United States where women could be prepared to teach theology and sacred scripture at the same level and with the same competence as profane subjects on college level. We have never had this priority of our school seriously questioned.

The graduate school of theology Regina Mundi was opened in Rome in 1954, ten years later, organized after careful consultation with members of our faculty here at Saint Mary's. Our entire program, texts, reference material and general plan, were taken from our office to Rome by the secretary of Reverend Arcadio Larraona, C.M.F., the representative of our Holy Father at the First National Congress of Religious in the United States, August 9 to 13, 1952. Graduates from the United States completing their studies at Regina Mundi have their credits validated by Saint Mary's School of Sacred Theology.[14]

In summary, the School of Sacred Theology commemorated its twentieth anniversary with the August commence-

ment of 1964. During this period 311 students have been
enrolled in its regular sessions; 1802, in summer sessions, as
shown in Table No. 14.

TABLE No. 14

Enrollment and Graduates of the School of
Sacred Theology: 1944-1964[15]

Year	Regular Session	Summer Session	Graduates Ph.D.	M.A.	Total
1944		45			
1945		50			
1946	6	54	4	10	14
1947	10	81			
1948	12	90	2	8	10
1949	13	102	7	7	14
1950	8	93	1	26	27
1951	8	79	1	1	2
1952	10	98	5	14	19
1953	18	108	5	16	21
1954	18	104	3	9	12
1955	28	102	5	18	23
1956	19	91	4	17	21
1957	18	78	4	18	22
1958	15	70	7	12	19
1959	19	66	3	15	18
1960	23	67	4	8	12
1961	23	77	5	8	13
1962	30	103	2	17	19
1963	18	109	0	18	18
1964	15	125	5	20	25
TOTAL	311	1802	67	242	309

Total Religious Graduates: 53 Ph.D.   230 M.A.
Total Lay Graduates: 14 Ph.D.   12 M.A.

By the end of the decade of 1940 to 1950 other religious communities were making efforts to implement formal programs for an integrated intellectual, religious, and cultural training of young teachers. A series of significant events, related and integrated, brought forth the Sister Formation Program in the United States and also in the Congregation of the Sisters of the Holy Cross, whose religious superiors and educational leaders played a part in its beginnings and development.

Mother M. Angela was *the* religious educator of the Sisters of the Holy Cross in the second half of the nineteenth century. Sister M. Madeleva was to achieve international and national status as an educator in the middle decades of the twentieth century. In an address given at the Philadelphia NCEA meeting, April 21, 1949, Sister M. Madeleva, president of Saint Mary's College, read a paper entitled, "The Education of Our Young Religious Teachers." It was an honest repudiation of the manner in which teachers had been educated in the past. It was a Utopian plan for sister education in the future. It was a plea for professional as well as religious formation. It was a cry for immediate, concerted action of all religious communities NOW.[16]

When one rereads *The Education of Sister Lucy,* fifteen years after its writing, it is clear that the problems which Sister M. Madeleva had forseen have been indigenous to all religious communities which have set up a program such as the hypothetical education of Sister Lucy. There have been acute shortages of teachers where sisters were retained until their professional training was completed. There have been objections of bishops and pastors to the cost of hiring lay teachers. There has been the staggering cost to religious communities of maintaining a five-year formation program.[17]

In March, 1948, the corporate efforts of the members of the Midwest College and University Department of the National

Catholic Educational Association were to set into action a series of events in the history of education of religious teachers in the United States. Concomitant in these same years of 1948 to 1950 there were to be events in the history of religious women in the church where the germ of this NCEA would find fertility and maturation. The part that Sister M. Madeleva played in the NCEA efforts is told in *The Education of Sister Lucy*. Sister tells it again in an interview:

However much Catholic education and educators may be credited with inertia, they have moved at times and moved significantly. At a meeting of the Midwest College and University Department of the National Catholic Educational Association on March 9, 1948, a paper on teacher preparation and education of our young sisters was presented. Because of its pertinence, an official committee on this subject was set up at the annual meeting of the NCEA in San Francisco, April 1 of that year. A committee was appointed, of which I was asked to be the chairman. We were given a place on the national meeting in Philadelphia, April 21, 1949, the last hour of the last afternoon, in a room that would scarcely seat thirty persons.

Well before the time of the opening of the meeting the room was filled and flowing into the halls. Immediately, we moved to the cafeteria of the building. By the time that we arrived there, its capacity, too, had been exhausted. We gravitated to the gymnasium, where with great expedition we set up our meeting with squealing microphones and an overflowing audience.

Papers had been prepared by members of six different religious communities and had been in the office of the chairman a month in advance of the meeting. I not only assured myself that good papers would be prepared, but there would be copies available, if necessary.

The response was overwhelming, even under the handicaps of time and place. When the last paper had been presented, there was an immediate request for the publication of the entire group. I offered to undertake the work of publishing but could not finance the expense. Again, the group called out spontaneously, "Let us pay."

As you see, I had the manuscripts all ready in my desk at home. We sent them to our printer, and within two weeks had the booklet, *The Education of Sister Lucy*, off the press and on sale for 50c apiece. The contents of the book are

The Education of Our Young Religious Teachers
Problems and Answers
The Diocesan Teachers' College Plan in Cleveland
The Ursuline Plan
The Educational Program of the School Sisters of Saint Francis
Teacher Training in Seminary and Scholasticate
The Preparation of Teachers of Religion in College

In one small brochure six possible and feasible programs for what has since grown into the Sister Formation movement were presented. Following this meeting, its impact and its influence, the entire body of teaching sisters has become organized or reorganized under what is now, one may well say, a world movement of the education of the religious teacher. Again and again at conventions the brochure, *The Education of Sister Lucy*, is cited as the Sister Formation movement in embryo, the valid, fertile and historic beginning of the thorough, Christian, professional preparation of religious women for their apostolate as Christian teachers.[18]

Historically, sister formation leads back to the movement from which it takes its vitality and which binds it to the Church: a world-wide program for adaptation and renovation publicly initiated by Pius XII and the Sacred Congregation of Religious. In the United States it was to see initial fruition in the First National Congress of the Religious of the United States, August 9–13, 1952. The congress met at the University of Notre Dame, Notre Dame, Indiana, called by Most Reverend Arcadio Larraona, C.M.F., at the direction of Pope Pius

XII. Two thousand religious—priests, brothers, and sisters—representing four hundred institutes in the United States, met to deepen and to strengthen the religious life throughout the world as an effective antidote against evils and dangers of these troubled times.[19]

The Sacred Congregation named a committee charged with the responsibility of organizing and promoting the congress. Four religious of Holy Cross were members of this committee of ten: Rev. John J. Cavanaugh, C.S.C., honorary chairman; Rev. Edward L. Heston, C.S.C., Rome, Italy, general secretary; Mother M. Rose Elizabeth, C.S.C., treasurer; and Sister M. Madeleva, C.S.C., publicity. Holy Cross members played a significant part in the program: Rev. Theodore Hesburgh, C.S.C., welcomed the delegates; His Excellency, Most Rev. John F. O'Hara, C.S.C., addressed the members in general assembly; and Sister M. Madeleva, C.S.C., eschewed theory and presented a program of theology for sisters, one that had been a reality for ten years at Saint Mary's College, Notre Dame, Indiana.[20]

Under the dynamic leadership of Sister M. Emil, I.H.M., chairman, the first national sister formation committee began a cooperative program of mutual understanding and assistance officially designated at the executive committee meeting of the College and University Department of the NCEA in Chicago, April 21, 1954.[21] An official publication, edited by Sister Ritamary, C.H.M., kept communication alive. A palpable metamorphosis has taken place in the years that followed. They saw a concerted effort of programs for the "formation of the integrated personality of the sister-teacher who regards professional preparation as a part of a way of life in reaching sanctity, and a life of sanctity as the framework into which specialization fits naturally and without ostentation.[22]

Major superiors of the Congregation of the Sisters of the Holy Cross continue to work closely with the Sister Formation

Program. Mother M. Rose Elizabeth has been a member of the planning committee since 1955. Mother Kathryn Marie, superior general, is at present national vice-chairman of the Conference of Major Superiors of Women's Institutes.

In August, 1958, a formal five-year program began. The sisters remained at the houses of formation for the Sisters of the Holy Cross, Notre Dame, for five years, enabling them to complete an integrated intellectual, spiritual, and cultural formation. In August, 1964, the first group to complete the five-year program went into parochial and private schools after a year's postulancy, a canonical year, a post-canonical year, and two years in the juniorate as temporarily professed sisters. After three years of mission experience they will be admitted to final profession. During these three years they pursue any additional classes needed to meet state certification requirements as they differ in the twenty states and the District of Columbia where the Sisters of the Holy Cross have schools.

A sister formation committee meets monthly, composed of the superior general, ex-officio; the director of education for the houses of formation, chairman; directresses in the houses of formation; the academic dean of Saint Mary's College; and the first and second assistants to the superior general, consultants for hospital education and missions abroad respectively. This group is consultative rather than deliberative, and works to coordinate and to integrate the threefold objectives of the intellectual, spiritual, and cultural religious teacher.[23]

Many candidates enter at the completion of their high school years. The average age of admission is eighteen years. Psychological tests, the postulants' interests, and the needs of the community determine the major and minor studies which are followed in the two years of the juniorate. A typical five-year course for a major in elementary education is outlined in Table No. 15.

TABLE No. 15

Typical Five-Year Course for Majors in Elementary Education[24]

First semester   *Second semester*

POSTULANCY

First semester		Second semester	
Old Testament 1	2 cdts.	Old Testament 2	2 cdts.
English 1	3	English 2	3
Gen. Psychology	3	Logic	3
Political Sci.	3	Intro. to Arts	3
	11 cdts.	Music Fundamentals	2
			13 cdts.

SUMMER SESSION

Liturgy and Holiness 102   2 cdts.
Philosophy of Nature   2
                           ———
                           4 cdts.

CANONICAL YEAR

First semester		Second semester	
New Testament 3	2 cdts.	New Testament 4	2 cdts.
Philos. Psychology	3	Metaphysics	3
Liturgical Music	1	Liturgical Music	1
	6 cdts.		6 cdts.

SUMMER SESSION

Basic Mathematics   5 cdts.

POST-CANONICAL YEAR

First semester		Second semester	
Dogmatic Theo.	2 cdts.	Moral Theo.	2 cdts.
Western Civiliz.	3	Western Civiliz.	3
English Lit.	3	Eng. and Amer. Lit.	3
Sociology 51	3	Intro. to Educat.	2
Language	4	Language	4
	15 cdts.	Music Literature	3
			17 cdts.

FIRST VOW SUMMER SESSION

The Sacraments	2 cdts.
Ethics	3
	5 cdts.

JUNIORATE—FIRST YEAR

Moral Theo. 123	2 cdts.	Contemp. Moral Theo.	2 cdts.
Biology 1	4	Biology 2	4
Geography	3	Math. for Teachers	3
Physical Sci.	3	Physical Sci.	3
The Child	5	The Curriculum	5
	17 cdts.		17 cdts.

SUMMER SESSION

Principles of Economics	3 cdts.
Basic Social Principles	3
	6 cdts.

JUNIORATE—SECOND YEAR

The Church	2 cdts.	Communication Arts	5 cdts.
U. S. History	2	U. S. History	2
Tests and Meas'nts.	2	Phil. of Education	3
Music Education	2	Children's Lit.	2
Art Education	2	Safety Education	1
Speech	2	Seminar	2
Health Education	1	Comprehensives	
	13 cdts.		15 cdts.

SUMMER SESSION

Student Teaching	6 cdts.

For a secondary school teacher a major in a content subject commences in the summer of the post-canonical year. The professional education required for a licensed secondary school teacher includes introduction to education, principles of secondary education, educational psychology, methods, and guidance. Both elementary and secondary teachers earn six hours in student teaching either at the Campus School or at Saint Joseph's High School.

The Campus School was opened in 1950 to meet two needs: parishes without schools and student teaching opportunities for members of the community. At present it accommodates children from two parishes, Pius X and Little Flower of South Bend. In principle it is an ungraded school with homogeneous groupings in arithmetic, reading, and spelling. The first grade is kept together, but a child who knows how to read before coming to school is usually started in a second-grade reading group. A superior faculty to meet state teacher certification characterizes the school. All supervising teachers are approved by Saint Mary's College. Mrs. Joseph McGuire is the supervisor of all student teachers, lay or religious.

Secondary student teaching is done at Saint Joseph's High School, especially during the summer session in small classes with opportunities for experimentation. The same scholastic requirements of the state prevail. The summer school is accredited by the state of Indiana. The supervising teachers are validated by Saint Mary's College, a member of the National Council for the Accreditation of Teacher Education.

The academic program for sisters in the houses of formation is based on the following considerations:

1. Normally, postulants entering as college freshmen will complete requirements for their undergraduate degree from Saint Mary's College by June of their second juniorate year.
2. Generally, required courses and course sequences are determined by the academic requirements of Saint Mary's College and the special needs of sisters in view of the goals of formation.

The academic requirements of Saint Mary's College account for the distribution of lower-division courses among basic humanistic, scientific, mathematical, philosophical, and theological studies. The special needs of sisters dictated stronger sequences in theology, philosophy, and the social sciences than are required in the standard college program.[25]

In addition, sequences in theology and philosophy extend to the final profession summer[26] and the tertianship summer.[27] Courses in sacred scripture on the graduate level are projected for these two summer sessions and also courses in history of modern philosophy (final profession summer) and history of contemporary philosophy (tertianship summer). Formal courses in the fine arts are supplemented by a planned co-curricular program.

Postulants who enter with a degree follow in the revised program the courses that may be lacking in their preparation or that may be needed for professional requirements. During the juniorate, other things being equal, these sisters have good prospects of completing a master's program (or in some instances of advancing beyond this point) at the University of Notre Dame, or, in special cases, elswhere.[28]

Besides its own program of sister formation, the Congregation of the Sisters of the Holy Cross has planned a program to aid other communities to prepare their religious teachers. At a Sister Formation Conference in 1959, Mother Kathryn Marie, superior general of the Sisters of the Holy Cross, and Sister M. Madeleva, president of Saint Mary's College, Notre Dame, agreed to set up and to sponsor a Religious Education Program. The purpose of the graduate program was to meet the need of those religious engaged in sister formation work in their respective communities.

Under the direction of Sister M. Emil, I.H.M., Sister Maria Pieta (Scott), C.S.C., planned a series of twenty-six lectures on asceticism conducted by eminent scholars and theologians. Eighty-four religious from thirty-five communities attended the first session in January, 1960, when Rev. Raphael Simon,

O.S.C.O., presented the first in the series, "Psychology and Asceticism."

The program in religious education is divided into twenty-six concentrated short courses consisting of thirteen lectures each and a two-hour examination for each course. A thesis earns four credits toward the degree. Proficiency in Latin and a modern language is required.

Distinguished theologians have supported the program from its inception: Rev. Walter Farrell, S.J.; Rev. Charles D. J. Corcoran, O.P.; Rev. Charles Schleck, C.S.C.; Rev. Godfrey Diekmann, O.S.B.; Rev. Leo Armoult, O.P.; Rev. Paul Augustine Hennessy, C.P.; Rev. Carroll Stuhlmueller, C.P.; Rev. William Coyle, C.S.S.R.; Rev. James Mark Egan, O.P.; and Rev. Juniper Cummings, O.F.M.

After fulfillment of its commitment to the group now pursuing the course, the program terminated in March, 1965. Those who pursued this experimental course did so at a time when there was an urgent need for greater effectiveness in the important task of training young religious who in turn will teach the Christian youth in our schools today.[29]

To calculate the cost of educating a teacher in the Congregation of the Sisters of the Holy Cross only in dollars and cents could be debilitating to the concept of religious life, a communal, dedicated life built on sacrifice. But since the purpose of the study is in part to reveal the fiscal problem of a religious community educating its teachers to meet the needs of contemporary society, an explanation of the accompanying annual cost for the year 1962–1963 is in place.[30]

A summary of administrative, educational, and retirement costs of the Sisters of the Holy Cross from May 31, 1956, to May 31, 1963, shows the impact of the rise in the cost of living and in the selection of personnel. The sister formation requirements and the increased state requirements contribute significantly. From an average annual cost of $1625 per sister living at the General House in 1956 to $3696 in 1963 there is a differential of $2071. To meet this expense an average of $963 must come from each teacher in a parochial school. Actually, the average contribution toward total cost is $207 per sister in parochial school, making a differential of $756. Sixty-seven percent of the total number of the Sisters of the Holy Cross are assigned to parochial schools. Table No. 16 gives the community cost in an eight-year perspective.

TABLE No. 16

Summary of Administrative, Educational, and Retirement Costs
Congregation of the Sisters of the Holy Cross[31]

	1955–56	1960–61	1961–62	1962–63
Expense (after crediting farm, Campus School, and rent income) including depreciation of General and Provincial Houses	$578,422	$895,616	$991,138	$1,143,309
Sisters assigned:				
Retired sisters and staff				
Provincial Houses	75	46	60	49
General House	153	175	158	171
Houses of formation	128	157	171	204
	356	378	389	424
Average annual amount required from each sister on mission to meet above costs	$489	$719	$802	$963
Income received from parochial school sisters				
Average contribution per sister in parochial schools	$187	$226	$230	$207
% of sisters assigned to parochial schools	65%	66%	67%	67%
% of income from parochial schools	13%	17%	18%	16%

The greatest number of members of the Sisters of the Holy Cross teach in ninety-eight elementary parochial schools in the United States. The community retains one private elementary school in 1964, the Academy of Saint Catherine, Ventura, California. With 67% of its total membership in the parochial school where salaries are lower than in secondary schools or colleges, and a differential of $756 per teacher, the community must turn to other sources for income. Nineteen per cent of the members teach in community-owned schools. The average income per sister is 14.6% of the administrative, educational, and retirement costs of the Congregation of the Sisters of the Holy Cross, or an average of $655. Again there is a differential between ordinary income and ordinary expense[32] of $963−655 = $308. It is evident from the graph "Income Distribution: 1961–1962" (Appendix, page 193) that the income of 86.5% of the teachers meets 32.8% of the cost of operation at the general house.[33] The imbalance between the ordinary expense of administration, education, and retirement, and the ordinary income from schools of the Sisters of the Holy Cross is given in the graph "Average Cost and Income per Sister in Parochial Schools" (Appendix, page 194).[34]

From the total of administrative, educational, and retirement costs of the Congregation of the Sisters of the Holy Cross, of the year 1962 to 1963, the cost of the formation program has been isolated. Over a period of five years the total cost of educating a teacher in the formation program is approximately $13,710 per sister as shown in Table 17.

TABLE No. 17

Estimated Costs of Formation Program[35]

Annual Cost	Total	Per Sister
Tuitions and fees	$160,000.	
minimum of $1000 per year for four years		
divided by five years in program		$ 800.

Amortization of new building	86,000.	430.
Share of General expenses, based on percentage of Sisters in Formation to Total Sisters and Priests in General House (54.5%)		
Administration and General	21,800.	109.
Dietary	99,299.	496.
Plant Operation	119,355.	597.
Chapel	2,180.	11.
Housekeeping (excluding nurse aide salaries)	22,236.	111.
Laundry	10,000.	50.
Sisters' Personal Maintenance— Clothing, postage, telephone, travel, books, medical, dental, optical, hospital, and Community expenses (excluding $20,000. from total medical and hospital expenses)	43,600.	218.
Total Annual Expense	$564,470.	$ 2,822.
Less Income— Postulant's fee—$400. per Sister		80.
NET ANNUAL EXPENSE		$ 2,742.
Five-year Expense per Sister		$13,710.[36]

The annual cost in tuition and fees at a minimum of $1000 per year for four years (divided by five because the program requires this number of years to complete) gives the average yearly cost of $800 per teacher. The Holy Cross Postulate and Holy Cross Juniorate building completed and occupied in 1964 costs the Congregation of Holy Cross $86,000 per year in amortization, an average of $430 per teacher.[37] The figures shown for administration, dietary, plant operation, chapel, housekeeping, laundry, and personal maintenance[38] represent 45.5% of the total cost of operation, i.e., $564,470, an average of $2822 per teacher. If a postulant is financially able, she brings a fee of $400 when entering the Congregation of the Sisters of the Holy Cross. An average of $80 per year is deducted, bringing the net annual expense of the total cost of a year of the sister formation to $2742. Projecting a five-year cost, allowing no increase in the cost of living, the prognostic cost of the formation program is approximately $13,710 per sister.[39]

The reasons why higher superiors initiated and maintained the formation program of the sisters may well be stated in the summary appeal which Sister M. Madeleva made at the national convention of the NCEA in Philadelphia, April 21, 1949:

Two years, three years, (five years) is only a breath in the history of education, or even in the life of a generation. We can never spare them (young sisters) better than now. . . . The education of Sister Lucy and of every young sister is our great privilege, our great responsibility. Will we superiors general, provincials, supervisors insist upon it? Will we pastors demand it? Will we bishops and archbishops, the great leaders and protectors of Catholic education, make the fulfillment of these conditions a requirement? . . . They (young sisters) think and move with the instancies of aviation and television. They think in terms of super-atomic power. We must form and educate them in terms of these potencies. We must not frustrate the magnificence of their qualities by our low-geared Victorian traditions and training.

God knows we need ten thousand young Lucys in our novitiates this minute. When He sees that He can trust us with their education and their training, He will send them to us. Our teachers made us, in large part, what we are. We archbishops and bishops, we pastors and superiors, we school administrators and teachers can make Lucy in large part the kind of religious teacher that she should be. Will we?[40]

When Saint Mary's College commemorated the hundredth birthday of its founding on July 16, 1944, Sister M. Madeleva suggested that the college "go to school." In the spirit of the first meaning and connotation of the word "school," the president planned a series of lectures for the scholastic year 1944–

1945.[41] Teachers, students, alumnae, and friends "went to school."[42] In the twenty years which have passed since the first centenary, the teachers in the Congregation of the Sisters of the Holy Cross have continued to "go to school," but not in the pristine sense of the word.

An inservice teacher-training impetus that has involved every teacher in the schools of Holy Cross parallels the sister formation movement for young teachers. The Sisters of the Holy Cross have also written and published articles, books, music, and art during this period of intensified retraining. In a survey conducted by the Fine Arts Committee under the chairmanship of Sister M. Ceciliana (Honor), C.S.C., is a list of 92 members of the congregation who have published works during the years 1950–1964.[43] The return to school is not unique. Educators in public and private schools dedicated to education of quality for every child in the schools of the United States have returned to school.

The sisters attended undergraduate and graduate classes conducted in the colleges of the community: Saint Mary's, Notre Dame, Indiana; Saint Mary-of-the-Wasatch, Salt Lake City, Utah;[44] Dunbarton College of Holy Cross, Washington, D.C.; and Cardinal Cushing College, Brookline, Massachusetts. The sisters in the midwest province attended the following universities: Notre Dame; Marquette; Detroit; Teachers' College, Columbia; DePaul; Laval; Wisconsin; Saint Louis; Illinois; Rochester; Yale; Michigan; Fordham; American Conservatory of Music; Chicago; Radcliffe; Western Reserve; Catholic University; and the Art Institute, Chicago, for graduate study.[45] The sisters in the eastern province studied at Manhattan College; Catholic University; Johns Hopkins; Rutgers; Harvard University; Western Reserve; Villanova; Boston College; Middlebury; Incarnate Word College, San Antonio, Texas; Regis College, Boston; and the Universities of Illinois, Pennsylvania, Utah, and Boston.[46] Graduate study in the western province continued at the University of San Francisco; University of Berkeley; Portland; Loyola, Los Angeles; Creighton; Southern California; Montreal; Stanford; and Utah. Colleges included: Holy Names, Oakland; Mount St. Mary's, Los Angeles; San Francisco College for Women; San Jose State College; Catholic University Extension, San Raphael; and San Diego College for Women.[47]

Complex factors have necessitated the return to graduate study. State requirements for teacher certification have changed. The latest revision in the state of Indiana, effective September, 1963, makes graduate study imperative for the elementary as well as the secondary school teacher.[48] Increased enrollment, disproportionate to the increase of teachers, challenges administrators, principals, and faculty to creative solutions.

Teachers have studied the use of audio-visual aids, experimentation with radio, television, and closed circuit. Ungraded primaries, departmental teaching in elementary as well as secondary schools, team teaching, experiments in scheduling, programmed learning—all require either a return to study, attendance at workshops, institutes, conferences, or programs of inservice study directed through the community supervisor or the principal.

On both the high-school and grade-school level all sisters involved with teaching mathematics have been retrained in the methodology as well as the content of modern mathematics. Science developments required teachers even with doctoral studies completed to take new courses or to do research. In the summer of 1963, in the midwest province alone, 90% of all secondary science teachers returned to school. Elementary teachers of science of the midwest province have had recourse to TV science programs.[49] Modern languages taught by direct method and the use of language laboratories evoked the sisters' participation in this country and abroad. Teachers need to study scripture, morals, and dogma to meet the developments of research in these subjects. The society that has evolved in the last two decades requires study of new content and methodology in social studies. In the elementary schools social studies, together with mathematics and English, have been departmentalized to permit teacher specialization. The Commission of English under the College Entrance Examination Board has a five-year evaluation study in progress. Project English Committees have been set up in twenty centers. The study of linguistics is a part of the development. Every English teacher must study the new content. Guidance programs have sent teachers and administrators back to school. Elementary and secondary library facilities have improved. Proper training of personnel for the libraries is necessary. Every teacher is affected by the significant changes in knowledge, pupil population, advanced curricula, proliferation of publications, teaching aids, and experimentation.

To finance a general continuation of and return to study of this magnitude taxes a religious community heavily. Tuition costs for university study in summer school programs is the same as the tuition of lay persons.[50] Travel, board and room, and books compound the cost.

In general, the cost of inservice education of the teachers in parochial and secondary schools is met by the particular house in which the sister lives. It is a community local expenditure. In the case of sisters released for advanced study during a scholastic year the cost is met on the provincialate level.

As indicated in the sister formation cost, tuition for a bachelor's degree, exclusive of board, room, travel, books, and sundries, is $4000.[51] To release a teacher for study in a master's program costs from $4000 to $5000; doctoral candidate study, $4500 to $6500.[52] The cost excludes replacement if the community must employ a lay teacher. The cost of a degree earned in the long process of summer schools and Saturday and night classes is more than the cost of a degree earned in the sister formation program or in released study time.[53]

In recent years, grants, aids, fellowships, and scholarships have alleviated some of the expenditure for inservice teacher training and for graduate study. A survey conducted by Sister Marie Angele (Yamamoto) in November, 1964, revealed that 77 Sisters of the Holy Cross had received scholarships, fellowships, and grants for graduate study during the years 1963 to 1964.[54] Teachers of science and mathematics have received the greatest amount of financial aid for advanced study. Such sources include the National Science Foundation, the Oak Ridge Institute of Nuclear Studies, the Arthur J. Schmitt Science Foundation, the Atomic Energy Commission, the Federal Government Traineeship (mathematics), and post-doctoral fellowships to the University of Notre Dame.

Aid to graduate study in the humanities comes from the Lilly Foundation (history), the Ford Foundation (non-Western studies); Catholic University scholarship (classical languages); University of Notre Dame scholarship (education, history, philosophy, and English); the Carnegie Study of Catholic Education grant (history of education); and the Esso Foundation (language and linguistics). The McCue-Slavin Scholarship and the John Quigley Scholarship are exclusively for the education of the Sisters of the Holy Cross.

The data in Table No. 18 indicate the number of teachers who completed their studies for a degree in a two-year period. The statistics exclude junior professed who during these years have been in the five-year sister formation program. These were years when the number of replacements did not balance the deceased and the drop-outs among teachers in the schools of the Sisters of the Holy Cross. They were difficult years about which all religious communities had been forewarned in *The Education of Sister Lucy*. With the completion of the formation program the community will have established a

pattern of study and training completed in a given time. They
will have the same number of sisters to send out each year,
with the incalculable difference that they will be adequately
prepared.[55]

TABLE No. 18

Inservice Survey of Sisters; Distribution of Degrees: 1962–1964[56]

	Doctors '62–'64		Masters '62–'64		Bachelors '62–'64		Total[57] '62–'64	
Administration[58]	3	5	11	13	9	7	23	25
(General and provincial)								
Missions Abroad			10	12	13	17	23	29
General House[59]	3	4	12	14	45	47	60	65
Midwest	22	25	105	121	154	150	281	296
East	8	10	61	65	151	155	220	230
West	2	2	71	72	164	174	237	248
Grand Total							844	893

Despite the dearth of replacements, magnified by increased
enrollments, the teachers have increased by 5.45% the number of degrees completed in a two-year period. As the sister
formation program continues, the yearly increase will be
significant.[60] The sisters engaged in teaching will continue
inservice study.

Throughout the province (Eastern) study plus teaching has
become the regular way of life with thirty-four sisters taking
classes at Dunbarton; eight at Fordham; eight at Saint Edward's
University, Austin, Texas; four at Saint Mary-of-the-Springs,
Columbus, Ohio; three at Catholic University of America, Washington, D.C.; five at the Catholic University of Dallas, Texas;
and one each at the University of Pennsylvania, Georgetown University, and the Drexel Institute, Philadelphia.[61]

Supervisors of the three provinces list enrollments and
faculty—lay and religious, men and women—in statistics for

the years 1955 to 1961. As indicated in Table No. 19, enrollments have increased. Priests have been added to faculties on the secondary level at an increase of 218% in five years; laymen, 121%. (See complete breakdown in Appendix, page 000.)

TABLE No. 19

Roman Report of Enrollments and Faculties: 1955–1961[62]

School	Enrollment	Religious Faculty		Lay Faculty	
		Men	Women	Men	Women
Elementary	22%		4%		130%
Secondary	31%	218%	9%	121%	88%
College	27%		2%	71%	6%
School of					
Sacred Theology	32%	50%			

Statistics drawn up for the provincial chapter of July, 1963, show that enrollment in the elementary school is leveling (1.8%) with no increase in religious teachers and an 18% increase in lay faculty. The secondary schools have increased enrollment by 13%, the religious faculty by 6½%, and the lay faculty by 28½%. The college enrollment is 5% higher, with the religious faculty decreased 2%. The midwest province opened in September, 1963, its first new parochial school in seven years;[63] the eastern province has opened no schools since 1957,[64] the western province assigned two sisters to a central high school in 1962 and four to another diocesan high school in 1960. The last new school opened in the West in 1957.[65]

In a period of twenty years the training of religious teachers in the United States and in the Congregation of the Sisters of the Holy Cross has had both renovation and renewal. Historically the sister formation movement is twelve years old. In this brief time *The Education of Sister Lucy* has become a reality. Great new sources of knowledge have been discovered.

Teachers have returned to school en masse. If a religious community of teachers cannot afford a sister formation program and inservice teacher training, it can less afford to shorten or to neglect them.

Mother Kathryn Marie, superior general, along with the Holy Cross sister formation committee, continues to study and to improve the present formation plan to educate intellectually, spiritually, and culturally the religious teacher of Holy Cross. Mother M. Verda Clare, midwest provincial superior; Mother M. Loretto (Conway), eastern provincial superior; and Mother M. Mauricita (Conway), western provincial superior, continue plans to meet the needs of the teachers, the needs of the schools, and the needs of the community. Between 1946 and 1961 public school enrollment increased 68%; Catholic school enrollment, 110%. Enrollments have increased, but the community has not committed itself to more new schools in an effort to staff adequately those it already operates. Given a few more years, the advantages of educating the young teachers in a definite program will offset the disadvantages felt when no replacements for the teachers in the parochial and private schools of the community were available. The times call for creative solutions of problems that are perennial ones, old, yet strangely new.

References

[1] *Saint Mary's Chimes,* 1897, p. 10.
[2] G-3, 3, AGH.
[3] Saint Mary's College and Academy, Notre Dame, Indiana, *Fifty-eighth Year Book* (Notre Dame, Indiana, 1913) n.p.
[4] Mother M. Vincentia to Sister M. Lauretana, 1932, AGH.
[5] Mother M. Rose Elizabeth to Sister Maria Concepta, 1964, AGH.
[6] Scholasticate: term formerly used for the second canonical year.
[7] Mother M. Rose Elizabeth to Sister Maria Concepta, *op. cit.*
[8] *Ibid.*
[9] *Ibid.*

[10] "Educational Report: Sisters of the Holy Cross, 1943 to 1949," AGH.

[11] *Ibid.*

[12] *Ibid.*

[13] *Ibid.*

[14] Interview with Sister M. Madeleva, March 24, 1964.

[15] The following data are the result of a survey made by the dean of the School of Sacred Theology in 1962: 99 graduates teaching: primary grades, 22; secondary school, 40; and college, 37; 40 graduates non-teaching: directresses in houses of formation, 17; prioresses, 2; provincial superiors, 3; deans, 6; students, 2; and 1 each: editor, college administrator, directress of education, director of public relations, education consultant, superior, head mistress-editorial assistant, catechetical instructor, and librarian. Data from the Office of the Dean of the School of Sacred Theology, Saint Mary's College, Notre Dame, Indiana, 1964.

[16] National Catholic Educational Association, *The Education of Sister Lucy: a Symposium on Teacher Education and Teacher Training* (Notre Dame, Holy Cross, Indiana, 1949).

[17] *Ibid.*, pp. 7ff. See chart No. 16 for necessary support from parochial schools to maintain a formation and retirement program.

[18] Interview with Sister M. Madeleva, March 24, 1964.

[19] National Congress of Religious of the United States, Sisters' Section, *Religious Community Life in the United States* (New York, 1952), pp. 9ff. Hereafter cited as *Religious Community Life.*

[20] Sister M. Madeleva, C.S.C., "Theology for Sisters," *Religious Community Life,* p. 45.

[21] Brother Bonaventure Thomas, F.S.C., "Cooperation of Communities in Problems of Sister-Formation," *Sister-Formation Bulletin,* I (October, 1954), 1.

[22] *Sister-Formation Bulletin* (Reprint edition of vol. V, no. 1 and vol. VIII, no. 4), p. ix.

[23] Interview with Sister M. Monica (Wagner), C.S.C., director of education, March 8, 1964. Present members of this committee (1965) include: Mother Kathryn Marie, Sister M. Monica, Sister Joseph Marie (Cumiskey), Sister M. Gertrude Anne (Otis), Sister Marianna (Heppen), Sister M. Alma (Peter), Sister M. Hilary (Farrelly), and Sister M. Olivette (Whalen).

[24] Program of Study, Office of the Dean, Saint Mary's College, Notre Dame, Indiana.

[25] National Catholic Educational Association, Sister Formation Conferences, *Report of Everett Curriculum Workshop,* Everett, Washington, June 1 to August 30, 1956 (Seattle, 1956).

[26] Eight years after admission.

[27] Eighteen years after admission.

[28] In the 1964 term nine sisters from the formation program are in graduate school at the University of Notre Dame; one, attending the University of Montreal. For the 1964–1965 term sisters in the formation program qualified to do graduate study will attend University of Notre Dame, University of Montreal, Duquesne University, and Loyola University.

[29] Interview with Sister Maria Pieta, director, Religious Education Program, Saint Mary's College, Notre Dame, Indiana, March, 1964.

[30] Everyone within a religious community is mindful of the cost in terms of personal sacrifice of the young aspirant who enters into the sister formation program of five years duration. To those who know the discipline of study, this is understandable. To those who know the discipline required for youth to harness her eagerness to enter the "active" apostolate, this is equally appreciable. But to those who understand the abandon of modern youth to cost, her sacrifice is comprehensible.

To the teacher in the parochial or private secondary school with an added class and no study period, to the teacher in the elementary school with larger classes, to the teacher retaining extracurricular activities more generally enjoyed by her younger counterpart, and to the teacher who has had a plethora of "extras" added to her school routine, sister formation has meaningful cost.

The retired teacher knows from experience the price of an education obtained in after-school college sessions, Saturday classes, and summer schools. She has shared with the sisters in the formation program renewal and renovation of the liturgical life. She would be the last to measure sister formation only in fiscal terms.

[31] Report of Sister M. Bertrand, general treasurer, Saint Mary's Convent, Notre Dame, Indiana.

[32] Fiscal terms used in canonical quinquennial report of a religious community to the Holy See through the Sacred Congregation of Religious.

[33] Report of Sister M. Bertrand, op. cit.

[34] Summary of "Report on Representative Houses in Provinces of Sisters of the Holy Cross," part of a study of the Sister Formation Committee, Conference of Major Superiors of Women's Institutes, 1963.

[35] Report of Sister M. Bertrand, op. cit.

[36] Saint Mary's College gives a discount on the tuition cost. This reduces the five-year expense per sister to approximately $12,000.

[37] A gift of $2,000,000 from friends and benefactors greatly reduced the amount borrowed to build the Holy Cross Postulate and Holy Cross Juniorate. The amortization figure will decrease yearly but not significantly to change the approximate total average where the figure is kept low. All avoidable cost has been eliminated. Report of Sister M. Bertrand, op. cit.

[38] Classifications used are those in the national study of the average cost and income per sister in parochial schools, Finance Committee, Conference of Major Superiors of Women's Institutes, 1963.

[39] The total figures are on the basis of two hundred members in the Sister Formation Program for the years 1961–1964.

[40] NCEA, *The Education of Sister Lucy,* p. 10.

[41] *A College Goes to School; Centennial Lectures* (Notre Dame, Holy Cross, Indiana, 1945), p. v. School "derives from the Greek *Schole,* a word for leisure, that in which leisure is employed, or lecture."

[42] The centennial lectures included Moral Education, by Jacques Maritain; Idea of a Catholic University, by Leo R. Ward, C.S.C.; Education for Freedom, by Robert M. Hutchins; Character and Intelligence, by Mortimer J. Adler; Collective Security vs. Isolationism, by William Bolger, C.S.C.; Can Peace Endure? by William Agar; The College Chapel, by Matthew Schumacher, C.S.C.; A Citadel of Western Culture, by Hugh O'Donnell, C.S.C.; Pioneers and the Liberal Arts, by Robert I. Gannon, S.J.; and Education, by Sister M. Madeleva, C.S.C., *Ibid.*

[43] Sister M. Ceciliana (Honor), C.S.C., Fine Arts Committee, Third Annual Conference on Education, "Publications of the Sisters of the Holy Cross 1950–1964."

[44] The College of Saint Mary-of-the-Wasatch closed in 1960. It continues a summer school session, an extension of Portland University. Archives of Saint Mary-of-the Wasatch, 1960–1961, p. 1, AGH.

[45] Degrees held by Sisters of the Holy Cross, Midwest Province, 1963. Report to the Superior General, Mother Kathryn Marie, C.S.C., Office of the Superior General, Sisters of the Holy Cross Generalate, Saint Mary's Convent, Notre Dame, Indiana (hereafter cited as Generalate), April, 1964.

[46] Degrees held by Sisters of the Holy Cross, Eastern Province, 1963. Report to the Superior General, Mother Kathryn Marie, C.S.C., Office of the Superior General, Generalate, April, 1964.

[47] Degrees held by Sisters of the Holy Cross, Western Province, 1963. Report to the Superior General, Mother Kathryn Marie, C.S.C., Office of the Superior General, Generalate, April, 1964.

[48] Certification in Indiana, State of Indiana, Division of Teacher Training, Indianapolis, Indiana, 1963.

[49] Interview with Sister M. Matthew (Betz), C.S.C., supervisor of elementary education, Midwest Provincialate, South Bend, Indiana, April 19, 1964.

[50] Sisters receive a discount on tuition at some Catholic colleges. The cost varies from thirty dollars to sixty dollars per credit hour.

[51] See p. 174.

[52] A 1961–1964 average computed by Sister Mary George (Sommer),

C.S.C., secretary-treasurer, Midwest Provincialate, South Bend, Indiana, April, 1964.

[53] A degree and a teacher's license earned in fifteen summers (ninety credits) with one Saturday class yearly (forty-five credits) could conceivably cost the same per credit hour, but board, room, and travel over the protracted time could obviously be more. The cost of a long-term degree has the comparable fiscal strength and weakness of a house bought on time.

[54] Sister Marie Angele (Yamamoto), Survey of Scholastic Honors Awarded Sisters of the Holy Cross, 1963–1964. AGH.

[55] NCEA, *The Education of Sister Lucy*, p. 9.

[56] Degrees: Midwest, Eastern, and Western Provinces, Office of the Superior General, Generalate, April, 1964.

[57] Total excludes deceased, drop-outs, and replacements of teachers.

[58] Survey, AGH.

[59] Annual Roman Report, 1962, 1964, Office of the Assistant Superior, Sister M. Agnes Claudia (Redman), C.S.C., General House, Saint Mary's, Notre Dame, Indiana, April, 1964. The figures represent inservice teacher study completed in 1962–1964.

[60] Report of probable date for completion of degrees, Midwest, Eastern, and Western Provinces, Report to the Superior General, Mother Kathryn Marie, C.S.C., Generalate, April, 1964.

[61] *Tidings: The Eastern Province* (November, 1961), p. 3.

[62] Six Year Report of Education: 1955–1961, Midwest, Eastern, and Western Provinces, Office of the General Secretary, Sister M. Davida (McKenna), C.S.C., Generalate, April, 1964.

[63] *Residence Directory of the Sisters of the Holy Cross:* 1963–1964. p. 18.

[64] *Ibid.,* p. 30.

[65] *Ibid.,* p. 44.

APPENDIX

Comparative Rise of Parochial Schools and Decline of Community-Owned Academies

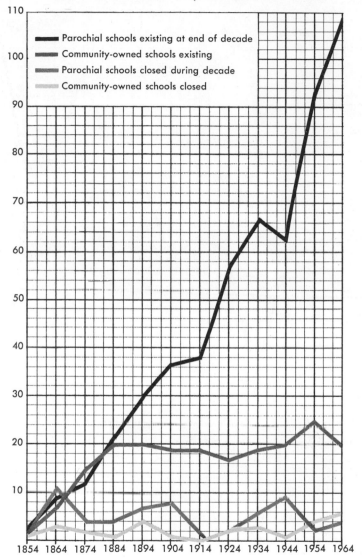

Parochial schools existing at end of decade
Community-owned schools existing
Parochial schools closed during decade
Community-owned schools closed

Persistency of Sisters of the Holy Cross

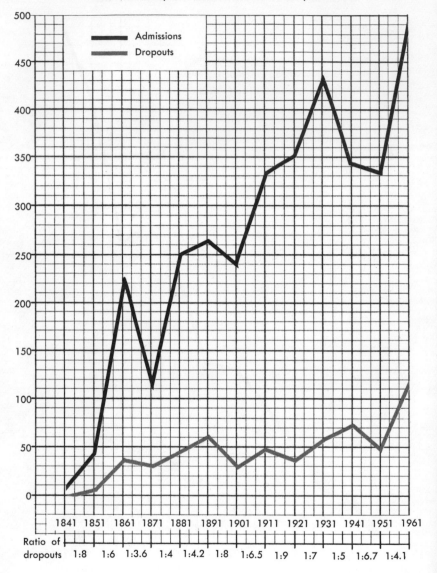

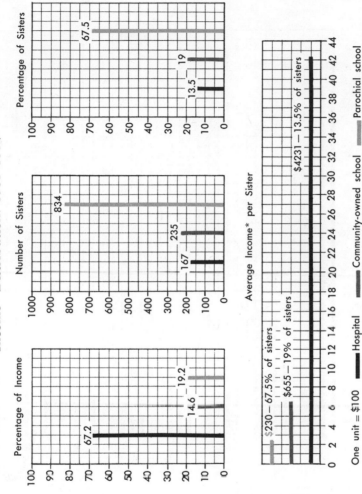

Income* Distribution: 1961–1962

Percentage of Sisters

Number of Sisters

Percentage of Income

Average Income* per Sister

One unit = $100 ■ Hospital ▬ Community-owned school ▬ Parochial school

*Income from sisters to the motherhouse for items 1, 2, and 3 of graph following on p. 194.

Average Costs and Income

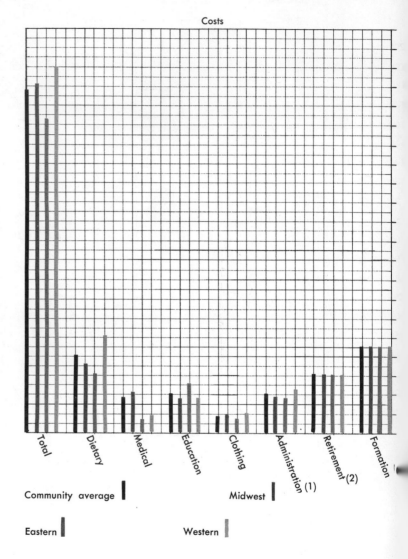

Costs

Total Dietary Medical Education Clothing Administration (1) Retirement (2) Formation

Community average   Midwest

Eastern   Western

)er Sister in Parochial Schools*

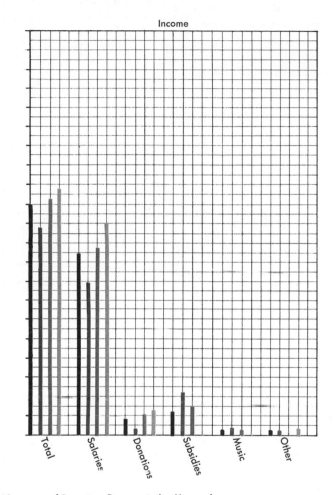

Income

*Summary of Report on Representative Houses in

Provinces of Sisters of the Holy Cross: 1961–1962

Longevity of Sisters of the Holy Cross: 1847–1963

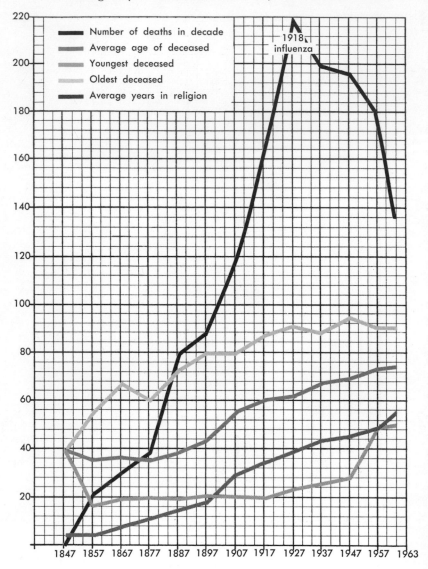

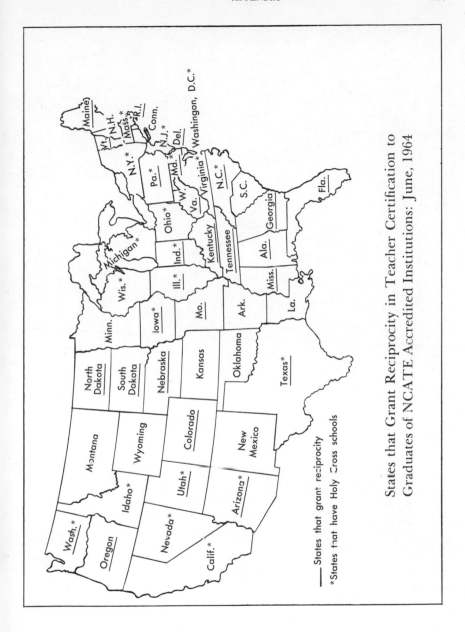

States that Grant Reciprocity in Teacher Certification to Graduates of NCATE Accredited Institutions: June, 1964

——— States that grant reciprocity
*States that have Holy Cross schools

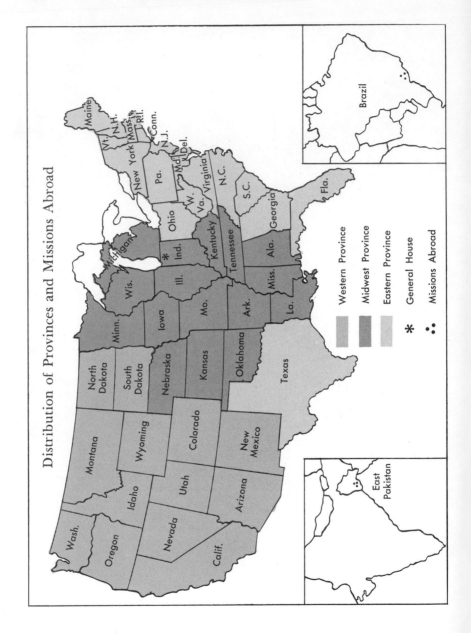

Distribution of Provinces and Missions Abroad

Roman Report of Enrollments and Faculties: 1955–61

Elementary Schools, Midwest Province

Scholastic Years

	Boys	Girls	Total
1955–1956	5926	5778	11,704
1956–1957	6283	6036	12,319
1957–1958	6639	6381	13,020
1958–1959	6935	6631	13,548
1959–1960	7247	6959	14,206
1960–1961	7305	6997	14,302
Increase over six-year period			2,598
Per cent of increase over six-year period			22%

	Religious		Faculty Lay		Music
	M	W	M	W	
1955–1956		196		53	13
1956–1957		199		70	11
1957–1958		201		86	9
1958–1959		209		98	9
1959–1960		206		107	9
1960–1961		204		122	7
Increase over six-year period		8		69	(6)
Per cent of increase over six-year period		4%		130%	(45.3%)*

* Music teachers were once a source of income for a religious community. These teachers have been placed in parochial schools to help both the bishops and pastors in those dioceses and parishes where lay teacher salaries are difficult to meet.

Elementary Schools, Western Province

Scholastic Years

	Boys	Girls	Total
1955–1956	5517	5406	10,923
1956–1957	6017	5912	11,929
1957–1958	6297	6131	12,428
1958–1959	6507	6544	13,051
1959–1960	6631	6552	13,183
1960–1961	6907	6678	13,585
Increase over six-year period			2,662
Per cent of increase over six-year period			24%

	Religious		Faculty Lay		Music
	M	W	M	W	
1955–1956		182		52	23
1956–1957		196		52	21
1957–1958		197	7	73	13
1958–1959		209		79	12
1959–1960		206		84	12
1960–1961		206		84	11
Increase over six-year period		24		32	(6)
Per cent of increase over six-year period		13%		61.5%**	(46%)*

* Music teachers have been placed in parochial schools.

** The western province have had a larger increase of sisters than the midwest province; their per cent of lay teachers is lower than the midwest.

High Schools, Midwest province

Scholastic Years

	Boys	Girls	Total
1955–1956	1145	2048	3193
1956–1957	1349	2297	3646
1957–1958	1283	2355	3638
1958–1959	1373	2401	3774
1959–1960	1468	2575	4043
1960–1961	1497	2672	4169
Increase over six-year period			976
Per cent of increase over six-year period			31%

	Religious		Faculty Lay		Music
	M	W	M	W	
1955–1956	11	80	14	17	5
1956–1957	17	83	18	21	5
1957–1958	23	84	22	27	5
1958–1959	30	84	26	25	3
1959–1960	39	84	26	31	3
1960–1961	35	87	31	32	3
Increase over six-year period	24	7	17	15	(2)
Per cent of increase over six-year perod	218%*	9%	121%	88%	(40%)**

* Bishops in the midwest dioceses where Sisters of the Holy Cross have secondary schools have assigned priests to high-school faculties.

** Music teachers have given up private lessons to teach school music.

High Schools, Western Province

Scholastic Years

	Boys	Girls	Total
1955–1956	470	1052	1522
1956–1957	642	1238	1880
1957–1958	529	1282	1811
1958–1959	522	1449	1971
1959–1960	458	1512	1970
1960–1961	758	1658	2416
Increase over six-year period			894
Per cent of increase over six-year period			58.7%*

	Religious		Faculty Lay		Music
	M	W	M	W	
1955–1956	9	54	10	9	7
1956–1957	11	56	7	6	8
1957–1958	9	67	10	11	9
1958–1959	15	72	10	14	11
1959–1960	16	80	7	17	11
1960–1961	16	84	7	21	11
Increase over six-year period	7	30	(3)	12	4
Per cent of increase over six-year period	77.7%	55.5%*	(30%)	130%	57%

* The increase in secondary enrollment (58.7%) is accompanied by a significant increase in sisters (55.5%).

St. Mary's College, Notre Dame, Indiana

Scholastic Years

College	Total	Religious		Faculty Lay		Music
		M	W	M	W	
1955–1956	882	3	44	21	33	126
1956–1957	971	1	42	21	23	171
1957–1958	1010	1	39	27	26	155
1958–1959	1053	1	43	30	37	158
1959–1960	1057	1	43	30	37	172
1960–1961	1119	1	45	36	35	208
Increase over six-year period	237	2	1	15	2	82
Per cent of increase over six-year period	27%	66⅔%	2%*	71%	6%	65%

* The Sisters of the Holy Cross have continued as a policy to send teachers to parochial schools to meet the current problem of teacher shortage. Hence the low 2% increase of religious on the college faculty.

Schools and Orphanages of the Sisters of the Holy Cross

Name	Year Opened	Year Closed	Classification
Holy Cross Convent Notre Dame, Indiana	1843		Community
Saint Mary's Academy Bertrand, Michigan	1844	1855	Private
Potowatamie Indian Mission Pokagon, Silver Creek, Michigan	1845	1852	Mission
Saint Mary's College Notre Dame, Indiana	1855		Private
Holy Angels Academy Mishawaka, Indiana	1848	1859	Private

Name	Year Opened	Year Closed	Classification
Saint Mary's Orphan Boys Asylum New Orleans, Louisiana	1849	1849	Diocesan
Saint John's School Lake County, Indiana	1849	1864	Parochial
Mackinac, Michigan	1852	1853	Parochial
Saint Alexis School became	1854	1857	Parochial
Academy of the Assumption, Lowell, Indiana became	1867	1890	Private
Saint Joseph's School South Bend, Indiana	1890		Parochial
Saint Mary's School became	1854	1864	Parochial
Saint Rose's Academy	1864	1919	Private
Saint Peter's School LaPorte, Indiana	1919		Parochial
Saint Ambrose's Academy became	1871	1886	Private
Saint Mary's School	1854	1897	Parochial
Saint Mary's School re-opened Michigan City, Indiana	1934		Parochial
Manual Labor School New York City, New York	1855	1856	Industrial
Saint Mary's Academy Susquehanna, Pennsylvania	1856	1858	Parochial
Saint Joseph's Orphan Asylum Washington, D. C., became	1856	1904	Diocesan
Saint Joseph's Home	1856		
Manual Labor and Day School Philadelphia, Pennsylvania	1856	1857	Diocesan, Industrial

Name	Year Opened	Year Closed	Classification
Orphan Asylum Buffalo, New York	1856	1857	Diocesan, Industrial
Saint Mary's of the Lake (Saint Mary's University) North Chicago, Illinois	1856	1861	Private
Holy Name School Chicago, Illinois	1856	1861	Parochial
Dolan Aid Asylum Baltimore, Maryland	1874	1959	Private
Saint Patrick's Asylum Baltimore, Maryland	1857	1875	Diocesan
Immaculate Conception	1857	1864	Parochial
Saint James School West Philadelphia, Pennsylvania	1861	1864	
Immaculate Conception Morris, Illinois	1857		Parochial
Saint Angela's Academy Morris, Illinois	1857	1958	Private
Saint Paul's School Philadelphia, Pennsylvania	1857	1864	Parochial
Saint Philomena's School Bourbonnais, Illinois	1858	1860	Parochial
French Settlement College Bourbonnais, Illinois	1858	1860	Private
Saint Augustine's School Philadelphia, Pennsylvania	1859	1865	Parochial and Private
Saint Patrick's Academy became	1859	1870	Private
Academy of the Holy Cross became	1870	1887	Private
Saint Patrick's School Baltimore, Maryland	1859		Parochial

Name	Year Opened	Year Closed	Classification
Academy New Orleans, Louisiana	1860	1869	Private
Manual Labor School New Orleans, Louisiana	1860	1869	Industrial
Saint Vincent's Academy became	1863	1871	Private
Holy Angels Academy (High School closed)	1871	1924	Parochial
Saint Vincent's School Logansport, Indiana	1863		Parochial
Saint Charles' School Crawfordsville, Indiana	1865	1944	Parochial and Private
Saint Joseph's Academy became	1865	1952	Private
Saint Joseph's High School South Bend, Indiana	1952		Diocesan
Saint Teresa's School Joliet, Illinois	1865	1880	Parochial
Academy of Our Lady of the Sacred Heart	1866	1934	Private
Saint Vincent's School Fort Wayne, Indiana	1866	1866	Parochial
Saint Joseph's Asylum Rensselaer, Indiana	1867	1887	Diocesan
Academy of the Holy Cross Washington, D. C., now Kensington, Maryland	1868 1956	1955	Private
Saint Cecilia's Academy Washington, D. C.	1868		Private
Saint Matthew's School became	1868	1905	Parochial
Calvert School Washington, D. C.	1905		

Name	Year Opened	Year Closed	Classification
Saint Peter's School Washington, D. C.	1868		Parochial
Saint Michael's School Plymouth, Indiana	1869		Private Parochial
Saint Mary's Academy Alexandria, Virginia	1869		Private
Saint Bernard's School Watertown, Wisconsin	1872	1903	Parochial
Sacred Heart Academy	1873	1958	Private
Saint Anthony's School Lancaster, Pennsylvania	1873		Parochial
Saint Mary's Academy Austin, Texas	1874		Private
Dolan Aid Asylum Baltimore, Maryland	1874	1959	Private
Saint Joseph's Asylum Lafayette, Indiana	1874	1893	Diocesan
Saint Bridget's School West Logan, Indiana	1875	1893	Parochial
Saint Mary-of-the-Wasatch Academy Salt Lake City, Utah	1875		Private
Saint Catherine's Normal Institute Baltimore, Maryland	1875	1929	Private
Saint Augustine's School Washington, D. C.	1875	1895	Parochial, Negro
Saint Mary's School Union City, Indiana	1877	1941	Parochial
Saint Agnes' School Catonsville, Maryland	1877	1881	Parochial
Sacred Heart School Ackley, Iowa	1878	1884	Parochial

Name	Year Opened	Year Closed	Classification
Sacred Heart Academy Ogden, Utah	1878	1937	Private
Sacred Heart Academy Clarksville, Texas	1879	1883	Parochial
Saint Mary's School Anderson, Indiana	1879		Parochial
Saint Joseph's School Marshall, Texas	1880		Parochial
Saint Mary's Academy Marshall, Texas	1880	1957	Private
Saint John's School Goshen, Indiana	1881	1917	Parochial
Saint Joseph's School Akron, Ohio	1881	1885	Parochial
Saint Vincent's School Elkhart, Indiana	1881		Parochial
Saint Mary's School Park City, Utah	1882	1933	Parochial
Holy Cross School Salt Lake City, Utah	1882	1896	Private
Saint Edward's Academy Deadwood, South Dakota	1883	1897	Parochial
Parish School Grand Junction, Colorado	1884	1885	Parochial
Saint Ann's School Lake Linden, Michigan	1885	1889	Parochial
Saint Mary's School South Bend, Indiana	1884	1933	Parochial, German
Saint Hedwige's School South Bend, Indiana	1885	1936	Parochial, Polish
Holy Rosary Academy Woodland, California	1886	1953	Private

Name	*Year Opened*	*Year Closed*	*Classification*
Saint Paul's Academy Washington, D. C.	1887	1952	Parochial
Saint Pius School Baltimore, Maryland	1888	1929	Parochial
Saint Teresa's Academy Boise, Idaho	1889	1964	Private
Bishop Kelly High School	1964		Diocesan
Saint Ann's School Akyab, India	1889	1896	Diocesan
Saint Gregory's School Dacca, India	1889	1891	Diocesan
Saint Patrick's School	1891		Parochial
Saint Mary's Academy Danville, Illinois	1891	1912	Private
Saint Joseph's School Eureka, Utah	1891	1941	Parochial
Saint Ann's Orphanage Salt Lake City, Utah	1891	1953	Diocesan
Saint Patrick's School Lead City, South Dakota	1891	1892	Parochial
Saint Joseph's School Pocatello, Idaho	1892		Parochial
Saint Augustine's Academy Fresno, California	1893	1952	Private
became			
Saint John's School	1952		Parochial
Saint Charles' School San Francisco, California	1894		Parochial
Saint Mary's School Alexandria, Virginia	1894		Private
Saint Joseph's School Ogden, Utah	1895		Parochial

Name	Year Opened	Year Closed	Classification
Sacred Heart School South Bend, Indiana	1896	1898	Parochial, Belgian
Saint Patrick's School Chatsworth, Illinois	1899	1941	Parochial
Saint Joseph's School Boise, Idaho	1900		Parochial
Saint Patrick's School South Bend, Indiana	1900		Parochial
Saint Stephen's School South Bend, Indiana	1900	1902	Parochial
Saint Paul's School Valparaiso, Indiana	1901		Parochial
Saint Vincent's Academy became	1901	1904	Private
Saint Patrick's Academy Washington, D. C.	1904		Parochial
Saint Mary's School Davenport, Iowa	1902		Parochial
Saint Mary's School Westville, Illinois	1902	1914	Parochial
Sacred Heart School Lancaster, Pennsylvania	1902	1909	Parochial
Saint Paul the Apostle School New York City, New York	1904		Parochial
Saint John's School Saint John's School reopened Peoria, Illinois	1906 1923	1915	Parochial
Saint Patrick's School Cairo, Illinois	1906	1939	Parochial
Saint Agnes' School Los Angeles, California	1914		Parochial
Saint Mary's School Woodstock, Illinois	1916		Parochial

Name	Year Opened	Year Closed	Classification
Saint Joseph's School Harvard, Illinois	1916		Parochial
Saint Alphonsus' School Fresno, California	1916		Parochial
Saint Theodore's School Chicago, Illinois	1917		Parochial
Saint Mary's School Austin, Texas	1918		Parochial
Our Lady of Guadalupe School Austin, Texas	1920		Parochial
Holy Rosary School Idaho Falls, Idaho	1921		Parochial
Saint Edward's School Twin Falls, Idaho	1921	1939	Parochial
Sacred Heart School Cheyenne Wells, Colorado	1921	1933	Parochial
Saint Paul's School Los Angeles, California	1922		Parochial
Holy Cross School Ventura, California	1922		Parochial
Saint Patrick's School East Chicago, Indiana	1923		Parochial
Our Lady of Lourdes' School Colusa, California	1923		Parochial
Bishop Conaty Memorial High School Los Angeles, California	1923		Diocesan
Blessed Sacrament School Washington, D. C.	1923		Parochial
Holy Trinity School Norfolk, Virginia	1924		Parochial
Saint Michael's School Fairbury, Nebraska	1924	1939	Parochial

Name	Year Opened	Year Closed	Classification
Saint Peter's School Washington, D. C.	1924		Parochial
Saint Thomas the Apostle School Washington, D. C.	1926		Parochial
Saint Anthony's School Hegeler, Illinois	1927	1932	Parochial
Judge Memorial High School Salt Lake City, Utah	1928	1964	Parochial
Judge Memorial Grade School Name changed to Our Lady of Lourdes School in 1962	1927		Parochial
Academy of Saint Catherine Ventura, California	1927		Private
Saint Mary's School Toomiliah, Dacca, India	1927	1952	Diocesan
Saint Columba's School Cairo, Illinois	1928	1963	Parochial, Negro
Catholic High School Lancaster, Pennsylvania	1928		Diocesan
Saint Paul's School Nampa, Idaho	1929	1939	Parochial
Holy Cross School South Bend, Indiana	1929		Parochial
Saint Bernard's School Oakland, California	1930		Parochial
Immaculate Conception School Sacramento, California	1930		Parochial
Good Shepherd School Beverly Hills, California	1930		Parochial
Saint Catherine's School Columbus, Ohio	1931		Parochial

Name	Year Opened	Year Closed	Classification
Saint Anthony's School Nagari, Dacca, India	1931	1952	Grade and Middle, English
Saint Matthew's School San Mateo, California	1931		Parochial
Catholic Central High School, now Bishop Noll Institute Hammond, Indiana	1933		Diocesan
Dunbarton College of Holy Cross Washington, D. C.	1935		Private
Saint Didacus' School San Diego, California	1939		Parochial
Saint Ignatius' School Austin, Texas	1940		Parochial
Most Holy Redeemer School Evergreen Park, Chicago, Illinois	1942		Parochial
Saint Angela Hall Rockville, Maryland	1944	1961	Preschool
Saint Jude's School East Chicago, Indiana	1944	1950	Parochial, Negro
Holy Rosary Convent Tejgaon, Dacca, East Pakistan	1945		Private Orphanage
Holy Redeemer School Flint, Michigan	1946		Parochial
Saint Barnabas' School Long Beach, California	1946		Parochial
Schlarman High School Danville, Illinois	1946		Diocesan
Our Lady of Sorrows' School McAllen, Texas	1946		Parochial

Name	Year Opened	Year Closed	Classification
San Joaquin Memorial High School Fresno, California	1947		Diocesan
Stella Maris Academy LaJolla, California	1947		Parochial
Vila Betania Sao Paulo, Brazil	1947		Ginasio, colegio, and primario
Holy Cross Academy Brookline, Massachusetts	1948		Private
Saint Stanislaus' School Modesto, California	1948		Parochial
Sacred Heart School Fort Wayne, Indiana	1949		Parochial
Blessed Sacrament School Alexandria, Virginia	1949		Parochial
Cathedral School Salt Lake City, Utah	1949		Parochial
Saint Hugh's School Greenbelt, Maryland	1949		Parochial
Saint Mary of the Lake School Gary, Indiana	1949		Parochial
Holy Cross College Tejgaon, Dacca, East Pakistan	1950		English grade school; I.A., I.Sc., and B.A. college Parochial
Saint Ambrose School Anderson, Indiana	1950		Parochial
Saint Mary's Campus School Notre Dame, Indiana	1950		Private and Parochial
Assumption School Washington, D. C.	1951		Parochial
Saint Thomas the Apostle School Elkhart, Indiana	1951		Parochial

Name	Year Opened	Year Closed	Classification
Cardinal Cushing College Brookline, Massachusetts	1952		Private
Notre Dame High School	1952		Parochial
Saint Mary's School Batavia, New York	1952		Parochial
Saint Bernard's School Riverdale, Maryland	1952		Parochial
Saint Cyril's School Tucson, Arizona	1952		Parochial
Saint Joseph's Grade School Mountain View, California	1952		Parochial
Holy Rosary School Woodland, California	1953		Parochial
Pius X High School Compton, California	1953		Diocesan
Saint Pius V School Redwood City, California	1953		Parochial
Bishop Gorman High School Las Vegas, Nevada	1954		Diocesan
Our Lady Help of Christians School Abington, Pennsylvania	1954		Parochial
Christ the King School South Bend, Indiana	1954		Parochial
Our Lary of Lourdes School Raleigh, North Carolina	1954		Parochial
Queen of All Saints' School Michigan City, Indiana	1954		Parochial
Saint Aloysius' School Palo Alto, California	1954		Parochial
Saint Anne's School Las Vegas, Nevada	1954		Parochial
Saint Paul's School Seattle, Washington	1954		Parochial

Name	Year Opened	Year Closed	Classification
Saint Philip Neri School Compton, California	1954		Parochial
Bishop Glass School Salt Lake City, Utah	1955		Parochial
Sacre Coeur School Creve Coeur, Illinois	1955		Parochial
Notre Dame School Michigan City, Indiana	1955		Parochial
Santa Cruz School Tucson, Arizona	1955		Parochial
Saint Matthew's School Seattle, Washington	1955		Parochial
Saint Louis' School Austin, Texas	1956		Parochial
Saint Paul's School Danville, Illinois	1956		Parochial
Holy Cross High School Riverside, New Jersey	1957		Diocesan
Holy Cross High School Mountain View, California	1957		Private
Saint Paul the Apostle School Richardson, Texas	1957		Parochial
Marian Central Catholic High School Woodstock, Illinois	1959		Diocesan
Mater Dei High School Santa Ana, California	1960		Diocesan
Holy Cross Grade School Garrett Park, Maryland	1961		Parochial
Convento Sao Jose Sao Paulo, Brazil	1962		Parochial
Saint Joseph's Convent Raninkong, East Pakistan	1963		Parochial

Comparative Enrollments, Saint Mary's Academy and College: 1844–1964 †

Saint Mary's Academy, Bertrand, Michigan: 1844–1855

Year	Enrollment
1844*	4
1845	6
1846	8
1847**	50
1848***	20
1849****	18
1850*****	30
1851	27
1852	46
1853	68
1854	69
1855******	70

Enrollment figures include only boarders, although the sisters taught children in the Bertrand-Niles-Buchanan area.

* Source: G-II, AGH, p. 9. Day students are excluded.
** Letter: Sorin to Moreau, 1847, AUND.
*** Sister M. Emerentiana's "Memoirs," p. 61.
**** Rev. Victor Drouelle, "Visits: Bertrand, #3," p. 2.
***** Ledger A (Financial Day Book of expenses and tuition. Boarders only). ASMC.
****** Rev. Victor Drouelle, "Visits: Bertrand, #3," p. 7. Visitor reported that of these 70 only 17 paid tuition.
† Compiled by Sister M. Rose Estelle (Hopfinger), C.S.C.

Saint Mary's Academy, Notre Dame, Indiana: 1856–1868

Year	Enrollment	Graduates
1856*	97	
1857	83	
1858	91	
1859	96	
1860	100	6
1861	90	0
1862†	92	0
1863	132	2

Year	Enrollment	Graduates
1864	187	3
1865	265	3
1866	253	6
1867	212	4
1868	213	9

* Source: Pupils' Register, ASMC.
† Source: Saint Mary's Academy Catalogues, ASMC.

Saint Mary's Academy, Notre Dame, Indiana: 1869–1887

Year	Senior Dept.	Junior	Total	Graduates
1869*	167	55	222	6
1870	169	50	219	11
1871	138	56	194	10
1872	159	70	229	11
1873	149	84	233	11
1874	165	100	265	11
1875	138	67	205	12
1876	118	67	185	10
1877	105	40	145	14
1878	105	42	147	10
1879	107	54	161	8
1880	124	70	194	11
1881	128	77	205	15
1882	119	64	183	6
1883	145	71	216	9
1884	104	66	170	4
1885	104	48	152	6
1886	122	48	170	6
1887	132	62	194	13

* Source: Saint Mary's Academy Catalogues, ASMC.

Saint Mary's Academy, Notre Dame, Indiana: 1888–1897

Year	College	Academy & Prep	Total	Graduates
1888*	155	57	212	13
1889	164	86	250	17

Year	College	Academy & Prep	Total	Graduates
1890	153	78	231	7
1891	164	74	238	12
1892	166	70	236	10
1893	176	80	256	8
1894	138	63	201	11
1895	143	57	200	16
1896	134	51	185	9
1897	144	52	196	13

* Source: Saint Mary's Academy Catalogues, ASMC. Between the years 1888–1897 students were classified under the college and academy. The latter included a preparatory department.

Saint Mary's Academy, Notre Dame, Indiana: 1898–1910

Year	College	Academy & Prep	Total	Graduates Col.	Acad.	Total
1898*	118	39	157	1	8	9
1899	127	50	177	1	12	13
1900	153	61	214	0	7	7
1901	173	61	234	2	10	12
1902	187	33	220	3	16	19
1903	197	63	260	0	15	15
1904	217	57	274	3	16	19
1905	202	51	253	2	13	15
1906	192	46	238	20	2	22
1907	190	50	240	21	1	22
1908	228	68	296	12	13	25
1909	205	79	284	10	14	24
1910	252	85	337	13	12	25

* Source: Saint Mary's Academy Catalogues, ASMC.

Saint Mary's College and Academy: 1911–1921

Year	Total	College	Graduates Academy	Total
1911*	345	16	14	30
1912	314	16	20	36
1913	283	19	24	43

			Graduates	
Year	Total	College	Academy	Total
1914	316	23	12	35
1915	284	20	16	36
1916	250	18	27	45
1917	273	17	21	38
1918	255	16	15	31
1919	277	17	19	38
1920	432	15	30	45
1921	446	33	29	62

* Two students graduated at the end of summer school, 1919; one at the end of 1920.

Saint Mary's College and Academy: 1922–1945

	Enrollments					Graduates			
Year	Col.	S.S.†	Acad.	S.S.	Total	Col.	Acad.	S.S.	Total
1922	193	189	193		386	28	27	16	71
1923	195		161		356	34	29	22	85
1924	204		150		354	39	25	30	94
1925	229	147	143		372	47	23	28	98
1926	272	183	146		418	38	42	19	99
1927	281	184	118***		583	45	32	7	84
1928	323	228	100		651	50	32	8	90
1929	347	279	102		780	57	26	4	87
1930	357	149	128		634	50	25	5	80
1931	363	293	90		746	70	29	12	111
1932	310	284	67		661	55	17	6	78
1933	212	289	71		572	49	11	11	71
1934	193	197	77		467	42	22	4	68
1935	310	259	89		658	48	30	9	87
1936	369	254	80	40	743	34	25		59
1937	371	209	89		669	37	30	6	73
1938	459	200	102	28	789	49	22		71
1939	451	228	104	15	798	53	28	5	86
1940	485	256	87	13	841	66	31	5	102
1941	435	233	75	12	755	64	16		80
1942	520	244	115	9	888	56	32		88

		Enrollments				Graduates		
Year	Col.	S.S.†	Acad.	S.S.	Total	Col.	Acad.	S.S.	Total
1943	506	203	113	6	828	64	22		86
1944*	529	195	75	10	809	52	20		72
1945**	539	200	100	21	860	45	16		61

As a result of the great depression, enrollment decreased. South Bend students who could not afford to go away to college were able to come to Saint Mary's Academy and College on a tuition basis. The first day students were admitted in 1933.

* Theology figures are not included. For enrollment and degrees from the School of Sacred Theology see Table No. 14.
** Saint Mary's Academy figures no longer included.
*** Saint Mary's Preparatory School figures no longer included. The depression affected enrollments, 1933–1934.
† Summer School.

Saint Mary's College: 1946–1964

		Enrollments		
Year	Coll.	S.S.	Total	Graduates
1946	733	225	958	78
1947	646	201	847	73
1948	701	200	901	91
1949	661	267	928	98
1950	646	306	952	92
1951	658	336	994	82
1952	668	337	1005	115
1953	720	341	1061	107
1954	757	341	1098	99	Honorary
1955	807	326	1133	100	Degrees
1956	897	374	1271	140	11
1957	956	370	1326	138	3
1958	1010	399	1409	170	4
1959	1053	370	1423	155	3
1960	1057	425	1482	189	4
1961	1119	548	1667	183	4
1962	1141	481	1622	198	3
1963	1174	461	1635	215	3
1964	1134	434	1568	223	4

Programme of Studies
of
Saint Mary's Academy, Notre Dame, Indiana (c.1851)

PRIMARY COURSE

Third Junior Class

Spelling, Reading, Writing, Oral Arithmetic, and Object lessons.

Second Junior Class

Spelling, Reading, Writing, Arithmetic (Stoddard's Combination), Primary Geography, Harvey's Elements of Grammar, (Taught Orally.)

First Junior Class

Harvey's Grammar, Excelsior Geography (Number Two), Spelling, Arithmetic, Reading.

PREPARATORY COURSE

Third Class

Bullions' School Grammar, Stoddard's Arithmetic, Excelsior Geography (Number Two), Third Reader, Orthography, and Penmanship.

Second Class

Bullions' Analytic and Practical Grammar (To Syntax), Excelsior Geography (Number One), and use of Globe, Davies' Practical and Stoddard's Mental Arithmetics, Spelling, Dictation, Fourth Reader.

First Class

Bullions' Analytic and Practical Grammar (Continued), Barnes' Series, United States History, Stoddard's Mental and Davies' Complete Arithmetic, Physiology, Either of the following Languages Commenced, viz; Arnold's Course Latin, Fasquelles' French, Ahn's German.

Third Class

— 1st Session. —

Bullion's Grammar (Rules and Syntactical Analyses, finished) Ganot's Philosophy, Davies' University Arithmetic (to Alligation), Fredet's Ancient History, Latin, French, or German.

— 2nd Session. —

Quackenbos' Rhetoric, Davies' Arithmetic and Algebra, Ancient History and Philosophy (finished).
Languages as above.

Second Class

— 1st Session. —

Rhetoric (to style), Algebra to Quadratic Equations, Wells' Chemistry, Fredet's Modern History.
Languages as above.

— 2nd Session. —

Rhetoric (finished), Algebra, Modern History and Chemistry (finished).
Languages as above.

First Class

— 1st Session. —

Jevon's Logic, Davies' Geometry, Gray's Botany, Brocklesby's Astronomy, Jenkins' Literature, Latin (Harkness' Grammar and Caesar), French (Telemaque), German (Meusen's Course).

— 2nd Session. —

Logic, Geometry, Botany, Astronomy, Literature (continued), History of France and England.
Languages as above.

Graduating Class

— 1st Session. —

Dana's Geology, Davies' Trigonometry (optional), Mental Philosophy, General Literature, Latin (Virgil), French (Literature), German (Meusen's Course).

— 2nd Session. —

Mental Philosophy, Criticism of English Authors, Botany, Review of General History, Languages as above, with the addition of Bonneau and Lucau's Academy Grammar, Translation of Mme. de Sevigne and Eugenie de Geurin.

_____

Christian Doctrine, Penmanship, Elocution, and Composition taught through the whole course.

Tuition, Board, and Room, Saint Mary's, Bertrand, Michigan, and Saint Mary's, Notre Dame, Indiana: 1844–1963

Year	Cost
1844	$ 73
1854	$ 85
1861	$ 110
1866	$ 160
1867	$ 200
1873	$ 220
1893	$ 250
1902	$ 260
1903*	$ 350, $300, $260
1910	$ 350, $300, $300
1915	$ 400, $400, $350
1920	$ 500, $500, $450
1923	$ 600, $600, $550
1925	$ 600, $600, $500
1930	$ 750
1934**	$ 660
1936	$ 750
1939	$ 800
1944	$ 850
1945	$ 750
1947	$ 900
1948	$ 950
1949	$1000
1950	$1100

Year	Cost
1951	$1300
1953	$1400
1955	$1600
1958	$1800
1960	$2000
1962	$2100
1963	$2200

* First figure is college cost; the second, academic; the third, preparatory.
** Depression affected enrollment significantly.

Saint Mary's Students Who Became Religious Teachers

Years	Sisters of the Holy Cross		Other Religious Communities	
1844–1865	0*	3**	0*	0**
1866–1875	14	5	0	2
1876–1885	4	3	1	7
1886–1895	6	8	1	6
1896–1905	2	7	1	3
1906–1915	5	11	0	2
1916–1925	26	17	1	14
1926–1935	14	7	2	11
1936–1945	4	2	1	11
1946–1955	12	20	2	28
1956–1964	11	24	2	28
Totals:	98*	107**	11*	112*
GRAND TOTAL:	205		123	

* Graduated from Saint Mary's.
** Attended Saint Mary's but did not graduate.

Census of the Sisters of the Holy Cross, September 30, 1963

	Active	Retired
Teachers	1038	67
Nurses	112	16

	Active	Retired
Hospital Workers	53	7
Administration and Council	43	1
Diocesan Office	1	
Junior Professed	81	
Child Care	4	
Postulants	45	
Novices	87	
Domestic	116	17
	1564	107

Total	1671
Deceased	1468

National Profile of Age and Educational Status of Sisters, 1962

Elementary Schools

Ed.	<20	198	20–24	198 (36)
H.S.	10.6	0.0	1.3	0.0
<1 col.	28.3	0.0	4.2	0.0
1 col.	29.6*	0.0	9.1	2.8
2 col.	29.9	0.0	67.6*(6550)	94.4*(34)
B.S.	0.0	0.0	10.9	2.8
B.S.+	0.6	0.0	6.2	0.0
M.S.	0.0	0.0	0.1	0.0
M.S.+	0.0	0.0	0.0	0.0

Ed.	25–34	198 (173)	35–44	198 (105)
H.S.	0.6	0.0	0.9	0.0
<1 col.	1.2	0.0	1.1	1.0
1 col.	2.6	.6	1.7	0.0
2 col.	53.4	82.7*(143)	20.8	38.1
B.S.	16.9	4.6	20.7	16.2*
B.S.+	23.2	10.4	41.7*	32.4
M.S.	1.4	0.6	9.9	7.6
M.S.+	0.3	0.0	2.5	3.8

Ed.	45–54	198 (104)	55–64	198 (77)	
H.S.	1.4	0.0	2.5	0.0	
<1 col.	1.3	2.9	1.7	1.3	
1 col.	1.7	0.0	2.5	0.0	
2 col.	13.7	15.4	19.0	31.2	
B.S.	19.9	16.3	19.6	20.8*	
B.S.+	45.0*	48.1*	40.1*	33.8	
M.S.	11.7	15.4	8.5	7.8	
M.S.+	4.4	1.9	3.7	3.9	

Ed.	65–69	198 (22)	>69	198 (11)	
H.S.	3.8	4.5 (1)	5.8	0.0	
<1 col.	3.7	0.0	3.1	9.1	1
1 col.	3.6	0.0	4.4	0.0	
2 col.	26.1	31.8	29.2	54.5*	6
B.S.	18.5*	4.5	19.0*	36.4	4
B.S.+	33.1	45.5*	29.0	0.0	0
M.S.	5.6	13.6	3.4	0.0	0
M.S.+	2.3	0.0	2.0	0.0	0

National norms are in the first column. Code *198* represents the norms of the Sisters of the Holy Cross, a religious community with a sister formation program. Hence, the number of teachers younger than twenty-four years of age is small. Numbers in parentheses indicate the base in a given group. The base is necessary to interpret statistics properly; e.g., if a 66⅔% increase represents two teachers, the sample is too small to be significant. An asterisk (*) marks the class in which the median falls.

Secondary Schools

Ed.	<20	198	20–24	198
H.S.	0.0	0.0	0.0	0.0 (3)
<1 col.	14.3	0.0	0.6	0.0
1 col.	28.6	0.0	1.5	0.0
2 col.	0.0	0.0	26.9	66.7*(2)
B.S.	0.0	0.0	33.6*	0.0
B.S.+	14.3*	0.0	33.8	33.3 (1)
M.S.	28.6	0.0	1.4	0.0
M.S.+	14.3	0.0	2.2	0.0

Ed.	25–34	198	35–44	198
H.S.	0.0	0.0	0.0	0.0
<1 col.	0.1	0.0	0.1	0.0
1 col.	0.2	0.0	0.1	0.0
2 col.	14.3	20.8	2.6	7.4
B.S.	12.3	8.3	6.3	3.7
B.S.+	57.6*	58.3*	40.1	44.7*
M.S.	11.2	8.3	36.1*	37.0
M.S.+	3.9	4.2	14.6	7.4

Ed.	45–54	198	55–64	198
H.S.	0.1	0.0	0.2	0.0
<1 col.	0.2	0.0	0.2	0.0
1 col.	0.0	0.0	0.1	0.0
2 col.	1.2	0.0	1.4	2.1
B.S.	4.3	7.3	5.7	8.5
B.S.+	28.6	36.6	29.3	34.0
M.S.	39.2*	29.3*	35.5*	34.0*
M.S.+	26.3	26.8	27.2	21.3

Ed.	65–69	198	>69	198
H.S.	0.1	0.0	0.7	0.0
<1 col.	0.2	0.0	0.1	0.0
1 col.	0.3	0.0	0.1	0.0
2 col.	1.7	6.3	3.3	0.0
B.S.	7.6	12.5	8.5	0.0
B.S.+	35.3	31.3*	36.5	70.0*
M.S.	31.2*	12.5	28.1*	20.0
M.S.+	22.7	31.3	22.0	10.0

The profile of a province in a community can likewise be practical in pointing out regional needs, differences, and policies. The Study of Catholic Education, University of Notre Dame, has released the figures of the national profile. An asterisk (*) marks the class in which the median falls.

Educational Status of Teaching Sisters in the Midwest Province: 1964–1965

Elementary Level

Number of Sisters	Percentage	Level of Education
38	19%	Master's Degree
81	40%	Bachelor's Degree
43	21%	More than 100 semester hours
17	9%	More than 80 semester hours
8	4%	Indiana Life License without degree
14	7%	Less than 80 semester hours
Total 201	100%	

Secondary Level

Number of Sisters	Percentage	Level of Education
3	3%	Doctorate
52	55%	Master's Degree
39	42%	Bachelor's Degree plus
0	0%	Less than Bachelor's Degree
Total 94	100%	

GLOSSARY

BAND: Religious congregations receive new members once or twice a year. Persons who enter before a certain date in a given year are said to be members of the same band.

CANONICAL VISIT: A visit made by the superior general at least once during her term of office, and by the provincial superior each year. The superior general visits all the houses of the congregation, whereas the provincial visits the houses in her province. Often referred to as a *regular visit*.

CANON LAW: The body of ecclesiastical laws governing the church.

CONGREGATION: A religious institute whose members take the simple vows of poverty, chastity, and obedience.

CONSTITUTION: The fundamental law determining the governing of a religious congregation.

COMMUNITY: A group of sisters under the authority of the same superior general, having the same general purpose and interests, and living the same rule.

GENERALATE: House in which the superior general and members of the general administration reside.

GENERAL HOUSE: A collective term for the group of community establishments at Saint Mary's, e.g., the church, convent, juniorate, novitiate, and postulancy. (Saint Mary's College, a mission of the Midwest Province, is to be excluded in this connection.)

HABIT: The distinctive garb worn by the sisters.

HORARIUM: A reasonably uniform order of the day followed by all the houses of a congregation in regard to common exercises of prayer, assigned obediences, and leisure.

JUNIORATE: A period of religious formation that follows both the postulancy and novitiate and prepares the young religious

231

for their apostolic work. It lasts for two years. During this time the religious are under vows for two one-year periods.

MISSION: A house of the congregation to which a sister may be assigned.

MOTHER HOUSE: The cradle of a religious community. For the Congregation of Holy Cross it is LeMans, France; for the American province of the Sisters of the Holy Cross it is Bertrand, Michigan.

NOVITIATE: The second period of formation, which lasts for two years, the first of which is called the canonical year. This begins with the ceremony of investiture and ends when the candidate takes vows.

OBEDIENCE: One of the three vows (solemn promises) taken by religious. They oblige themselves to obey the commands of the lawful superiors in everything concerned directly or indirectly with the life of the congregation, that is, to observe the vows and the constitutions. Sometimes used to refer to a particular assignment.

ORDER: Canon law reserves this name to religious institutes in which the members take solemn vows. They consist principally of all the "old orders" (of monks, canons, nuns, and friars) and the Jesuits. In common parlance, however, any of the societies that canon law calls religious institutes are referred to as orders.

POSTULANT (ASPIRANT): A candidate who undergoes at least six months of probation, the purpose of which is to initiate her into religious life and to test her vocation.

POSTULANCY: The period of formation in which the candidate first begins her training. The time can vary from six months to a year.

PROFESSED: Those members of the congregation who have taken the three vows of poverty, chastity, and obedience. These vows are temporary for five years and then perpetual. During the period of temporary vows, the sisters are referred to as junior professed.

PROVINCE: A geographical area such as the Midwest, East, or West under the general supervision of the mother provincial of that province.

PROVINCIAL SUPERIOR: A religious acting under the superior general of a congregation and exercising general supervision over all houses in a province.

RULE: Order of life followed by members of religious orders.

SACRED CONGREGATION OF THE PROPAGATION OF THE FAITH: A department of the papal administration charged with the spread of Catholicism and with the regulation of church affairs in non-Catholic countries.

SCHOLASTICATE: A term formerly used for the years of post-canonical study.

SISTER FORMATION: Program of studies and activities adopted by a religious community through which it endeavors to form its members integrally and completely from every point of view—human, religious, and apostolic.

SUPERIOR GENERAL: Person in a religious congregation who, together with a council, exercises authority over all provinces, regions, houses, and members of the congregation. The superior general is elected by delegates of the congregation at a general chapter. The council is elected in the same manner. The superior general of a religious congregation of men is called father general; of a religious congregation of women, mother general.

VOWS: Solemn promises made to God alone for the attainment of a higher good. In other words, there is a supernatural end in view in the making of these vows, which is union with God.

BIBLIOGRAPHY

I. Manuscripts

Accounts, 1868–1943 (Microfilm reels 1–8b); 1943–1964. Archives, Saint Mary's Convent, Notre Dame, Indiana.

Angela (Gillespie), C.S.C., Mother M. Letters: Mother M. Angela to Orestes Brownson, Oct. 21, 1858; Jan 2, 1860; April 24, 1860. Brownson Papers, University of Notre Dame Archives. Mother M. Angela to Edward Sorin, 1869. Mother M. Angela to the sisters, 1870. P. Farrelly to Mother M. Angela, 1854. Henry Kennedy to Mother M. Angela, 1855. Robert Harves to Mother M. Angela, Jan. 17, 1856. Charles Chaney to Mother M. Angela, April 24, 1864. Ada Woods to Mother M. Angela, 1879. Archives, Saint Mary's Convent, Notre Dame, Indiana.

Annunciata (McSheffry), C.S.C., Mother M. Circular Letters. Archives, Saint Mary's Convent, Notre Dame, Indiana.

Archives: Saint Catherine's Normal Institute, Baltimore, Maryland. Saint Mary-of-the-Wasatch, Salt Lake City, Utah. Saint Mary's Academy, Alexandria, Virginia. Saint Mary's Academy, Austin, Texas. Saint Mary's Academy, Morris, Illinois. Saint Mary's Convent, Notre Dame, Indiana. Archives located at Saint Mary's Convent, Notre Dame, Indiana.

Armstrong, W. Earl. To Sister Mary Alma (Peters), July 13, 1962. Office of the Academic Dean, Saint Mary's College, Notre Dame, Indiana.

Articles of Incorporation, 1851, 1855, 1903. Archives, Saint Mary's College, Notre Dame, Indiana.

Assignments, 1868–1952 (Microfilm reels 15–16).

Binswanger, Robert B. "The Dilemma Facing Roman Catholic Schools in the United States with Respect to Current Financial Considerations." Unpublished doctoral dissertation. Graduate School of Education, Harvard University, 1961.

Brown, Ella Ewing. "Memoirs of Eliza Gillespie: Mother Mary Angela." Archives, Saint Mary's Convent, Notre Dame, Indiana.

————. "Memoirs of Sister M. Elizabeth Lilly." Archives, Saint Mary's Convent, Notre Dame, Indiana.

Ceciliana (Honor), C.S.C., Sister M. Fine Arts Committee, Third Annual Conference on Education, "Publications of the Sisters of the Holy Cross 1950–1964."

Certification Data File. Office of the Academic Dean, Saint Mary's College, Notre Dame, Indiana.

A Chronicle of Community History Written at Saint Mary's Convent, Notre Dame, Indiana, 1834–1879. Archives, Saint Mary's Convent, Notre Dame, Indiana.

A Chronicle of Community History, 1841–1908. Written at Holy Cross Convent, Notre Dame, Indiana. Archives, Saint Mary's Convent, Notre Dame, Indiana.

Class Meeting Minutes, 1855–1880. Archives, Saint Mary's College, Notre Dame, Indiana.

Cointet, Francois. To Basil Moreau, 1848. University of Notre Dame Archives.

Community Register. 2 vols. Archives, Saint Mary's Convent, Notre Dame, Indiana.

Compassion (Gleason), C.S.C., Mother M. Diary, May 6, 1845–March 13, 1913. Archives, Saint Mary's Convent, Notre Dame, Indiana.

————. "Life of Mother M. Angela." Archives, Saint Mary's Convent, Notre Dame, Indiana.

Connolly, Mary Elizabeth. "Schools in California Conducted by the Sisters of the Congregation of the Holy Cross." Unpublished master's thesis. Department of Education, San Francisco College for Women, 1953.

Coquillard, Alexis. To Sister M. Columba (Sweeney), 1858. Archives, Saint Mary's Convent, Notre Dame, Indiana.

Council Minutes, Saint Mary's Academy, Bertrand, Michigan, 1850–1855. Archives, Saint Mary's Convent, Notre Dame, Indiana.

"Educational Report: Sisters of the Holy Cross, 1943–1949." Archives, Saint Mary's Convent, Notre Dame, Indiana.

Egan, William. To Directress of Studies, Saint Mary's Academy, Bertrand, Sept. 17, 1852. Archives, Saint Mary's Convent, Notre Dame, Indiana.

Elizabeth (Lilly), C.S.C., Sister M. "Memoirs of Mother M. Angela." Archives, Saint Mary's Convent, Notre Dame, Indiana.

Emerentiana (Nowlan), C.S.C., Sister M. "Important Events in the Annals of the Congregation of the Sisters of the Holy Cross–Dating from July, 1895 to" [June, 1918]. Archives, Saint Mary's Convent, Notre Dame, Indiana.

————. "Notes on Deaf Mutes." Archives, Saint Mary's Convent, Notre Dame, Indiana.

————. "The Origin of the Congregation of the Holy Cross." Archives, Saint Mary's Convent, Notre Dame, Indiana.

Euphrosine (Pepin), C.S.C., Sister M. Diary. Archives, Saint Mary's Convent, Notre Dame, Indiana.

Family Tree of Neal Gillespie, Sr. Ewing Papers, University of Notre Dame Archives. Ewing File, Archives, Saint Mary's Convent, Notre Dame, Indiana.

Flanagan, F. J. To Directress of Studies, Saint Mary's Academy, Bertrand, Michigan, Feb. 1853. Archives, Saint Mary's Convent, Notre Dame, Indiana.

Flynn, F.F.C., Brother Austin. "The School Controversy in New York, 1840–1842, and Its Effect on the Formulation of Catholic Elementary School Policy." Unpublished doctoral dissertation. Department of Education, University of Notre Dame, 1962.

Foy, Patrick, and Foy, Bridget. Contract made with Sister M. Charles (Flynn), July 28, 1866. Archives, Saint Mary's Convent, Notre Dame, Indiana.

Gage, Harry Morehouse. To Mother M. Pauline (O'Neill), May 13, 1922. Office of the Academic Dean, Saint Mary's College, Notre Dame, Indiana.

Greathouse, Charles A. To Mother M. Pauline, March 12, 1915, and May 8, 1915. Office of the Academic Dean, Saint Mary's College, Notre Dame, Indiana.

Hodges, Dorothy. To Sister M. Frederick (Eggleston), Sept. 1, 1937. Office of the Academic Dean, Saint Mary's College, Notre Dame, Indiana.

Kennedy, Henry. To Sarah Kennedy, 1855. Archives, Saint Mary's Convent, Notre Dame, Indiana.

Laurence, C.S.C., Brother. To Sister M. Columba (Sweeney), Sept. 6 and 7, 1858. Archives, Saint Mary's Convent, Notre Dame, Indiana.

Ledger of Student Accounts, Saint Mary's Academy, 1849–1864. Archives, Saint Mary's College, Notre Dame, Indiana.

Lemonnier, Auguste, C.S.C. "The Report of the Prefect of Studies of Notre Dame University to the General Prefect of Studies, June 5, 1872." University of Notre Dame Archives.

Louppe, Joseph Nicolas. Contract made with Sisters of the Holy Cross, May 22, 1851. Archives, Saint Mary's Convent, Notre Dame, Indiana.

"Le Registre de la Mission de Saint Joseph, (Bertrand, Michigan), Dioceses de Bardstown et de Cincinnati," Saint Mary's Church, Niles, Michigan.

"Liber Confirmatorum" (1847–1855), Saint Mary's Church, Niles, Michigan.

"Liber Conjugatorum—1846–1856," Saint Mary's Church, Niles, Michigan.

"Liber Defunctorum—1844–1859," Saint Mary's Church, Niles, Michigan.

"Liber Status Animarum, Ecclesiae Parochialis S. (sic) Joseph, Civitatis Bertrand, (incceptus die 18 mensis Decembris anno 1847)" Saint Mary's Church, Niles, Michigan.

Marie Angele (Yamamoto), C.S.C., Sister. Survey of Scholastic Honors Awarded Sisters of the Holy Cross, 1963–1964. AGH.

Monsimer, Urban. To Sarah Kennedy, 1855. Archives, Saint Mary's Convent, Notre Dame, Indiana.

Murray, C. L. To Sister M. Frederick, Feb. 18, 1935; Sept. 10, 1935. Office of the Academic Dean, Saint Mary's College, Notre Dame, Indiana.

North Central Association. Report of the Visiting Team of the North Central Association to Sister Mary Alma, June, 1961. Office of the Academic Dean, Saint Mary's College, Notre Dame, Indiana.

Novitiate Record Book, 1877–1893. Archives, Saint Mary's Convent, Notre Dame, Indiana.

Pabst, Robert L. To Sister Mary Alma, April 18, 1958. Office of the Academic Dean, Saint Mary's College, Notre Dame, Indiana.

Personnel Files, 1843–1952 (Microfilm Reels 9–14) ; 1953–1964. Archives, Saint Mary's Convent, Notre Dame, Indiana.

Reception Register. 3 vols. Archives, Saint Mary's Convent, Notre Dame, Indiana.

Records of Annual Statistics, 1844–1964. 4 vols. Archives, Saint Mary's Convent, Notre Dame, Indiana.

Records of Bertrand Administration. Vol. I: "Provincial Council Verbal Processes." Vol. II: "Establishments and Conditions of Foundations, Province of Indiana." Vol. III: "Visits." Vol. IV: "Catalogue of the Deceased." Vol. V: "Contracts." Vol. VI: "Dignitaries." Vol. VII: "Benefactors—Friends of the House." Vol. VIII: "Ordinances and Decrees." Vol. IX: "Favors of the H. [oly] See and of the Bishops." Archives, Saint Mary's Convent, Notre Dame, Indiana.

Reisert, John E. To Sister Mary Alma, June 21, 1963. Office of the Academic Dean, Saint Mary's College, Notre Dame, Indiana.

Roberts, Eunice C. To Sister M. Madeleva (Wolff), C.S.C., March, 1950; Dec. 20, 1955. Office of the Academic Dean, Saint Mary's College, Notre Dame, Indiana.

Rose Elizabeth (Havican), C.S.C., Mother M. To Sister Maria Concepta (McDermott), C.S.C., 1964. Archives, Saint Mary's Convent, Notre Dame, Indiana.

Sadlier Publishing Company. "Articles of Agreement" between Sister Mary Angela and D. S. Sadlier & Co., March 7, 1870.

————. Letters: William H. Sadlier to Mother M. Collette (Cunnea), Feb. 22, 1877. Annie Sadlier to Mother M. Collette, June 1, 1879; Dec. 27, 1879. Mrs. William H. Sadlier to Mother M. Angela, Jan. 15, 1881. Annie Sadlier to Mother M. Collette, Jan. 1, 1882. Mrs.

William H. Sadlier to Mother M. Collette, Feb. 11, 1884; Feb. 2, 1889. F. Sadlier Dinger to Sister Maria Concepta, Jan. 30, 1964. Sadlier File, Archives, Saint Mary's Convent, Notre Dame, Indiana.

Saint Mary's Academy Register, 1854. Archives, Saint Mary's Convent, Notre Dame, Indiana.

Sorin, Edward. Agreement with Mother M. Angela concerning royalties from Sadlier Publishing Company, Oct. 19, 1869. Sadlier File, Archives, Saint Mary's Convent, Notre Dame, Indiana.

————. Letters: Edward Sorin to Pierre Chappe, 1844. Edward Sorin to Basil Moreau, 1847. University of Notre Dame Archives. Edward Sorin to Pastor of St. Philomena's Parish, Bourbonnais, Illinois, 1858; 1859. Victor Douelle to Edward Sorin, 1850. J. O'Reilly to Edward Sorin, 1854. Patrick Donahoe to Edward Sorin, Oct. 29, 1856. Archives, Saint Mary's Convent, Notre Dame, Indiana.

Starr, Eliza Allan. "A Great Educational Center." Archives, Saint Mary's Convent, Notre Dame, Indiana.

Survey of the Educational Status of the Congregation of the Sisters of the Holy Cross (1844–1964). Archives, Saint Mary's Convent, Notre Dame, Indiana.

Vincentia (Fannon), C.S.C., Mother M. To Sister M. Lauretana (Unrich), 1932. Archives, Saint Mary's Convent, Notre Dame, Indiana.

Whisler, H. M. To Mother M. Pauline, June 14, 1927; Nov. 30, 1927; Aug. 15, 1930; Sept. 16, 1930. To Sister Mary Alma, Aug. 9, 1956. Office of the Academic Dean, Saint Mary's College, Notre Dame, Indiana.

Williams, Oscar H. To Mother M. Pauline, July 27, 1920; Dec. 16, 1921; March 8, 1922; Sept. 8, 1923. Office of the Academic Dean, Saint Mary's College, Notre Dame, Indiana.

II. Published Primary Materials

Alerding, Rev. Herman Joseph. Report of the Superintendent of the Catholic Schools of the Diocese of Fort Wayne. Privately printed, 1905–1908.

American Council of Education. Commission on Teacher Education. The Improvement of Teacher Education: a Final Report by the Commission on Teacher Education. Washington, D. C.: The Council, 1946.

Aquina (Kirwan), C.S.C., Sister M. Course of Study: Grades 1 through 8. Privately printed, no date.

Baltimore Sun, June 13, 1925.

Catalogue of Saint Catherine's Normal Institute, Baltimore, Maryland, June, 1887. Baltimore: Andrew J. Conlon, 1887.

Catalogue of Saint Mary's Academy, Notre Dame, Indiana. 1860–1923; 1925–1964. (Published first by Saint Mary's Academy, later jointly by Saint Mary's College and Academy, still later separately by each. None published in 1924.)

Chicago Sun, June 1875.

The Chimes, Saint Mary's College, Notre Dame, Indiana, July, 1895.

Holy Cross, Congregation of. *General Directory of Houses and Religious.* Rome, Italy: Curia Generalizia di Santo Croce, 1962.

————. Congregation of the Sisters of the Holy Cross. *Constitutions of the Congregation of the Sisters of the Holy Cross.* Notre Dame, Ind.: Ave Maria Press, 1962. (Earlier editions of the *Rules and Constitutions* were published in 1870, 1895, and 1933.) For the first French edition see Société des Marianites.

An Illustrated Historical Atlas of St. Joseph's Co., Indiana. Chicago: Higgins Belden and Company, 1875.

Indiana. Department of Public Instruction. *The Education of Indiana Teachers.* State of Indiana Division of Teacher Education and Certification Bulletin 400. Indianapolis: State Department of Public Instruction, 1963.

————. *Handbook on Teacher Education in Indiana.* State of Indiana Department of Public Instruction, Division of Teacher Training and Licensing Bulletin 192. 2nd rev. ed. Indianapolis, State Department of Public Instruction, 1954.

————. *Laws, Rules, Regulations and General Information Governing Teacher Training & Licensing.* Education Bulletin No. 94. Indianapolis: Department of Education, 1937.

John XXIII, Pope. "Il Tempio Massimo," Encyclical Letter, June 2, 1962. *Sister Formation Bulletin,* X (Autumn, 1962), 1–9.

Kuhlmann, Charles. Editorial, (Marshall, Illinois) *Church Progress,* May 1, 1886, p. 4.

Moreau, Basile-Antoine-Marie. *Circular Letters of the Very Reverend Basil Anthony Mary Moreau.* 2 vols. Translated by Edward L. Heston, C.S.C., Notre Dame, Ind.: Ave Maria Press, 1943.

————. *Etrennes spirituelles offertes aux Associées du Bon Pasteur et de Saint-Joseph.* LeMans: Gallienne, 1840–1851.

————. *[La]Pédagogie Chrétienne à l'usage des Joséphites de la Congrégation de Sainte-Croix.* LeMans: Imprimerie Julien, Laniel et Cie., 1865.

————. *Nouveau, livre de lectures à l'usage de la jeunesse Chrétienne.* 7 ieme ed. LeMans: Imprimerie Beauvais, 1865.

National Catholic Educational Association. *The Education of Sister Lucy;* a Symposium on Teacher Education and Teacher Training, April 21, 1949. Holy Cross, Ind.: Saint Mary's College, Notre Dame, 1949.

New World, Sept. 14, 1901.

Reisert, John E., and Patterson, Anne. *99 Most Common Questions*

Concerning Indiana Teacher Certification. Indianapolis: Indiana Department of Public Instruction, Division of Teacher Education and Certification, 1964.

Saint Mary's Chimes. Vol. I-LXXVI, 1892–1964.

Saint Mary's College, Notre Dame, Holy Cross, Indiana. *A College Goes to School: Centennial Lectures.* Paterson, N. J.: St. Anthony Guild Press, 1945.

The Scholastic Annual. University of Notre Dame, Indiana. 1876–1964.

Sister Formation Bulletin; Official Publication of the Sister Formation Conference. Reprint ed. Milwaukee: Marquette University Press, 1959–1963.

Société des Marianites. *Règles particulières aux Marianites, à l'usage des professes.* Edition approuvée par le chapitre. LeMans: Gallienne, Imprimeur-Libraire, 1854.

Sorin, Edward. *Circular Letters of the Very Rev. Edward Sorin, Superior.* 2 vols. Notre Dame, Ind.: Ave Maria Press, 1885–1894.

Teachers' Guide for the Use of the Sisters of the Holy Cross. Privately printed, no date. Rev. ed., 1909.

Tidings; the Eastern Province (Sisters of the Holy Cross). November 1961.

United States Bureau of Education. *Biennial Survey of Education* (1928-1960). Washington, D. C.: Government Printing Office, 1932–1962.

United States Department of Health, Education and Welfare. Division of Educational Statistics. Bureau of Educational Research and Development. *Digest of Educational Statistics.* United States Office of Education Bulletin, No. 10 (1963). Washington, D. C.: Government Printing Office, 1962.

Textbooks

Angela (Gillespie), C.S.C., Mother M. *The Metropolitan Fourth Reader.* New York: D. & J. Sadlier and Company, 1875.

_____. *The Metropolitan Sixth Reader: The Book of Oratory.* New York: D. & J. Sadlier and Company, 1867.

_____. *Sadlier's Excelsior Catholic Readers, No. 6.* New York: William H. Sadlier, 1878.

_____. *Sadlier's Excelsior Compendium of Literature and Elocution, No. 6.* New York: William H. Sadlier, 1878.

_____. *Sadlier's Excelsior Complete Speller,* New York: William H. Sadlier, 1879, 1880, 1885.

_____. *Sadlier's Excelsior Fifth Reader.* New York: William H. Sadlier, 1877, 1904.

_____. *Sadlier's Excelsior First Reader.* New York: William H. Sadlier, 1876, 1887; Annie M. Sadlier, 1904.

————. *Sadlier's Excelsior Fourth Reader.* New York: William H. Sadlier, 1876, 1886; Annie M. Sadlier, 1904.

————. *Sadlier's Excelsior Geography Number Three* (New York Edition) Revised Edition of the First Catholic Geography in America. New York: Frank X. Sadlier, 1917.

————. *Sadlier's Excelsior Introduction to Geography* (Designed for Junior Classes). New York: William H. Sadlier, 1866.

————. *Sadlier's Excelsior Second Reader.* New York: William H. Sadlier, 1876; Annie M. Sadlier, 1904.

————. *Sadlier's Excelsior Third Reader.* New York: William H. Sadlier, 1876; Annie M. Sadlier, 1904.

————. *Sadlier's New Excelsior Geography, Number Two, for Elementary and Intermediate Classes.* New York: William H. Sadlier, 1875, 1880, 1891, 1896; Frank X. Sadlier, 1914.

The Brothers of the Christian School. *The Third Book of Reading Lessons.* New York: D. & J. Sadlier and Company, 1853.

Davies, Charles. *Elementary Algebra: Embracing the First Principles of the Science.* New York: A. S. Barnes and Co., 1856.

Fredet, Peter. *Ancient History from the Dispersion of the Sons of Noe to the Battle of Actium.* 5th ed. Baltimore: John Murphy and Company, 1851.

Fulton, Levi S., and Eastman, George W. *A Practical System of Bookkeeping by Single and Double Entry.* 7th ed., rev. New York: A. S. Barnes and Co., 1856.

Hervey, George Winifred. *The Rhetoric of Conversation: Bridles and Spurs for the Management of the Tongue.* New York: Harper Brothers, 1863.

Olmsted, Denison. *A Compendium of Natural Philosophy.* New Haven: S. Babcock, 1851.

Olney's School Atlas and Supplement. New York: Pratt, Woodford and Co., 1844.

III. Secondary Materials

A. Books

Alerding, Right Reverend Herman Joseph. *The Diocese of Fort Wayne: a Book of Historical Reference, 1669–1907.* Fort Wayne, Ind.: Archer Printing Company, 1907.

Altrocchi, Julia Cooley. *Wolves Against the Moon.* New York: Macmillan Company, 1940.

Annales de la Congrègation des Soeurs de Sainte-Croix et des Sept Douleurs. 4 vols. Saint-Laurent, P. Q.: Privately printed, 1930.

Armstrong, W. Earl, and Stinnett, Timothy M. *Certification Requirements for School Personnel in the United States.* Washington, D. C.: National Education Association, 1959.

Bachman, Frank P. *Training and Certification of High School Teachers.* Division of Surveys and Field Studies, Field Studies No. 2. Nashville, Tenn.: George Peabody College for Teachers, 1930.

Baldwin, Leland Dewitt. *The Stream of American History.* 2 vols. New York: American Book Company, 1952.

Ballard, Ralph. *Old Fort St. Joseph.* Niles, Mich.: Fort St. Joseph Historical Society, 1949.

————. *Tales of Early Niles.* Niles, Mich.: Fort St. Joseph Historical Society, 1947.

Bertrande (Meyers), Sister. *The Education of Sisters; a Plan for Integrating the Religious, Social, Cultural and Professional Training of Sisters.* New York: Sheed & Ward, 1941.

Blauch, Lloyd E. (ed.) *Accreditation in Higher Education.* Washington, D. C.: Government Printing Office, 1959.

Boone, Richard Gause. *History of Education in Indiana.* New York: D. Appleton and Company, 1892.

Borromeo (Brown), Sister Mary. *History of the Sisters of Providence of Saint Mary-of-the-Woods.* 2 vols. New York: Benziger Brothers, Inc., 1949.

Bowden, W. T. (ed.). *The National Crisis in Education.* United States Bureau of Education, No. 29. Washington, D. C.: Government Printing Office, 1920.

A Brief History of the University of Notre Dame du Lac, Indiana, 1842–1892. Chicago: Werener Company, 1895.

Brown, Elmer E. *The Making of Our Middle Schools: an Account of the Development of Secondary Education in the United States.* 3rd ed. New York: Longmans, Green and Company, 1907.

Burns, James A., C.S.C., and Kohlbrenner, Bernard J. *History of Catholic Education in the United States.* New York: Benziger Brothers, 1937.

Catta, Etienne, and Catta, Tony. *Basil Anthony Mary Moreau.* 2 vols. Translated by Edward L. Heston, C.S.C. Milwaukee: Bruce Publishing Company, 1955.

————. *Mother Mary of the Seven Dolors and the Early Origins of the Marianites of Holy Cross (1818–1900).* Translated by Edward L. Heston, C.S.C. Milwaukee: Catholic Life Publications, Bruce Press, 1959.

Cavanaugh, John William, C.S.C. *The Priests of Holy Cross.* Notre Dame, Ind.: University of Notre Dame Press, 1904.

Cicognani, Amleto Giovanni. "A State Held in Honor," *Addresses and Sermons (1951–1955).* Paterson, N. J.: St. Anthony Guild Press, 1955, pp. 59–69.

Conant, James B. *The Education of American Teachers.* New York: McGraw-Hill Book Company, 1963.

Cook, Katherine M. *State Laws and Regulations Governing Teachers' Certificates.* United States Bureau of Education Bulletin 22. Washington, D. C.: Government Printing Office, 1920.

Coolidge, Orville W. *A Twentieth Century History of Berrien County, Michigan.* Chicago: Lewis Publishing Company, 1906.

Corrigan, Anthony B. *Financial Support of Roman Catholic Colleges and Universities in the United States.* New York: Fordham University Press, 1954.

Cowles, Edward B. (comp.). *Berrien County Directory and History.* Niles, Michigan: Edward B. Cowles, 1871.

Cubberley, Ellwood P. *The Certification of Teachers.* 5th Yearbook of the National Society for the Scientific Study of Education, Part 2. Chicago: University of Chicago Press, 1906.

————. *Publication Education in the United States; a Study in Interpretation of American Educational History.* Boston: Houghton Mifflin Company, 1934.

Cunningham, Wilbur M. *The Land of Four Flags: an Early History of the St. Joseph Valley.* Grand Rapids, Michigan: William B. Eerdmans Publishing Company, 1961.

Deferrari, Roy J. *Some Problems of Higher Education in the United States.* Boston: Daughters of St. Paul, 1963.

Dunn, Jacob P. *A History of Indiana: Supplement to Gordy's History of the United States.* New York: Charles Scribner's Sons, 1916.

Dunn, William Kailer. *What Happened to Religious Education? The Decline of Religious Teaching in the Public Elementary, 1776–1861.* Baltimore: The Johns Hopkins Press, 1958.

Eleanore (Brosnahan), C.S.C., Sister M. *On the King's Highway.* New York: D. Appleton and Company, 1931.

Elsbree, Willard S. *The American Teacher.* New York: The American Book Company, 1939.

Evenden, Edward S., Gamble, Gary C., and Blue, Harold G. *Teacher Personnel in the United States: National Survey of the Education of Teachers,* Vol. II. United States Office of Education Bulletin, No. 10 (1933). Washington, D. C.: Government Printing Office, 1935.

Francesca (McDougal), C.S.C., Sister M. *Our Mother House: Centenary Chronicles of the Sisters of the Holy Cross, 1841–1941,* Vol. IV. Hammond, Ind.: W. B. Conkey Company, 1941.

Francis Jerome (O'Laughlin), C.S.C., Sister M. *This Is Mother Pauline: Centenary Chronicles of the Sisters of the Holy Cross,* Vol. VII. Paterson, N. J.: St. Anthony Guild Press, 1945.

Frazier, Benjamin W. *Education of Teachers as a Function of State Departments of Education.* United States Office of Education Bulletin, No. 6. Washington, D. C.: Government Printing Office, 1941.

————. et al. *Special Survey in Nine Parts: National Survey of the*

Education of Teachers, Vol. V. United States Office of Education Bulletin, No. 10 (1933). Washington, D. C.: Government Printing Office, 1933.

Goebel, Edmund J. *A Study of Catholic Secondary Education During the Colonial Period up to the First Plenary Council of Baltimore, 1882.* Washington, D. C.: Catholic University of America Press, 1937.

"History of Teacher's Training," *Cyclopedia of Education.* Edited by Paul Monroe. New York: The MacMillan Company, 1911–1913. Vol. V, 515–523.

Hodenfield, G. K., And Stinnett, Timothy M. *The Education of Teachers; Conflict and Consensus.* Englewood Cliffs, N. J.: Prentice-Hall, Inc., 1961.

Holy Cross, Congregation of the Sisters of the. *Our Provinces: Centenary Chronicles of the Sisters of the Holy Cross, 1841–1941,* Vol. V. Privately printed, 1941.

————. *Pioneers and Builders: Centenary Chronicles of the Sisters of the Holy Cross, 1841–1941,* Vol. III, Hammond, Ind.: W. B. Conkey Company, 1941.

————. *Residence Directory of the Sisters of the Holy Cross.* Published yearly. Notre Dame, Ind.: Ave Maria Press, 1952–1953.

————. *Songs of the Rood: Centenary Chronicles of the Sisters of the Holy Cross.* Vol. I. Paterson, N. J.: Saint Anthony Guild Press, 1941.

————. *A Story of Fifty Years: 1855–1905.* Notre Dame, Ind.: Ave Maria Press, 1941.

————. *Superior Generals: Centenary Chronicles of the Sisters of the Holy Cross,* 1841–1941. Vol. II. Paterson, N. J.: St. Anthony Guild Press, 1941.

Inglis, Alexander James. *Principles of Secondary Education.* Boston: Houghton Mifflin Company, 1918.

The Juniorate in Sister Formation; Proceedings and Communications from the Fourth Series of Regional Meetings of the Sister Formation Conference, 1957–1958. Edited by Sister Ritamary, C.H.M. New York: Fordham University Press, 1961.

Kandel, Isaac L. *History of Secondary Education: A Study in the Development of Liberal Education.* Boston: Houghton Mifflin Company, 1930.

Kershaw, Joseph A., and McKean, Roland N. *Teacher Shortages and Salary Schedules,* New York: McGraw-Hill Book Company, 1962.

LaFontaine, A. E. *Report of the Superintendent of Catholic Schools of the Diocese of Fort Wayne for the Year 1905–1906; 1906–1907; 1907–1908.* Fort Wayne, Ind.: Press of Journal Gazette, 1906, 1907, 1908.

Lathrop, George Parsons, and Lathrop, Rose Hawthorne. *A Story of Courage; Annals of the Georgetown Convent of the Visitation of the Blessed Virgin Mary.* Boston: Houghton Mifflin Company, 1894.

Lieberman, Myron. "Teacher Education and the Secondary Curriculum—U. S. A.," *The Yearbook of Education,* 1958. New York: Harcourt, Brace, and World, Inc., 1958, pp. 318–325.

The Life of the Rev. F. Cointet: Priest and Missionary of the Congregation of Holy Cross. Cincinnati: John P. Walsh, 1855.

McAllister, Anna Shannon. *Ellen Ewing; Wife of General Sherman.* New York: Benziger Brothers, 1936.

————. *Flame in the Wilderness; Life and Letters of Mother Angela Gillespie, C.S.C., 1824–1887, American Foundress of the Sisters of the Holy Cross: Centenary Chronicles of the Sisters of the Holy Cross,* Vol. VI. Paterson, N. J.: St. Anthony Guild Press, 1944.

McCandless, Marion. *Family Portraits: History of the Holy Cross Alumnae Association of Saint Mary's College, Notre Dame, Indiana, 1879–1949.* Hammond, Ind.: W. B. Conkey Company, 1952.

MacEoin, Gary. *Father Moreau: Founder of Holy Cross.* Milwaukee: Bruce Publishing Company, 1962.

Madeleva (Wolff), C.S.C., Sister M. *My First Seventy Years.* New York: Macmillan Company, 1959.

Martin, Michael, and Gelber, Leonard. *The New Dictionary of American History.* New York: Philosophical Library, 1952.

Mathews, Alfred. *History of Cass County, Michigan.* Chicago, Privately Printed, 1882.

The Mind of the Church in the Formation of Sisters; Selections from Addresses Given during the Six Regional Conferences and the First National Meeting of the Sister Formation Conference, 1954–1955. Edited by Sister Ritamary, C.H.M. New York: Fordham University Press, 1956.

Moffitt, John Clifton. *In-Service Education for Teachers.* Washington, D. C.: Center for Applied Research in Education, Inc., 1963.

Moreau, Charles. *Le très Révérend Pére Basile-Antoine Moreau, prêtre du Mans, et ses oeuvres.* 2 vols. Paris: Firmon-Didot, 1900.

National Catholic Educational Association. *Sister Formation Conferences. Report of Everett Curriculum Workshop, Everett, Washington, June 1 to August 30, 1956.* Seattle, Wash.: Heiden's Mailing Bureau, 1956.

National Commission on Teacher Education and Professional Standards. *The Education of Teachers; New Perspective.* Bowling Green, Ohio: The Commission, 1958.

National Congress of Religious of the United States. Sisters' Section. *Religious Community Life in the United States.* New York: The Paulist Press, 1952.

National Education Association of the United States. National Commission of Teacher Education and Professional Standards. *New Horizons for the Teaching Profession.* Edited by Margaret Lindsey. Washington, D. C.: The Association, 1961.

Norris, William, C.S.C. "Fr. Moreau and the Apostolate of Education," *Basile Moreau.* LeMans: L'Imprimerie Jean Viliare, 1962.

Paré, George. *The Catholic Church in Detroit, 1701–1888.* Detroit: Gabriel Richard Press, 1951.

Pius XI, Pope. *The Christian Education of Youth—Divini Illius Magistri.* New York: The Paulist Press, 1929.

Planning for the Formation of Sisters; Studies on the Teaching Apostolate and Selections from Addresses of the Sister Formation Conference, 1956–1957. Edited by Sister Ritamary, C. H. M. New York: Fordham University Press, 1958.

Progress of Public Education in the United States of America, 1960–1961. Washington, D. C.: United States Department of Health, Education, and Welfare, 1962.

Public Education in Indiana. New York: General Education Board, 1923.

Sheedy, Morgan. *The Parochial Schools in the United States.* Report of the Commissioner of Education for 1903. Washington, D. C.: Government Printing Office, 1905.

Smith, Elmer Reid (ed.). *Teacher Education: A Reappraisal.* New York: Harper and Row, 1962.

Spiritual and Intellectual Elements in the Formation of Sisters; Selections from Addresses and Communications on Discussion Topics from the Six Regional Meetings of the Sister Formation Conference, 1955–1956. Edited by Sister Ritamary, C. H. M. New York: Fordham University Press, 1957.

Suhrie, Ambrose L. (ed. and comp.). *Problems in Teacher Training.* Proceedings of the 1929 Spring Conference Conducted by the Normal-School and Teachers-College Section of the New York Society for the Experimental Study of Education, Vol. 4. New York: New York University Press, 1929.

Swenson, E. J. "Teacher Preparation," *National Social Study Educational Yearbook,* I (1961), 287–304.

Trahey, James J., C.S.C. *The Brothers of Holy Cross.* Notre Dame, Ind.: University Press, 1909.

Weslet, Edgar B. *NEA: The First Hundred Years.* New York: Harper & Brothers Publishers, 1957.

Woody, Thomas. *A History of Women's Education in the United States.* 2 vols. New York: The Science Press, 1929.

Wooster, George F. *Teaching in Indiana and Ohio.* Los Altos, Cal.: Howard Chandler, 1958.

B. Dissertations

Angelica (Velardi), Sister. *Aspects of the Preparation of Sisters for Teaching in Secondary Schools.* New York: Fordham University Press, 1959.

Antonia (Durkin), B.V.M., Sister. *The Preparation of the Religious Teacher.* Washington, D. C.: Catholic University of America Press, 1926.

Austin (Schirmer), O.S.B., Sister M. *An Evaluation of Teacher Education Programs in a Selected Group of Catholic Liberal Arts Colleges for Women.* Washington, D. C.: Catholic University of America Press, 1959.

Benedict (Murphy), R.S.H.M., Mother M. *Pioneer Roman Catholic Girls Academies: Their Growth, Character, and Contributions to American Education; A Study of Roman Catholic Education for Girls from Colonial Times to the First Plenary Council of 1852.* New York: Columbia University Press, 1958.

Brideen (Long), O.S.F., Sister. *An Evaluation of Catholic Elementary School Teachers' Pre-Service Education.* Washington, D. C.: Catholic University of America Press, 1952.

Carol (Schroeder), O.S.F., Sister Mary. *The Catholic Church in the Diocese of Vincennes, 1847–1877.* Washington, D. C.: Catholic University of America Press, 1946.

Clarissa (Doyle), Sister M. *Teacher Education in the Catholic Colleges and Universities of the United States.* New York: Fordham University Press, 1955.

Cody, Conall Alfred. *Education for Secondary School Teaching in Religious Communities of Men.* Washington, D. C.: Catholic University of America Press, 1960.

Dumas, Alexander A. *The Competence Required in Secondary School Teaching and Their Implications for Teacher Education.* Washington, D. C.: Catholic University of America Press, 1955.

Etheldreda (Heard), C.PP.S., Sister. *A Critical and Constructive Study of the Organization, Control, and Administration of Teacher Training Programs for Religious Teachers in Catholic Elementary Schools.* St. Louis: St. Louis University Press, 1938.

Margaret Marie (Doyle), C.S.C., Sister. "*The Curriculum of the Catholic Women's College.*" Unpublished doctoral dissertation. Department of Education, University of Notre Dame, 1932.

Nona (McCreal), O.P., Sister M. *The Role of a Teaching Sisterhood in American Society.* Washington, D. C.: Catholic University of America Press, 1951.

Ralph (Fahey), Sister Mary. *The Inservice Training of Religious Secondary School Teachers in the Congregations of Women in the*

United States. New York: Fordham University Press, 1960.

Rose Matthew (Mangini), I.H.M. *Professional Problems of Sister Teachers in the United States.* New York: Fordham University Press, 1958.

C. Periodical Literature

Barosse, Thomas, C.S.C. "Father Moreau and the Question of a Holy Cross Education," *Bulletin of the Educational Conference of the Priests of Holy Cross,* XXX (Dec., 1962), 68–78.

"Bibliography on Teacher Personnel," *Review of Educational Research,* VII (1937), 316–318.

Bonaventure, Thomas, F.S.C., Brother. "Cooperation of Communities in Problems of Sister-Formation," *Sister Formation Bulletin,* I (Oct., 1954), 1–3.

Ei, J. C. "Difficulties Encountered by Religious Superiors in the Professional Training of Their Teachers," *National Catholic Educational Association Bulletin,* X (Nov., 1913), 367-379.

Gordon, Leon M. "The Influence of River Transformation," *Indiana Magazine of History,* XLVI (1950), 284–289.

Harcar, George A., C.S.Sp. "Orienting the Lay Teacher into the Catholic Philosophy of Education and Its Objectives," *National Catholic Educational Association Bulletin,* LII (1955), 273–277.

Hickey, Augustine F. "The Responsibility of the Superintendent in Fostering Spiritual Ideals in Education," *National Catholic Educational Association Bulletin,* XXII (1925), 395–400.

Hinsdale, Burke A. "Early Views and Plans Relating to a National University," *Report of the United States Commissioner of Education,* II (1893), 1293–1312.

———, et al. "The Certification of College and University Graduates as Teachers of the Common Schools," *The School Review,* VII (1899), 331–371.

Johnson, C. C. "A Plan of Teacher Certification," *National Catholic Educational Association Bulletin,* XVIII (Nov., 1921), 388–394.

Lambert, Sam M. "Educational Growth and Change Lie Ahead in the 1960's," *National Education Association Journal,* XLIX (Dec., 1960), 45–47.

Long, Winifred R., and Enzler, Carol E. "281 Dissertations on Catholic Education," *National Catholic Association Bulletin,* LX (May, 1964), 20–23.

McAvoy, Thomas T., C.S.C. "Notre Dame, 1919–1922: the Burns Revolution," *Review of Politics,* XXI (Oct., 1963), 431–450.

McNeill, Leon A. "The Diocesan Superintendent and the Religious Instruction of Public-School Pupils," *National Catholic Educational Association Bulletin,* XXIX (Nov., 1932), 488–496.

Macelwane, Francis J. "The Superintendent's Responsibility for the Professional Advancement of His Teachers," *National Catholic Educational Association Bulletin*, XXVIII (Nov., 1931), 566–588.

"Michael Hyde—Early-Day King of Owyhee Cattle Empire," *Scenic Idaho*, XII:4 (1959), 31–32.

Newell, M. A. "Contributions to the History of Normal Schools in the United States," *Report of the Commissioner of Education*, II (1898–1899), 2275–2295.

Peckham, Howard H. "Recent Documentary Acquisitions to the Indiana Historical Society Library Relating to Fort Wayne," *Indiana Magazine of History*, XLIV:4 (1948), 225–228.

Shields, Thomas E. "Some Relations Between the Catholic School System and the Public School System," *National Catholic Association Bulletin*, XII (Nov., 1916), 51–62.

Starr, Eliza Allan. "Mother M. Angela of Holy Cross," *New York Freeman's Journal*, Mar. 26, 1887.

Verhalen, David H., C.S.C. "Father Moreau's 'Christian Pedagogy,'" *Bulletin of the Educational Conference of the Priests of Holy Cross*, XXX (Dec., 1962), 57–67.

D. Map

Ballard, Ralph. Map of Indiana Trails. Niles, Mich.: Fort St. Joseph Historical Society, 1939.

IV. Interviews

Interview with Miss Marion McCandless, Secretary Emeritus of Holy Cross Alumnae Association, Saint Mary's College, Notre Dame, Indiana, Feb., 1964.

Interview with Mother Kathryn Marie (Gibbons), C.S.C., Superior General, Sisters of the Holy Cross Generalate, Saint Mary's Convent, Notre Dame, Indiana, Feb., 1964.

Interview with Mother M. Verda Clare (Doran), C.S.C., Provincial Superior, Midwest Provincialate, South Bend, Indiana, May, 1964.

Interview with Rev. Thomas T. McAvoy, C.S.C., Archivist, University of Notre Dame, Notre Dame, Indiana, Feb., 1964.

Interview with Sister M. Benedictus (Kern), Dec. 20, 1964.

Interview with Sister M. Madeleva (Wolff), C.S.C., Saint Mary's College, Notre Dame, Indiana, Mar., 1964.

Interview with Sister Maria Pieta (Scott), C.S.C., Saint Mary's College, Notre Dame, Indiana, Mar., 1964.

Interview with Sister M. Matthew (Betz), C.S.C., Supervisor of Elementary Education, Midwest Provincialate, South Bend, Indiana, April, 1964.

Interview with Sister M. Monica (Wagner), C.S.C., Director of Education, Sisters of the Holy Cross Generalate, Saint Mary's Convent, Notre Dame, Indiana, Mar., 1964.

Interview with Sister M. Rhoda (Hyde), C.S.C., Saint Mary's Convent, Notre Dame, Indiana, Mar., 1964.

INDEX OF NAMES